JOHN DOWLAND

John Dowland: A Research and Information Guide offers the first comprehensive guide to the musical works and literature on one of the major composers of the English Renaissance. Including a catalogue of works, discography of recordings, extensive annotated bibliography of secondary sources, and substantial indexes, this volume is a major reference tool for all those interested in Dowland's works and place in music history, and a valuable resource for researchers of Renaissance and English music.

K. Dawn Grapes is Associate Professor of Music History at Colorado State University.

ROUTLEDGE MUSIC BIBLIOGRAPHIES

RECENT TITLES

COMPOSERS

Isaac Albéniz, 2nd Edition (2015)
Walter A. Clark

William Alwyn (2013)
John C. Dressler

Samuel Barber, 2nd Edition (2012)
Wayne C. Wentzel

Béla Bartók, 3rd Edition (2011)
Elliott Antokoletz and Paolo Susanni

Alban Berg, 3rd Edition (2018)
Bryan R. Simms

Leonard Bernstein, 2nd Edition (2015)
Paul R. Laird and Hsun Lin

Johannes Brahms, 2nd Edition (2011)
Heather Platt

William Byrd, 3rd Edition (2012)
Richard Turbet

John Cage (2017)
Sara Haefeli

Frédéric Chopin, 2nd Edition (2015)
William Smialek and Maja Trochimczyk

Miles Davis (2017)
Clarence Henry

John Dowland (2019)
K. Dawn Grapes

Edward Elgar, 2nd Edition (2013)
Christopher Kent

Gabriel Fauré, 2nd Edition (2011)
Edward R. Phillips

Alberto Ginastera (2011)
Deborah Schwartz-Kates

Fanny Hensel (2019)
Laura K.T. Stokes

Gustav Holst (2011)
Mary Christison Huismann

Charles Ives, 2nd Edition (2010)
Gayle Sherwood Magee

Quincy Jones (2014)
Clarence Bernard Henry

Alma Mahler and Her Contemporaries (2017)
Susan M. Filler

Bohuslav Martinů (2014)
Robert Simon

Felix Mendelssohn Bartholdy, 2nd Edition (2011)
John Michael Cooper with Angela R. Mace

Olivier Messiaen, 2nd Edition (2017)
Vincent P. Benitez

Claudio Monteverdi (2018)
Susan Lewis and Maria Virginia Acuña

Nikolay Andreevich Rimsky-Korsakov, 2nd Edition (2015)
Gerald R. Seaman

Gioachino Rossini, 2nd Edition (2010)
Denise P. Gallo

Pëtr Il'ich Tchaikovsky (2019)
Gerald R. Seaman

Ralph Vaughan Williams (2016)
Ryan Ross

Giuseppe Verdi, 2nd Edition (2012)
Gregory W. Harwood

Richard Wagner, 2nd Edition (2010)
Michael Saffle

Anton Webern (2017)
Darin Hoskisson

GENRES

Blues, Funk, R&B, Soul, Hip Hop, and Rap (2010)
Eddie S. Meadows

Chamber Music, 3rd Edition (2010)
John H. Baron

Choral Music, 3rd Edition (2019)
James Michael Floyd

Church and Worship Music in the United States, 2nd Edition (2017)
Avery T. Sharp and James Michael Floyd

Ethnomusicology, 2nd Edition (2013)
Jennifer C. Post

Free Jazz (2018)
Jeffrey Schwartz

The Madrigal (2012)
Susan Lewis Hammond

The Musical, 2nd Edition (2011)
William A. Everett

North American Fiddle Music (2011)
Drew Beisswenger

Popular Music Theory and Analysis (2017)
Thomas Robinson

The Recorder, 3rd Edition (2012)
Richard Griscom and David Lasocki

String Quartets, 2nd Edition (2011)
Mara E. Parker

Women in Music, 2nd Edition (2011)
Karin Pendle and Melinda Boyd

John Dowland
A Research and Information Guide

K. Dawn Grapes

Routledge
Taylor & Francis Group

NEW YORK AND LONDON

First published 2020
by Routledge
605 Third Avenue, New York, NY 10017

and by Routledge
2 Park Square, Milton Park, Abingdon, Oxon, OX14 4RN

First issued in paperback 2021

Routledge is an imprint of the Taylor & Francis Group, an informa business

Library of Congress Cataloging-in-Publication Data
A catalog record for this book has been requested

ISBN 13: 978-0-367-78493-5 (pbk)
ISBN 13: 978-1-138-29855-2 (hbk)

Typeset in Minion
by Apex CoVantage, LLC

Contents

Acknowledgments

First, I must offer my sincere thanks to Cristi MacWaters and Maggie Cummings of the Interlibrary Loan division at Colorado State University Libraries, without whom this volume could not have taken shape. You are my heroes and deserve much credit for your continuous and tireless fulfillment of my many requests. Thanks also to the librarians and staffs at Harvard University's Loeb Music and Isham Memorial Libraries, Northwestern University Music Library, Eastman School of Music Sibley Music Library, the British Library, Royal Academy of Music Library, Middle Temple Archives, Dublin Trinity College Library, Marsh's Library, University of Nottingham Libraries, Queen's University Belfast Library, New York Public Library for the Performing Arts, Princeton Scheide Library, the Staatsbibliothek zu Berlin, Stadtbibliothek Bautzen, Zentral- und Landesbibliothek Berlin, and to the Lancelyn Green Family of Poulton Hall. Appreciation also goes to Dean Ben Withers and the Colorado State University College of Liberal Arts for financial support to travel to a number of the archives and libraries listed previously, and to Genevieve Aoki, who enthusiastically encouraged my work on this research guide from its inception. To Jeremy L. Smith, my mentor and friend, who first handed me an opportunity to delve into John Dowland studies, I cannot fully express my gratitude for your support and trust in my abilities. Thanks also to Andrew Woolley and Katharyn Benessa for their expert advice and to Natalie Grapes and Chelsea Kendall for editorial assistance. Finally, special appreciation goes to Dan Goble and all of my School of Music, Theatre, and Dance faculty and staff colleagues for your on-going support; to Cary, Jim, Tom, Peter, Adam, John, Denise, and Kate for your humor, incessant encouragement, and, of course, lunches and tea breaks; to Natalie and David III for making my world a better place; and to David for, well, everything. *Nil sine numine.*

Figures

1

Introduction

John Dowland, English lutenist, composer, translator, entrepreneur, and poet, remains one of the most intriguing figures of the early modern period. The most internationally known English musician of his generation, he played at Danish and German courts and traveled throughout Italy and France. The musician also spent time at home, where he produced the most well-received London musical print of the time, *The First Booke of Songes or Ayres of fowre partes with Tableture for the Lute* (1597), which was reprinted at least four times. This groundbreaking anthology of songs, which could be performed by vocal soloist with lute accompaniment, four singers, or any combination of the aforementioned, stood at the forefront of an early seventeenth-century English lute song-air craze that was short-lived, but enthusiastically embraced by those in classes that valued courtly poetry and domestic music. The tablebook format of the volume, allowing performers to sit around a table and share one book, became the standard for lute song-airs that followed. Dowland himself produced three more printed songbooks, a volume of consort of music, and a translation of an earlier theoretical treatise. The composer's choice to set some lyrics that tapped into the early seventeenth-century trend toward melancholy helped shape his own public persona, one that encouraged visions of isolation and despair. Yet contemporaneous mentions of the composer suggest someone perceived as talented, vital, and savvy. Such a figure begs for further study.

Dowland left behind limited biographical information in the texts of a handful of letters sent and received. The prefatory material of his printed volumes allows additional glimpses into his life. Yet there remain large gaps in our knowledge of Dowland's biography, lacunae that have been evident since the seventeenth century, when the first brief sketches of the composer's life appear. In spite of the discovery of new archival material related to burial records and certain account ledgers and receipts in which he is mentioned, we do not know much more about Dowland than was known four hundred years ago. Perhaps we know less. Maybe it is *because of* what we do not know that he remains such an enigma, placing him as an object of interest for scholars, students, and performers. Further, it is not unreasonable to think that this is just the way Dowland would have wanted it, for he was a man who seems to have encouraged the air of mystery that surrounds him even today.

Where *was* the composer born? In what manner did he receive his early training to become one of the most internationally known performers, composers, scholars, and publishers of his day? Was he a spy? For whom? Did he truly convert to Catholicism while on the continent? If so, did he ever sincerely re-embrace the faith of the Church of England? And how did his view of the religious divide within England affect his life choices, his career, and his music? Or did they? These are the sorts of issues that have plagued Dowland scholars for centuries. Other researchers have concentrated on myriad aspects of Dowland's works: his lyrics bring up questions of authorship, rhetorical choices, and textual-musical association; primary source textual application informs historical performance, aiding in interpretations of the composer's compositions, regardless of instrumentation; and Dowland's music itself, which many have deemed the most outstanding of its kind, gains appreciation through analytic inspection.

Interest in Dowland and his works has blossomed in the twentieth and twenty-first centuries, during which time the number of articles, editions, and dissertations exploring the musician and his music has increased decade-by-decade. Research guides on Dowland are scarce. Those that exist are either intentionally limited in size or out-of-date. This current volume is intended to aid future researchers by providing a complete guide to previously produced materials, both primary and secondary, from which new scholarship can emerge.

WORKS

The music catalogue and source list chapters have several aims. The first attempts to deliver a complete list of all known Dowland compositions, regardless of instrumentation or genre. The second is an inventory that collates and clarifies the many sixteenth- and seventeenth-century sources in which compositions written by the composer, or that were inspired by his music, are found. Compiling these catalogues proved a monumental task for, though previous scholars have created such lists, they are often limited by genre or instrument, and the few sources that attempt comprehensive coverage are now quite old. Creating a comprehensive works list for John Dowland is fraught with issues stemming from a variety of sources, starting with the composer himself. Dowland composed for different forces: lute solos, lute songs and dialogues for voice with lute accompaniment, versions of those same songs for multiple voice parts with or without accompaniment, consort settings for various combinations of instruments, and traditional four-part metrical psalm harmonizations. Sometimes the composer set the same piece for more than one of these combinations, using identical musical source material to create works previously composed for different musical combinations. In a number of cases, he gave different titles to works that share the same musical source material, with one label for instrumental works and another for vocal works (usually based on the words of the first line of text, which were sometimes added later to pieces first conceived as instrumental music). Further, more Dowland works, both attributed and unattributed, survive in manuscript copies than in prints authorized by the composer. Few of these appear in Dowland's hand or feature his signature. As such, they may or may not reflect the original compositional thought of the musician, and titles appear in many variants, if at all. Some pieces are close approximations of versions found in Dowland's print books or in manuscripts written in his own hand, some vary slightly, and some are completely new arrangements, based on Dowland's original material. Concordances have helped identify some Dowland pieces and others have been put forth as the composer's by experts, based on stylistic features, and then questioned by others.

Perhaps these complications have discouraged the creation of a complete, numbered Dowland catalogue. The closest semblance of one is found in the numbering of pieces in the 1974 Poulton-Lam volume of collected lute works (**221**), but that collection, as useful as it is, represents less than half of Dowland's compositions. The works list included with the *Grove Music Online* "Dowland" article is more complete, but unnumbered, and it does not immediately represent material presented in multiple forms. The catalogue in Chapter 2 assigns each Dowland work a unique "D" number. Organization proved complicated. Ordering sections by type of work is not a completely clear method, due to the multivarious nature of many Dowland compositions. A chronological ordering is impossible because many of the works cannot be dated accurately. In an attempt to maintain consistency with previous pieces of scholarship that rely on Poulton-Lam numbers, I have maintained that numbering system, re-using the already established list. For the many Dowland compositions without a "P" number, I first continued with lute pieces discovered or recognized after **221**, then unnumbered instrumental consort works, and finally with pieces including voice or voices, starting with those found in Dowland's published collections and concluding with sacred pieces found both in prints and in manuscripts. Variants are conflated with the piece on which they are based. The five Poulton-Lam numbers given to variant versions of previously numbered lute works (D88–D92) are maintained, but as with all other arrangements, sources for compositions counted in this group previously are included with the number assigned to the original version of each respective work. An alphabetical index is provided at the end of the works list for reader ease. This works list is in no way intended to authenticate or dis-authenticate any individual piece, but seeks to be as inclusive as possible. Both the works and source lists, of course, would not have been possible without the diligent identification and cataloguing done by previous scholars. Inventories are compiled from many primary and secondary sources, including those listed in the editions section and secondary source bibliographies that follow.

As mentioned previously, this new works catalogue consolidates as many variants as possible. Titles are cross-referenced as appropriate. Spellings have been modernized to reduce the impractical number of early English variants. Songs (for voice or voices in any combination) are indicated in quotation marks; instrumental music titles have no quotation marks. Each musical entry includes concordance references to the source lists that follow in the subsequent chapter. For this guide, concordance does not indicate an exact copy, for very rarely is this the case. Pieces categorized under the same number may appear with different titles, in alternate keys, with different instrumentations, and in many cases (such as all of the keyboard works and works for instruments with which Dowland is not personally identified), are likely arrangements based on Dowland's work, that belong as much to their arranger as to Dowland. Arrangers are indicated when known. Under each work listed, "† Primary:" indicates sources found in musical collections either initiated by the composer, appearing in print versions likely approved by Dowland, or existing in manuscripts in the composer's hand or featuring his signature; all other concordance lists are categorized by instrumentation, with versions that may or may not have been known to the composer, including arrangements that are perhaps more representative of preferences and needs of the copyist or another composer than of Dowland's. Though at times items may fit into more than one category, concordance references are placed within the category deemed most appropriate. Works with questionable authorship are marked with an asterisk (*). The source inventories include only volumes dated to the sixteenth or seventeenth centuries or (rarely) ones lost but appearing in later sources based on a sixteenth- or seventeenth-century original.

The number of concordances, and possibilities of newly discovered sources, makes omissions and inaccuracies unavoidable. For any such errors, I accept all responsibility and will work to catalogue new discoveries and to correct erroneous information in updates and future revised editions. Citations for published facsimiles are provided for ease of researcher access, and readers should also consider that many sources are now available through portals such as *Early English Books Online* (http://eebo.chadwyck.com, subscription-based) and the *International Music Score Library Project* (https://imslp.org, public domain). Digitized manuscript and print sources accessible through their holding institution websites are listed with hyperlinks. The very nature of the internet, however, assures that some of these addresses will change with time. Further, as more libraries and archives work to photograph their documents, surely there will be an increase in future electronic availability.

A contents title list of Dowland's printed volumes is included in the primary source list for easy reference. Descriptions of other sources feature content only by D number. The editions bibliography is made up only of critical collected editions of Dowland's music. An exception was made in the case of consort music, as there is no complete critical edition. Because of this, the two most useful performance editions are listed. The sheer number of modern performance editions of Dowland's music, for all combinations of instruments and/or voices, precludes a comprehensive bibliography of other Dowland-related scores at this time.

BIBLIOGRAPHIES OF MUSIC LITERATURE

Primary Sources

Much of the primary source information we have regarding Dowland comes from writings by the composer himself, through his famous surviving letter to Robert Cecil, the prefatory material included in his printed volumes, and in several theoretical-pedagogical tracts. The bibliography of primary source music literature and documentation will guide researchers to these sources. Some, such as the composer's printed musical collections, are included both in the works section and in the primary source bibliography of literature, which seems only appropriate, as they offer both music and extra-musical texts. Annotations in the primary source bibliography in Chapter 5 provide only basic information, as readers are encouraged to explore these primary sources themselves.

Secondary Sources

Although often cast within the musicological field, Dowland studies include a wide array of interdisciplinary subject areas, including but not limited to British and continental history, religious studies, English literature, rhetoric, and philosophy. The secondary source bibliographic chapters of this guide include annotations for: books about Dowland, as well as monographs on larger topics that devote copious space to or include important information regarding the musician; exceptional doctoral dissertations that examine Dowland and his works or contribute in significant ways to Dowland discourse; academic journal articles related to the composer and his works; exemplary reference articles; internet databases and bibliographies of note; and miscellaneous items of special interest. Textbook chapters and most dictionary articles are not included, nor are items that simply mention Dowland in passing. While the majority of secondary sources chosen for inclusion were published in English, publications in other languages are also considered, if readily available through conventional library services.

Secondary source entries are organized in clearly indicated topical sections, starting in Chapter 6 with overviews of the composer and his works, reference items, and works related to biography. Entries are alphabetized within sections by author last name, with the exception of the historical biographies section, which is presented chronologically. Chapters 7 and 8 consist of sources examining Dowland's works, source studies of original manuscripts and prints, and performance-related issues. The items in the section devoted to modern poetry are not research sources per se, but reflect contemporary perceptions of Dowland and his music.

Many entries fit well into more than one section. In these cases, each is included within the topical area that seems most appropriate, and then is cross-referenced in alternate sections. For this reason, it is important that readers rely not solely on annotations found in any given section, but refer to other listed suggestions. Further, certain items included in the overviews section, such as **264** and **265**, are relevant to most or all other sections, and should be kept close at hand for any Dowland-related project.

A discography concludes this volume. As there are thousands of recordings that include one or more Dowland works, in a diverse variety of instrumental and vocal combinations, the list provided herein is selective by necessity. Scope is limited to recorded collections focusing primarily on Dowland's music that use instruments common to the early modern period in England. Hopefully, the chapter will serve as a guide for those seeking aural representations of Dowland's music as it may have been presented in prints and manuscripts of the time.

ISBN and LC call numbers, as available, are included throughout the volume for ease of item location. Citations generally conform to guidelines of the *Chicago Manual of Style*. Song titles are standardized to modern English, though primary source titles of published volumes retain their original spellings, as do individual song titles listed under specific Dowland volumes in the printed volume contents lists. Indexes and all cross-references use numbers assigned to each bibliographic entry, rather than the pages on which they appear. Indexes at volume end catalogue items in critical editions, secondary source bibliographies, and recordings chapters only.

DOWLAND'S LIFE AND CAREER: A CHRONOLOGY

1562/1563	John Dowland is born, possibly in Westminster.
c. 1580	Travels to Paris in the company of Sir Henry Cobham, Ambassador to the French court. Remains at least through 1584.
1588	Awarded BMus from Christ Church, Oxford.
c. 1591	Son Robert is born. Sir Robert Sidney is named godfather.
1592	Six metrical psalm harmonizations are included in Thomas East's new edition of the *Whole Booke of Psalmes*.
1594	Unsuccessfully petitions for John Johnson's lutenist post in the court of Elizabeth I.
1594	Travels to the German states visiting, among others, Heinrich Julius, Duke of Brunswick-Lüneberg at Wolfenbüttel, and Moritz, the Landgrave of Hesse at Kassel.
1595	Journeys through the Italian lands, headed toward Rome. Abruptly abandons his travel plans and pens the famous "Cecil letter."
1596	Returns to the court of Moritz, Landgrave of Hesse.
1596	Compositions appear in William Barley's *New Booke of Tabliture*, without Dowland's approval.
1596	Receives letter from Sir Henry Noel, encouraging his return to London.
1596/1597	*Lamentio Henrici Noel*, a set of psalms, is composed upon the death of Henry Noel.
1597	*The First Booke of Songes or Ayres* is printed.
1598	Afforded royal appointment as lutenist to Christian IV of Denmark.
1598	Receives letter of esteem from the Landgrave of Hesse.
1600	First reprint of the *First Booke of Songes*.
1600	*The Second Booke of Songes or Ayres* is published.
1601–1602	Travels to England on business for Christian IV.
1602	English diplomat Stephen Lesieur writes to Dowland in September to request information on the Danish-English maritime situation.

1603	Second reprint of *The First Booke of Songes*.
1603	*The Third and Last Booke of Songes or Aires* issued.
1603–1604	Travels to England, gaining "access" in Winchester to the new queen, Anne of Denmark, wife of James I.
1604	*Lachrimae or Seaven Teares* is printed.
1606	Leaves position in Denmark in February and returns to England.
1606	Third reprint of the *First Booke of Songes*.
1608/1609	*Andreas Ornithoparcus, His Micrologus* translation is issued.
1610	Son Robert Dowland's *A Varietie of Lute Lessons* is printed. The volume features nine John Dowland pieces, as well as the essay "Other Necessary Observations belonging to the Lute."
1610	Printing of *A Musicall Banquet* (Robert Dowland), which includes three John Dowland works.
1612	*A Pilgrimes Solace*, Dowland's final songbook, featuring both secular and devotional songs in diverse musical combinations, is issued.
1612	Secures appointment as one of James I's lutenists.
1613	Fourth reprint of *The First Booke of Songes*.
1613/1614	*Teares or Lamentacions of a Sorrowfull Soule* by William Leighton is printed. The volume includes two Dowland songs and a dedicatory poem.
1620	Referred to as "Doctor" in Henry Peacham's *Thalia's Banquet*.
1621	Ravenscroft's *Whole Booke of Psalmes* includes a new Dowland setting of Psalm 100.
1626	Dies and is buried at St. Anne, Blackfriars. Replaced at court by son Robert.

A HISTORY OF DOWLAND SCHOLARSHIP

When Dowland died in 1626, he was never completely forgotten. His music continued to be copied in both English and continental manuscripts and printed in anthologies, especially within the German lands. As an individual musician, both as performer and composer, the lute master was also remembered. Details of the composer's life as found in several letters and the prefatory material of his printed works, however, were not closely studied until the early twentieth century. Yet the first biography of Dowland appeared less than forty years after his death, in Thomas Fuller's posthumous 1662 *The History of the Worthies of England*. Though not completely accurate, the information contained within provided a foundation for subsequent sketches that followed, such as the one in Anthony à Wood's *Athenae Oxonienses* of 1691. Well-known eighteenth-century writers John Hawkins and Charles Burney each included commentary on Dowland in their music histories, the first such endeavors published in English. Dowland's music also continued to appear in collections of English music, often as songs in four-part score. The nineteenth century continued this trend, and Dowland's music was printed in music periodicals and collections, capturing the interest of choral societies and others. The turn of the century brought a renewed interest in the musician. Through the 1930s, commentary on Dowland was included in larger surveys of English music and of lutenist composers. Several featured articles on the composer appeared in music journals, transcripts of Dowland's famous Cecil letter were printed, and scholarship from the first group of British Dowland experts emerged, authored by Philip Heseltine, William H. Grattan Flood, Edmund Fellowes, and others. While some of the information disseminated by these early pioneers has since been contradicted, these men did a great service in keeping Dowland's name and music relevant in musicological circles. Fellowes is also credited with the first complete editions of Dowland's songbooks, issued in series with other recognized lute song composers of the time.

By mid-century, scholars began specializing in Dowland studies, and sub-fields emerged. Thurston Dart revised Fellowes's editions, raising editorial standards. A new movement in lute studies assured that the composer assumed more historical importance. The early music revival of the 1960s and 1970s brought new attention to Dowland's music, in all genres. Experts in English literature, led by Edward Doughtie, looked more seriously at the texts of English ayres, including Dowland lyrics, anthologizing them, analyzing their literary content, and eventually moving toward closer examination of the relationship between the composer's music and the texts he chose to set. This time period also highlighted the monumental efforts of Diana Poulton and John M. Ward. In 1974, Poulton issued an edition of Dowland's complete lute music, filling a long-felt gap in the composer's bibliography of music. A few years earlier, the first edition of her now-iconic monograph on the composer's life and works was published. The friendly rivalry that developed between Poulton and Ward resulted in more accurate and complete scholarship, from which we benefit today. Emerging from this foundation, a young David Greer began his own Dowland studies, eventually producing the first critical editions of the songbooks that included all parts: cantus voice, lute accompaniment, and additional voices, providing scores that adhere to modern editorial standards while presenting the music with all the options the composer originally envisioned. All three of these giants of Dowlandia continued to contribute to Dowland studies throughout the remainder of the century, and for Ward and Greer, into the next. Their deaths in 1995, 2011, and 2017 marked deeply felt losses to the early music community—the end of an era really.

The late 1970s and 1980s also featured the emergence of a contingent of performer-scholars who specialized in Dowland's music. Robert Spencer, Anthony Rooley, and Lyle Nordstrom led a group who published articles and issued musical editions, offering performance guidance and studying contextual meaning within Dowland's music for decades to come. The same time period witnessed a rise in commentary on rhetoric within Dowland lyrics, featuring the scholarship of Robin Headlam Wells, Elise Bickford Jorgens, and Daniel Fischlin. The 1990s continued this trend, and the number of articles related to Dowland has not decreased since. Studies of Dowland's music continues to become more and more specialized, with examinations of single compositions, collections, and other primary sources. In 1999, Peter Holman produced a monograph on Dowland's 1604 *Lachrimae*, providing a new focus on the composer's consort music, which has long been overshadowed by his lute solos and songs. The *Lachrimae* debate, over hidden inspirations and meanings in the collection and associations with the musician's melancholic portrayal, was introduced more than a decade earlier, and continues to this day. The 1990s and early 2000s also saw the release of collected recordings of Dowland's music by performers such as Jakob Lindberg, Nigel North, and Paul O'Dette, as well as a multi-disc collection of Dowland works spearheaded by Anthony Rooley and the Consort of Musicke that brought together projects recorded over many years. These musicians and others who have recorded music and produced performing editions of Dowland compositions have provided a great service to researchers in making different interpretations of Dowland's music available to a wider public.

Interest in Dowland has not abated in the twenty-first century. New volumes on early instruments and the music written for them, by authors such as Douglas Alton Smith, Matthew Spring, Christopher Hogwood, Michael Fleming, and John Bryan, contribute more tidbits to our biographical and contextual knowledge of Dowland and other composers of the time. Considerations of Dowland's self-fashioned public persona and political implications found in archival material, by scholars such as Kirsten Gibson, David Pinto, and Peter Hauge, create new interest in the composer's life choices. And revelations of the print and manuscript cultures in which Dowland participated continue to illuminate the expectations of composers, printers, and publishers of the time. As more scholarship on Dowland is produced, it becomes clear that, though our base of primary source data on the composer has not increased substantially over multiple centuries, there are many avenues of the composer's music and life yet to explore. We owe a profound debt of gratitude to those who set such a solid foundation through their in-depth research and analysis. A knowledge and understanding of prior work opens doors for new studies that will no doubt enhance interest in a most intriguing historical figure.

Figure 1 Title page, *The First Booke of Songes or Ayres*. London: Peter Short, 1597. RB
59102. The Huntington Library, San Marino, CA.

Source: The Huntington Library, San Marino, California.

2

Music Catalogue

WORKS LIST

Each item provides title(s), previously assigned Poulton-Lam number (P), if applicable, and numbered references indicating in which sources (listed in Chapter 3) each composition is found.

† Primary = item likely printed with Dowland's knowledge, or found in manuscript in the composer's hand, or with signature

Song = voice or voices in any combination, with or without accompanying instruments, or parts intended to be sung (with or without text)

Lute = lutes only: solo, duo, or trio

Consort = two or more other instruments, in any combination, including those for instruments plus lutes

* = uncertain authorship

D1 fantasia (P1)
> † Primary: **7** (ff. H1r–2r)
> Lute: **14** (ff. 170v–171v), **55** (ff. 8v–9r), **89** (ff. 16v–17r), **102** (ff. 13v–14v), **107** (ff. 14v–15r), **109** (ff. 24v–25r), **194** (ff. 27v–31r)

D2 Forlorn Hope (fantasia) (P2)
> Lute: **29** (pp. 210–11), **31** (pp. 37–8), **64** (ff. 16v–17r), **199** (ff. 54v–56r)

D3 Farewell (fantasia) (P3)

† Primary: **63** (ff. 43v–44r, signature and title in Dowland's hand)
Lute: **20** (pp. 18–19), **31** (pp. 1–2), **89** (ff. 41v–42r), **199** (ff. 41v–43r)

D4 Farewell (fantasia) (P4)
Lute: **64** (ff. 41v–42r, 50v–51r)

D5 fantasia (P5)
Lute: **55** (ff. 17v–18r; 33v, incomplete)

D6 fantasia (P6)
Lute: **29** (pp. 208–10), **31** (pp. 30–1), **55** (ff. 7v–8r), **64** (ff. 43v–44r), **66** (ff. 32v–33r), **199** (ff. 39v–41r)

D7 fantasia (P7)
Lute: **64** (ff. 6v–7v), **89** (ff. 35r–36r)

D8 Captain Piper's Pavan/Piper's Pavan (P8)
Lute: **12** (ff. E3r–F1r), **27** (f. 37v), **55** (ff. 2v–3r), **57** (ff. 46v–47r), **89** (f. 29v), **102** (ff. 27v–28r), **109** (ff. 19v–20r), **135** (f. 21r), **164** (ff. 70v–71r). Pairs with galliard **D19**.
Song: **15** (p. 110), **104** (f. 22v)
Consort: **23** (XXIV, a5), **30** (no. 4), **61** (f. 3v, bass viol), **62** (f. 1v, recorder), **65** (f. 31v, cittern), **117** (f. 89r, bandora), **165** (no. 49)
Keyboard: **67** (pp. 298–9, arr. Peerson), **195** (f. 57r), **208** (p. 4)
Bandora: **57** (f. 82r)
Cittern: **60** (f. 27v)

D9 Semper Dowland, semper dolens (P9)
† Primary: **4** (8)
Lute: **27** (ff. 38v–39r), **89** (f. 25r), **109** (f. 31v), **134** (f. 14v), **141** (f. 40v)

D10 Solus cum sola (pavan) (P10)
Lute: **57** (f. 58v), **89** (ff. 27v–28r), **102** (ff. 14v–15r), **120** (ff. 10v–11r), **166** (pp. 104–5)
Keyboard: **151** (f. 76r, incomplete), **208** (p. 4)
Lyra Viol: **122** (no. 11, arr. Sumarte)
Orpharion: **12** (ff. B3v–4r)

D11 Mrs. Brigide Fleetwood's Pavan (P11)
Lute: **38** (II:110), **39** (f. III1r), **64** (ff. 33v–34r)

D12 Dr. Case's Pavan (P12)
Lute: **57** (f. 14v)

D13 Dowland's Adieu for Master Oliver Cromwell/Resolution (P13)
† Primary: **2** (f. N1v)
Lute: **66** (ff. 17v–18r, 18r–v)

D14 Mr. John Langton's Pavan/Sir John Langton, his Pavan (P14)
† Primary: **4** (10), **7** (ff. K1v–2v)

Lute: **20** (pp. 53–5, 62, arr T. K.), **27** (f. 36v), **31** (pp. 48–9), **63** (ff. 2v–3r)
Consort: **42** (XXI)

D15 "Flow my tears, fall from your springs"/Lachrimae/Lachrimae Antique/Lachrimae
Pavan (P15)
    † Primary: **2** (II), **4** (1)
    Lute: **12** (ff. E1r–2v), **14** (ff. 16v–17r; 30r, 30v–31r, arr. Besard), **20** (pp. 60–1, arr.
Strobelius), **26** (ff. 94r–95r), **27** (f. 2v, arr. van den Hove), **38** (II:91), **39**
(ff. GG5v–6r), **54** (ff. 5v–6r), **55** (ff. 4v–5r, 14v–15r; 36v–37r, arr. C.K.),
57 (ff. 75v–77r, 81v), **63** (ff. 9v, 21r), **68** (ff. 8v–9r), **89** (ff. 25v–26r), **90**
(ff. 225v–227v), **92** (f. 1r), **107** (ff. 22v–23r), **109** (ff. 16v–17r), **110** (f.
11v), **115** (ff. 21v–22v), **118** (f. 11r), **120** (ff. 11v–12r), **134** (f. 4v), **135**
(f. 11r), **145** (ff. 109v–110r), **155** (ff. 36v–38r), **158** (ff. 72v–74r), **159** (ff.
103v–104r), **161** (pp. 17–19, arr. van den Hove), **164** (ff. 5r–v, 55v–56r),
166 (pp. 78–9, 122–3, duet or consort part), **182** (f. 24v), **185** (ff. 388v;
389v, duet or consort part), **212** (ff. 18v–19r), **214** (ff. 24r–27r). Pairs
with galliard **D46**.
    Song: **15** (pp. 44–53), **18** (1662: no. 61; later editions: no. 55), **46** (f. 51r), **47**
(pp. 116, 217–18), **76** (p. 34), **77** (f. F4r), **82** (f. 1r–v), **84** (f. 6v), **86** (B:
p. 202), **96** (f. 14r), **97** (ff. 11v–12r), **103** (f. 86r), **104** (f. 22r), **128** (f. 30v),
131 (pp. 6–7), **132** (f. 51r–v), **187** (f. 1r)
    Consort: **13** (ff. D4v–E1r, arr. Besard), **28** (pp. 2, 7–8, arr. Schop), **30** (no. 7),
48 (III:17), **58** (ff. 16v–17v, lute), **61** (ff. 3v, 6v, 28v, bass viol), **62** (f. 3v,
recorder), **65** (f. 25r, cittern), **117** (ff. 17v, 92r), **156** (12), **165** (no. 42),
174 (no. 8, arr. Schermer), **175** (f. 8v, arr. Hausmann), **182** (f. 38v–41r,
consort bandora)
    Keyboard: **67** (pp. 222–3, arr. Byrd; 406–8, arr. Farnaby), **69** (ff. 75v–76r; 83r–
84r, arr. Randall), **101** (ff. 71r–72v), **113** (ff. 5v–7v, arr. Cosyn), **114** (ff.
167r–171r, arr. Byrd), **130** (f. 11r, incomplete), **137** (ff. 60v–61r, arr.
Scheidt; 224v–225r, arr. Scheidemann), **139** (pp. 27, 28, 32), **143** (ff. 2r–3v,
arr. Schildt), **144** (ff. 1r–4v, arr. Schildt, incomplete), **147** (pp. 322–7), **148**
(ff. 115v–116r), **149** (ff. 2v–3r), **170** (ff. 154v–157r), **173** (ff. 11v–12r, 12v–
13r), **177** (ff. 34v–36r, arr. Sweelinck), **180** (ff. 56v–57v), **184** (f. 19v, arr.
Schmidt), **195** (ff. 24v–25v), **196** (ff. 28v–29r, arr. Schildt, incomplete; 34v–
35r, arr. Schildt), **208** (pp. 186–7), **209** (f. 14r), **210** (ff. 2v–4v, arr. Cussen)
    Bandora: **57** (f. 84v)
    Lyra Viol: **74** (pp. 42–3), **102** (ff. 35v–36r), **122** (pp. 18–19, arr. Sumarte), **126**
(ff. 25v–26r)
    Recorder: **51** (ff. 11v–12v, 61v–63v, both arr. van Eyck), **52** (ff. 12r–13r, 62v–65r,
both arr. van Eyck)

D16 pavan (P16)
    Lute: **63** (ff. 47v–48r)

D17 Lady Russell's Pavan (P17)
    Lute: **55** (ff. 5v–6r), **57** (f. 38v), **63** (ff. 64v–65r), **64** (ff. 5v–6r), **89** (ff. 37v–38r)

D18 pavan (P18)

    Lute: **63** (ff. 51v–52r), **64** (ff. 1v–2r)

D19 Captain Digorie Piper's Galliard/Captain Piper, his Galliard/"If my complaints could passions move" (P19)/(P88*)

    † Primary: **1** (IV), **4** (18)

    Lute: **14** (f. 107v), **19** (f. 13r, arr. Francisque), **55** (ff. 3v–4r), **57** (f. 53r), **63** (ff. 21v, 10r), **64** (f. 73v), **89** (f. 28v), **90** (ff. 92v–93r), **102** (ff. 28v–29r), **110** (f. 11r), **120** (f. 21v), **164** (f. 92v). Pairs with pavan **D8**.

    Song: **69** (f. 62v), **73** (S: f. R2v, Q: ff. O2v, O3r), **84** (ff. 30v–31r), **94** (f. 15v), **97** (ff. 12v–13r), **100** (f. 14r), **104** (f. 22v), **105** (ff. 2r, 7v, 8r), **124** (f. 7r), **131** (pp. 52–3), **138** (pp. 2–3)

    Consort: **30** (no. 5), **117** (f. 89r)

    Cittern: **35** (f. D4v), **60** (f. 4v), **202** (f. 14r)

    Keyboard: **67** (pp. 299–303, arr./var. Bull), **114** (ff. 222v–224r), **129** (ff. 18v–19r, arr. Byrd), **130** (f. 10v, incomplete), **148** (f. 7v), **170** (ff. 173v–175r), **192** (ff. 8v–9r, 30v–31r, arr. Philips), **208** (p. 4)

    Lyra Viol: **17** (f. G1v)

D20 galliard (P20)

    Lute: **57** (f. 67v), **119** (f. 6v), **185** (f. 22r)

    Bandora: **117** (f. 10v)

D21 Captain Candish, his Galliard/galliard (P21)

    Lute: **54** (f. 6v), **57** (ff. 7v, 56r), **110** (f. 11v), **118** (f. 1r)

D22 galliard (P22)

    Lute: **57** (ff. 56r, 60r, 95r), **89** (f. 23r), **120** (f. 22v)

    Consort: **61** (f. 5r, bass viol), **62** (f. 5r, recorder), **65** (f. 33v, cittern)

    Cittern: **60** (f. 28r)

D23 Frog Galliard/"Now O now I needs must part" (P23)/(P90*)

    † Primary: **1** (VI), **212** (f. 12v, signed)

    Lute: **55** (ff. 42v–43r), **57** (ff. 40v, 93r), **89** (ff. 26v–27r), **135** (f. 100r), **158** (ff. 60v–62r), **160** (p. 134), **161** (pp. 144–5), **166** (pp. 198, 230), **169** (pp. 4–5), **172** (ff. 9v–10r, duet; 13v), **182** (ff. 21r, 22v), **185** (f. 28v), **193** (ff. 15v–16r), **194** (ff. 15v–16r), **215** (13)

    Song: **15** (pp. 24–6), **18** (no. 47), **47** (pp. 54–5), **69** (f. 63v), **70** (f. 2v), **73** (S: ff. O4r, Q4r, Q: f. N4r), **99** (f. 22r–v), **105** (ff. 2v, 7v, 8v), **124** (f. 5r), **131** (p. 45), **132** (ff. 38v–39r), **138** (pp. 6–7)

    Consort: **30** (no. 10), **182** (ff. 5v, consort lute; 40v, consort bandora)

    Cittern: **35** (f. G1r)

    Keyboard: **83** (ff. 29v–32v, arr. Wilbye), **116** (ff. 8r–9r), **133** (ff. 28v–30r, arr. Hall), **135** (f. 94v)

    Mandora: **80** (pp. 35–40), **135** (f. 102v)

D24 "Awake sweet love, thou art returned"/galliard/Fr. Cutting galliard* (P24)/(P92)

    † Primary: **1** (XIX)

Lute: **55** (f. 33v), **57** (f. 58r), **63** (f. 63r, arr. Cutting?)
Song: **18** (no. 23), **99** (f. 11r), **105** (ff. 3v, 9v), **132** (ff. 18v–19r)

D25 Melancholy Galliard (P25)
Lute: **57** (f. 12r), **89** (f. 24v)

D26 "My thoughts are winged with hopes"/Sir John Souch, his Galliard/Sir John Souch's Galliard (P26)
† Primary: **1** (III), **4** (13)
Lute: **63** (f. 26r)
Song: **124** (f. 9r)
Keyboard: **148** (f. 7r)
Bandora: **117** (f. 18v)

D27 galliard (P27)
Lute: **63** (f. 49v)

D28 galliard (on a galliard by Daniel Bacheler) (P28)
Lute: **20** (pp. 108–10), **63** (ff. 35v–36r), **68** (ff. 54v–55r), **89** (ff. 20v–21r), **107** (ff. 15v–16r), **120** (ff. 16v–17r), **164** (ff. 94v–95r)

D29 Giles Hoby's Galliard/Mr. Giles Hobies Galliard (P29)
† Primary: **4** (15)
Lute: **27** (f. 52v), **63** (ff. 16v–17r), **68** (f. 10r)

D30 galliard (P30)
Lute: **63** (ff. 25v–26r)

D31 galliard (P31)
Lute: **57** (f. 82v), **63** (f. 37r)

D32 Mrs. Vaux's Galliard (P32)
Lute: **20** (p. 108), **63** (ff. 18v–19r), **64** (f. 20r)

D33 Mr. Langton's Galliard (P33)
Lute: **64** (ff. 17v–18r), **89** (f. 18v)

D34 Mignarda/Mr. Henry Noel, his Galliard/"Shall I strive with words to move" (P34)
† Primary: **4** (14), **5** (V)
Lute: **57** (f. 77r), **63** (f. 31v), **64** (f. 29r), **71** (p. 123)

D35 galliard (P35)
Lute: **64** (f. 37v), **185** (f. 26v)

D36 Mr. Knight's Galliard (P36)
Lute: **63** (f. 56r), **64** (f. 19v)

D37 Galliard for Two to Play Upon One Lute/My Lord Chamberlain, his Galliard (P37)
† Primary: **1** (f. L2v)
Lute: **56** (f. 32v, variant), **64** (f. 90r)

D38 Mr. Bucton's Galliard/Galliard/The Right Honorable the Lord Viscount Lisle, his Galliard/Sir Robert Sidney's Galliard/Suzanna Galliard* (P38)/(P91)
  † Primary: **4** (19), **6** (f. B1r)
  Lute: **57** (f. 52r, variant)
  Consort: **21** (Galliard XVIII)

D39 Round Battle Galliard (P39)
  Lute: **212** (f. 6r, possible consort part)
  Consort: **61** (f. 5r, bass viol), **62** (f. 5v, recorder), **65** (f. 36v, cittern)

D40 Battle Galliard/King of Denmark's Galliard/The Most High and Mighty Christianus the Fourth, King of Denmark, his Galliard (P40)
  † Primary: **4** (11), **7** (ff. L2v–M1r)
  Lute: **20** (pp. 112–13), **64** (ff. 23r, 94v), **107** (ff. 12v–13r), **109** (ff. 17v–18r), **119** (f. 7v, misattrib. to Johnson), **120** (ff. 17v–18r), **134** (f. 5v), **155** (f. 239r), **166** (pp. 198, 202, 518), **182** (ff. 22v; 22v–23r, var.), **194** (f. 33r), **212** (ff. 10v–11r)
  Keyboard: **177** (ff. 50v–52r, arr. Scheidt)

D41 The Most Sacred Queen Elizabeth, her Galliard/K. Darcy's Galliard/Do. Re. Ha. Galliard (P41)
  † Primary: **7** (f. M1v)
  Lute: **57** (f. 59r)
  Consort: **61** (f. 5v, bass viol), **62** (f. 6r, recorder), **65** (f. 20r, cittern)

D42 "Can she excuse my wrongs"/Earl of Essex Galliard/Galliard Can She Excuse/The Right Honorable Robert, Earl of Essex, his Galliard (P42)/(P89)
  † Primary: **1** (V), **4** (12), **7** (f. M2r), **212** (f. 16r, signed)
  Lute: **20** (pp. 121, 122, var. Strobelius), **26** (f. 99r), **49** (pp. 36–40), **55** (f. 48r), **57** (ff. 40v, 62v), **68** (f. 55r), **89** (f. 24r), **110** (f. 11v), **135** (f. 41r), **145** (nos. 131, 152, melody only), **150** (p. 31), **155** (ff. 30r, 114r, 124v, 239r, 247v), **159** (ff. 136v–137r), **164** (ff. 2r, 2v, 56v–57r), **172** (ff. 6v, 7r–v, 7v–8r, 65v, 66r), **176** (f. 22v), **182** (ff. 22v–23r, 58v), **185** (f. 22v, duet)
  Song: **15** (pp. 66–9), **69** (f. 63r), **70** (ff. 1v–2r), **97** (f. 42v), **105** (ff. 2r, 7v, 8r), **124** (f. 8r), **138** (pp. 4–5)
  Consort: **23** (f. 46, a4), **25** (Galliarda II), **30** (no. 6), **66** (f. 37r, lute consort part)
  Cittern: **35** (ff. E2v, E3v), **60** (f. 28r)
  Keyboard: **67** (p. 306), **69** (ff. 79v–80r), **148** (ff. 8r, 117v), **170** (no. 71), **195** (ff. 62v–63r)
  Lyra Viol: **74** (pp. 67–7), **131** (p. 107)
  Orpharion: **12** (f. B4v)
  Recorder: **53** (f. 30r–v)
  Violin: **33** (p. 188)

D43 Lady Rich's Galliard/Dowland's Bells (P43)
  † Primary: **7** (f. N1r)
  Lute: **63** (f. 9r), **64** (f. 91v), **72** (pp. 190, 381), **74** (p. 37), **109** (f. 18r), **118** (f. 8r), **134** (f. 5r), **160** (p. 88), **161** (pp. 146–7), **166** (p. 147), **172** (f. 3r), **182** (ff. 21r, 21v, 56v), **185** (ff. 21v, 392v), **194** (ff. 25v–26r)

Consort: **95** (f. 30v)
Keyboard: **188** (pt. 2, no. 43, arr. Nörmiger)

D44 Earl of Derby's Galliard (P44)
† Primary: **7** (f. M2v)
Lute: **63** (f. 38r), **66** (ff. 1r, 2r), **89** (f. 21r), **119** (f. 13v), **134** (f. 7r), **161** (p. 142), **214** (ff. 39v–40v)

D45 K. Darcy's Spirit/The Right Honorable the Lady Clifton's Spirit* (P45)
† Primary: **7** (ff. N1v–2r)
Lute: **57** (f. 58r)

D46 Galliard to Lachrimae (P46)
† Primary: **5** (XXII)
Lute: **115** (ff. 44v–45r), **214** (ff. 27r–28r). Pairs with pavan **D15**
Keyboard: **113** (ff. 7v–8v, arr. Cosyn)

D47 Sir John Smith, his Almain (P47)
† Primary: **7** (ff. P2v–Q1r), **212** (ff. 13v–14r, signed)
Lute: **54** (f. 10r), **72** (p. 384), **74** (p. 7, duet part), **107** (f. 8v), **153** (f. 43v), **155** (f. 43r), **161** (p. 148), **163** (f. 21r), **185** (f. 503r), **194** (ff. 16v–17r)
Keyboard: **136** (no. 11)

D48 Lady Laiton's Almain (P48)
† Primary: **212** (f. 11v, signed)
Lute: **14** (f. 139v), **20** (p. 80), **27** (f. 59r), **54** (f. 10v), **57** (f. 48r), **118** (f. 10r), **134** (f. 5r), **135** (f. 28r), **161** (pp. 145–6), **166** (pp. 347, 367, 491, 498), **168** (p. 2), **172** (f. 36v), **182** (f. 66v), **185** (ff. 492r–493r), **189** (ff. 59v–60r), **205** (f. 17r)
Song: **15** (pp. 197–203)
Bandora: **117** (f. 11r)
Cittern: **65** (f. 28v), **202** (ff. 13v–14r)
Keyboard: **125** (ff. 6v, 5v–r), **148** (ff. 120v–121r), **195** (f. 10v)

D49 almain (P49)
Lute: **57** (ff. 38r, 47r), **166** (p. 479)

D50 Mrs. White's Choice/Mrs White's Thing (P50)
Lute: **54** (f. 6r), **57** (f. 63v), **107** (f. 2r), **109** (f. 19r), **119** (f. 7r), **145** (ff. 10v, 11r–v), **205** (f. 15r)
Cittern: **60** (f. 31v)

D51 almain* (P51)
Lute: **63** (f. 32r)

D52 Mistress Nichols Almand/Mrs. Nichols Almain (P52)
† Primary: **4** (20)
Lute: **27** (f. 58r), **57** (f. 100v), **89** (f. 24r), **155** (f. 46v), **166** (pp. 296, 448), **189** (f. 60v)
Consort: **24** (LXXI), **43** (IIX), **93** (ff. 9r, 64r)

D53 Mrs. Clifton's Almain (P53)
  † Primary: **212** (f. 23v, in Dowland's hand)
  Lute: **64** (f. 28v), **89** (f. 44r)

D54 Lady Hunsdon's Almain/Lady Hunsdon's Puffe (P54)
  † Primary: **212** (f. 22v, in Dowland's hand and signed)
  Lute: **63** (f. 7r), **64** (f. 38r), **92** (f. 2r), **153** (ff. 44v–45r), **166** (pp. 454, 499), **183** (f. 113v), **190** (ff. 59v–60r), **200** (f. 1v), **201** (f. 17r), **211** (pp. 26–7, 79), **213** (p. 78)
  Song: **37** (XI, opening melody only)
  Keyboard: **178** (f. 5r–v)

D55 Mrs. Winter's Jump/Courante (P55)
  Lute: **89** (f. 24v), **102** (f. 23r), **166** (p. 241), **169** (pp. 12–13), **212** (f. 5v)
  Consort: **34** (CLVII, CCC)
  Orpharion: **12** (f. D1r)

D56 Mrs. White's Nothing (P56)
  Lute: **57** (f. 22r)

D57 Mrs. Vaux's Jig (P57)
  Lute: **64** (f. 20v)

D58 The Shoemaker's Wife, a Toy (P58)
  Lute: **63** (f. 6v), **64** (f. 21v)

D59 Tarleton's Resurrection (P59)
  Lute: **205** (f. 11r)

D60 "Come again, sweet love doth now invite"/Come Away (P60)
  † Primary: **1** (XVII)
  Lute: **66** (f. 21v), **164** (ff. 1v, 64v), **166** (pp. 472, 502)
  Song: **18** (no. 60), **47** (p. 167), **73** (S: f. O3v, Q: f. N3v), **76** (p. 53), **84** (ff. 9r, 23v–24r), **86** (T: p. 183, B: p. 198), **97** (ff. 26v–27r), **99** (f. 11v), **103** (f. 85r), **105** (ff. 3v, 9r), **124** (f. 10v), **132** (ff. 49v–50v), **138** (pp. 14–15), **164** (f. 32v), **203** (ff. 75v, 86r)
  Consort: **61** (ff. 26v, 28r, bass viol)
  Cittern: **202** (f. 11r)
  Keyboard: **121** (ff. 16v–17r), **180** (ff. 54v–55v, 56r–57r), **209** (f. 14r)
  Recorder: **51** (ff. 36v–39r), **52** (ff. 38v–41r)

D61 Orlando Sleepeth (P61)
  Lute: **20** (p. 47), **26** (ff. 106r, 106v), **57** (f. 55v), **74** (p. 111), **118** (f. 5v), **120** (f. 1r), **140** (f. 22v), **150** (p. 50), **164** (ff. 23v, 38r), **185** (f. 399r)
  Consort: **182** (f. 1r, treble and bandora)
  Cittern: **65** (ff. 17v, 28v)

D62 Fortune my foe (P62)
  Lute: **12** (f. F3r–v), **26** (f. 106v), **50** (p. 8), **59** (f. 11v), **64** (f. 89r, duet part), **74** (pp. 14, 111), **89** (f. 27r), **115** (f. 79v), **118** (f. 9v), **134** (f. 2r), **135** (ff.

34r, 38r), **153** (ff. 11v–12r), **157** (ff. 158v, 159r, 159v, 160r–159v), **161** (pp. 20–4), **162** (ff. 8v–9r), **166** (p. 412), **167** (f. 45r–v), **169** (p. 13), **182** (ff. 7v, 20v, 27v, 60r), **185** (ff. 387r, 387v, 388r, 477r), **189** (f. 62r), **191** (f. 16r), **193** (ff. 13r–13v, 13v), **194** (f. 14r), **212** (f. 57r), **214** (ff. 18v–21r)

Song: **47** (pp. 132–3), **75** (pp. 49–50), **81** (pt. III, after p. 65)

Consort: **62** (f. 1r, recorder), **65** (f. 21v, cittern)

Keyboard: **41** (II, pp. 143–56, var.), **67** (pp. 123–5), **83** (ff. 14v–20r), **114** (ff. 127v–130r), **116** (f. 7r), **129** (ff. 20r–21v), **146** (pp. 174–81, 185), **148** (f. 24r), **152** (ff. 27v–28v), **171** (no. 47), **181** (ff. 132r–134r), **186** (ff. 34v–35r), **195** (f. 34r)

Lyra Viol: **16** (ff. F2v–G1r), **66** (f. 15r), **122** (p. 12, arr. Sumarte)

D63 Complaint (P63)
Lute: **57** (f. 56r)
Consort: **61** (f. 5r, bass viol), **62** (f. 5r, recorder), **65** (f. 21v, cittern)
Cittern: **60** (f. 23r)

D64 Go from my window (P64)
Lute: **36** (f. H1r, arr. Robinson), **63** (ff. 39v–40r), **89** (ff. 17v–18r), **109** (f. 29v)
Orpharion: **12** (ff. C2v–4r)

D65 Lord Strang's March (P65)
Lute: **57** (f. 58r)

D66 My Lord Willoughby's Welcome Home (P66)
† Primary: **212** (f. 9v, first part of duet, signed)
Lute: **14** (f. 134v), **26** (f. 107v), **36** (ff. K2v–L1v, arr. Robinson), **49** (pp. 47–8), **57** (ff. 14v, 58v), **63** (f. 28v), **89** (f. 38r), **109** (ff. 25r; 33v, arr. of Byrd arr.?), **118** (f. 1r), **119** (f. 11v, duet part), **140** (f. 21v), **142** (no. 8), **145** (f. 12v), **153** (f. 49v), **166** (p. 372), **176** (f. 36r), **182** (ff. 14v, 41r, 57r), **185** (f. 389r), **189** (f. 24r), **198** (pp. 331–2), **205** (f. 12r)
Song: **47** (p. 83, Dutch words added)
Keyboard: **67** (pp. 278–9, arr. Byrd), **101** (ff. 115v, 116r–v), **111** (ff. 146v–148v, arr. Byrd), **114** (ff. 13v–14v, arr. Byrd), **154** (pp. 280–2), **195** (f. 2r)
Consort: **40** (no. 28, arr. Strobelius)

D67 Walsingham (P67)
Lute: **64** (ff. 67v–68r, var.), **150** (p. 35), **182** (f. 24r), **205** (f. 17r)

D68 Aloe (P68)
Lute: **56** (f. 25r), **63** (ff. 38v–39r), **89** (ff. 21v–22r)

D69 Loth to Depart (P69, some versions of questionable authorship)
Lute: **57** (f. 9r), **64** (ff. 68v–69v), **89** (f. 31r), **109** (f. 33r), **120** (f. 7v)

D70 Robin (P70, some arrangements of questionable authorship)
Lute: **20** (pp. 114–15), **54** (f. 12r), **55** (f. 32v), **57** (ff. 53r, 66r), **64** (ff. 29v–30r), **74** (p. 113), **89** (f. 31r), **102** (f. 25r), **109** (ff. 22v, 35r), **118** (f. 8r), **120** (f. 12v), **164** (f. 3v), **182** (f. 6v), **212** (f. 16v)

Bandora: **64** (f. 81v)
Consort: **58** (f. 11r, consort lute)
Lyra Viol: **66** (ff. 19v–20r)

D71 fantasia* (P71)
Lute: **31** (pp. 28–9), **109** (ff. 23v–24r)

D72 fantasia* (P72)
Lute: **89** (ff. 42v–43r)

D73 fantasia* (P73)
Lute: **64** (ff. 44v–45v)

D74 fantasia* (P74)
Lute: **29** (pp. 226–8), **102** (f. 24r), **194** (ff. 27v–31r)

D75 A Dream* (P75)
Lute: **57** (f. 48r), **110** (f. 3r)
Cittern: **65** (f. 26v)

D76 galliard* (P76)
Lute: **64** (f. 19v), **89** (f. 42r)

D77 Mrs. Norrish's Delight* (P77)
Lute: **72** (p. 382)

D78 jig* (P78)
Lute: **89** (f. 26r)

D79 "What if a day"* (P79)
† Primary: **212** (f. 23r, in Dowland's hand)
Lute: **56** (f. 2r), **64** (f. 62v), **78** (p. 127), **109** (f. 19r), **155** (f. 186r), **197** (f. 19r), **212** (f. 87r)*
Song: **11** (XVII), **15** (pp. 146–9), **18** (no. 17), **22** (p. 140), **45** (p. 77), **47** (p. 248), **86** (C: p. 189, T: p. 178, B: p. 183), **97** (ff. 25v–26r, 69v–70r), **103** (ff. 81v–82r), **127** (f. 109v), **131** (p. 115), **203** (f. 34v)
Keyboard: **148** (f. 15r–v), **152** (f. 42r), **208** (pp. 70–1)
Cittern: **35** (f. K2r), **60** (f. 32r)
Mandora: **80** (pp. 113–14)
Lyra Viol: **122** (p. 12, arr. Sumarte)

D80 A Coy Toy* (P80)
Lute: **118** (f. 7r)

D81 Tarleton's Jig* (P81)
Lute: **57** (f. 56r)
Consort: **58** (ff. 17r, cittern; 53r, lute), **61** (f. 5r, bass viol), **62** (f. 5r, recorder)
Cittern: **60** (f. 25r)

D82 galliard* (P82)
Lute: **64** (f. 22r–v)

D83 My Lady Mildmay's Delight* (P83) [by Robert Johnson?]
  Lute: **66** (f. 11r), **107** (f. 16v), **118** (f. 12v), **134** (ff. 15v–16r), **212** (f. 22r)

D84 Hasellwood's Galliard* (P84) [arr. of consort work by A. Holborne]
  Lute: **64** (f. 17r, Holborne, arr. Dowland?), **110** (f. 5r)

D85 galliard* (P85)
  Lute: **54** (f. 7r), **57** (f. 71v), **72** (p. 386), **89** (f. 29), **102** (f. 34), **166** (pp. 218, 234),
    185 (f. 33r)

D86 pavan* (P86)
  Lute: **166** (p. 114)

D87 galliard* (P87)
  Lute: **166** (p. 195)

D88 Piper's Galliard variant (P88), see **D19**

D89 Can She Excuse variant (P89), see **D42**

D90 Frog Galliard variant (P90), see **D23**

D91 Suzanna Galliard (Lord Viscount Lisle variant, P91), see **D38**

D92 Galliard Fr. Cutting (galliard variant, P92), see **D24**

D93 Une jeune filette* (P93)
  Lute: **161** (pp. 25–8)

D94 pavan (P94)
  Lute: **161** (pp. 28–31)
  Consort: **43** (V)

D95 La mia Barbara (pavan) (P95)
  Lute: **161** (pp. 49–51)
  Consort: **42** (XI)
  Keyboard: **196** (ff. 1v–3r, arr. Siefert)

D96 almain (P96)
  Lute: **120** (f. 13r)

D97 Queen's Galliard (P97)
  Lute: **57** (f. 62r), **120** (f. 24r). Opening phrase based on same material as **D41**

D98 preludium (P98)
  Lute: **120** (f. 29r)

D99 Mr. Dowland's Midnight (P99)
  Lute: **120** (f. 26v)

D100 Coranto (P100)
  Lute: **120** (f. 30r)

D101 fantasia* (P101)
    Lute: **176** (f. 17r)

D102 prelude* (P102)
    Lute: **176** (f. 17r)

D103 galliard* (P103)
    Lute: **176** (f. 6v)

D104 galliard (P104)
    Lute: **57** (f. 41r), **110** (f. 7r)
    Cittern: **202** (f. 10v, arr. Sprignell)
    Bandora: **57** (f. 44r)

D105 galliard (P105)
    Lute: **172** (f. 4v)

D106 pavan
    Lute: **31** (pp. 52–3)

D107 pavan
    Lute: **31** (pp. 54–6)

D108 Galliard on Gregory Huet's Galliard
    Lute: **182** (f. 66r)

D109 Dowland's Allmaine
    Consort: **93** (ff. 6v, 61v)

D110 volta
    Consort: **43** (XXXIX)

D111 Sir Henry Guildford, his Almain*
    † Primary: **7** (f. P1r)

D112 Mrs. Jane Leighton's Choice*
    Lute: **118** (f. 6v)

D113 Monsieur's Almain*
    Lute: **54** (f. 12v), **58** (f. 35v, first part of duet), **59** (f. 12r), **64** (ff. 53v–54r), **161**
    (pp. 147–8), **179** (ff. 140r–139v), **182** (f. 1r), **212** (f. 13r)

D114 Lachrimae antiquae novae
    † Primary: **4** (2)
    Consort: **42** (III)

D115 Lachrimae gementes
    † Primary: **4** (3)

D116 Lachrimae tristes
    † Primary: **4** (4)

D117 Lachrimae coactae
　　† Primary: **4** (5)

D118 Lachrimae amantis
　　† Primary: **4** (6)

D119 Lachrimae verae
　　† Primary: **4** (7)

D120 Sir Henry Umpton's Funeral
　　† Primary: **4** (9)

D121 Mr. Nicholas Gryffith, his Galliard
　　† Primary: **4** (16)
　　Lute: **27** (f. 51v)

D122 Mr. Thomas Collier, his Galliard
　　† Primary: **4** (17)
　　Lute: **27** (f. 53v)

D123 Mr. George Whitehead, his Almand
　　† Primary: **4** (21)
　　Lute: **27** (f. 57v)

D124 Fuga
　　† Primary: **98** (f. 88r, signed)

D125 "Unquiet thoughts"
　　† Primary: **1** (I)
　　Song: **69** (f. 61v), **79** (f. 19r), **124** (ff. 3v–4r), **203** (f. 149r)
　　Keyboard: **148** (f. 6r)

D126 "Whoever thinks or hopes of love for love"
　　† Primary: **1** (II)
　　Song: **69** (f. 61v), **105** (ff. 2r, 8r), **124** (ff. 2v–3r)
　　Keyboard: **148** (f. 6v)

D127 "Dear if you change I'll never choose again"
　　† Primary: **1** (VII)
　　Song: **69** (f. 64r), **84** (f. 7r), **105** (ff. 3r, 9v), **124** (f. 9v), **138** (pp. 18–19)
　　Keyboard: **148** (f. 8v)

D128 "Burst forth my tears"
　　† Primary: **1** (VIII)
　　Song: **69** (f. 64v), **105** (ff. 2v, 8v), **124** (f. 11v), **138** (pp. 10–11)

D129 "Go crystal tears"
　　† Primary: **1** (IX)
　　Song: **69** (f. 65r), **124** (f. 10r)
　　Keyboard: **148** (f. 9r)

D130 "Think'st thou then by thy feigning"
    † Primary: **1** (X)
    Song: **87** (p. 44), **124** (f. 6r)
    Keyboard: **148** (f. 13v)

D131 "Come away, come sweet love"
    † Primary: **1** (XI)
    Song: **87** (p. 44), **105** (ff. 2v, 8v), **124** (f. 6v)
    Keyboard: **148** (f. 13v)

D132 "Rest awhile you cruel cares"
    † Primary: **1** (XII)
    Song: **70** (ff. 3v–4r), **73** (S: f. R3v, Q: ff. O3v, O4r), **105** (ff. 3r, 8v), **124** (f. 8v),
        207 (f. 8r)
    Keyboard: **148** (f. 9v)

D133 "Sleep wayward thoughts"
    † Primary: **1** (XIII)
    Song: **18** (no. 20), **32** (p. 41), **73** (S: f. R2r, Q: ff. O1v, O2r), **86** (C: p. 202, T: p. 184,
        B: p. 200), **87** (p. 44), **88** (p. 71), **94** (f. 7r), **95** (f. 4v), **97** (ff. 28v–29r), **100**
        (f. 2r), **103** (f. 85v), **105** (ff. 3r, 9r), **124** (f. 7v), **131** (p. 46), **132** (f. 16r), **138**
        (pp. 12–13), **203** (f. 67r)
    Lute: **85** (p. 6), **215** (f. 6v, index only)
    Lyra Viol: **108** (f. 91)
    Keyboard: **94** (f. 22v), **148** (f. 10v)
    Mandora: **80** (pp. 114–15)

D134 "All ye whom love or fortune hath betrayed"
    † Primary: **1** (XIV)
    Song: **105** (ff. 3r, 9r), **204** (ff. 12v, 12v, 28v)
    Keyboard: **148** (f. 10r)

D135 "Wilt thou unkind thus reave me of my heart"
    † Primary: **1** (XV)
    Song: **95** (f. 6r), **124** (f. 12r)
    Keyboard: **148** (f. 13r)

D136 "Would my conceit that first enforced my woe"
    † Primary: **1** (XVI)
    Song: **73** (S: f. S3v, Q: f. P3v)

D137 "His golden locks Time hath to silver turned"
    † Primary: **1** (XVIII)
    Song: **105** (f. 9r–v), **124** (f. 11r), **138** (pp. 16–17)
    Keyboard: **148** (f. 11r)

D138 "Come heavy sleep"
    † Primary: **1** (XX)
    Keyboard: **148** (f. 11v)

D139 "Away with these self-loving lads"
    † Primary: **1** (XXI)
    Song: **84** (f. 9), **87** (p. 44), **99** (f. 12r), **124** (f. 12v), **138** (pp. 8–9)
    Keyboard: **148** (f. 13r)

D140 "Praise God upon the lute and viol"/Psalm 150 (three-voice canon)
    † Primary: **2** (title)
    Song: **99** (f. 25v)

D141 "I saw my lady weep"
    † Primary: **2** (I)

D142 "Sorrow stay, lend true repentant tears"
    † Primary: **2** (III)
    Song: **96** (f. 9r, arr. Wigthorpe), **97** (ff. 31v–32r), **106** (C: ff. 58v–59r, Q: f. 57r–v,
        A: ff. 77v–78r, T: ff. 56v–57r, B: f. 61r), **131** (p. 70)
    Keyboard: **148** (ff. 77r–78r)

D143 "Die not before thy day"
    † Primary: **2** (IV)

D144 "Mourn, mourn, day is with darkness fled"
    † Primary: **2** (V)

D145 "Time's eldest son, old age" (Second part: "Then sit thee down," Third part: "When
    others sing")
    † Primary: **2** (VI–VIII)

D146 "Praise blindness eyes, for seeing is deceit"
    † Primary: **2** (X)
    Song: **138** (pp. 28–9)
    Keyboard: **148** (f. 58v)

D147 "O sweet woods, the delight of solitariness"
    † Primary: **2** (X)

D148 "If floods of tears could cleanse my follies past" (some feature lyrics set to the tune
    of "Sleep Wayward")
    † Primary: **2** (XI)
    Song: **18** (no. 13), **80** (pp. 114–15, words), **86** (C: p. 202, T: p. 184, B: p. 200), **103**
        (f. 85v, words), **132** (f. 11r–v), **138** (pp. 24–5), **203** (f. 74v)

D149 "Fine knacks for ladies"
    † Primary: **2** (XII)
    Song: **84** (ff. 30v–31r)

D150 "Now cease my wandering eyes"
    † Primary: **2** (XIII)
    Keyboard: **148** (ff. 58v–59r)

D151 "Come ye heavy states of night"
† Primary: **2** (XIV)
Song: **131** (p. 47)

D152 "White as lilies was her face"
† Primary: **2** (XV)
Song: **18** (no. 40), **132** (f. 33r–v)
Keyboard: **148** (f. 59r)

D153 "Woeful heart with grief oppressed"
† Primary: **2** (XVI)

D154 "A shepherd in a shade"
† Primary: **2** (XVII)
Song: **18** (no. 56), **132** (ff. 45v–46v), **138** (pp. 22–3)

D155 "Faction that ever dwells in court"
† Primary: **2** (XVIII)
Keyboard: **148** (ff. 59r–60v)

D156 "Shall I sue, shall I seek for grace"
† Primary: **2** (XIX)
Song: **87** (p. 44), **138** (pp. 30–1), **203** (f. 64r)
Keyboard: **148** (f. 77r)

D157 "Toss not my soul"
† Primary: **2** (XX)
Song: **138** (pp. 26–7)

D158 "Clear or cloudy, sweet as April showering"
† Primary: **2** (XXI)

D159 "Humor say what mak'st thou here"
† Primary: **2** (XXII)
Song: **94** (f. 12r), **138** (pp. 20–1, a5)

D160 "Farewell too fair"
† Primary: **3** (I)

D161 "Time stands still"
† Primary: **3** (II)

D162 "Behold a wonder here"
† Primary: **3** (III)
Song: **18** (no. 46), **132** (f. 38r)

D163 "Daphne was not so chaste as she was changing"
† Primary: **3** (IV)

D164 "Me, me, and none but me"
† Primary: **3** (V)

D165 "When Phoebus first did Daphne love"
    † Primary: **3** (VI)

D166 "Say Love, if ever thou didst find"
    † Primary: **3** (VII)

D167 "Flow not so fast ye fountains"
    † Primary: **3** (VIII)

D168 "What if I never speed"
    † Primary: **3** (IX)
    Song: **203** (f. 66v)

D169 "Love stood amazed at sweet Beauty's pain"
    † Primary: **3** (X)

D170 "Lend your ears to my sorrow, good people"
    † Primary: **3** (XI)

D171 "By a fountain where I lay"
    † Primary: **3** (XII)

D172 "O what hath overwrought my all amazed thought"
    † Primary: **3** (XIII)

D173 "Farewell unkind, farewell"
    † Primary: **3** (XIV)

D174 "Weep you no more, sad fountains"
    † Primary: **3** (XV)

D175 "Fie on this feigning, is love without desire"
    † Primary: **3** (XVI)

D176 "I must complain, yet do enjoy my love"
    † Primary: **3** (XVII)

D177 "It was a time when silly bees could speak"
    † Primary: **3** (XVIII)
    Song: **18** (no. 54), **94** (f. 21r), **132** (f. 44r–v)

D178 "The lowest trees have tops"
    † Primary: **3** (XIX)
    Song: **18** (no. 27), **132** (ff. 21v–22r)

D179 "What poor astronomers are they"
    † Primary: **3** (XX)

D180 "Come when I call or tarry till I come"
    † Primary: **3** (XXI)

D181 "Disdain me still that I may ever love"
    † Primary: **5** (I)

D182 "Sweet stay awhile, why will you rise"
  † Primary: **5** (II)

D183 "To ask for all thy love"
  † Primary: **5** (III)

D184 "Love those beams that breed"
  † Primary: **5** (IV)

D185 "Were every thought an eye"
  † Primary: **5** (VI)
  Consort: **43** (X)

D186 "Stay Time, awhile thy flying"
  † Primary: **5** (VII)

D187 "Tell me true Love"
  † Primary: **5** (VIII)

D188 "Go nightly cares, the enemy to rest"
  † Primary: **5** (IX)

D189 "From silent night, true register of moans"
  † Primary: **5** (X)

D190 "Lasso vita mia, mi fa morire"
  † Primary: **5** (XI)

D191 "In this trembling shadow cast"
  † Primary: **5** (XII)

D192 "If that a sinner's sighs be angel's food"
  † Primary: **5** (XIII)

D193 "Thou mighty God" (Second part: "When David's life," Third part: "When the poor cripple")
  † Primary: **5** (XIV–XVI)

D194 "Where sin sore-wounding"
  † Primary: **5** (XVII)

D195 "My heart and tongue were twins"
  † Primary: **5** (XVIII)

D196 "Up merry mates, to Neptune's praise"
  † Primary: **5** (XIX)

D197 "Welcome black night, Hymen's fair day"
  † Primary: **5** (XX)

D198 "Cease these false sports"
  † Primary: **5** (XXI)

D199 "Far from triumphing court"
    † Primary: **6** (VIII)

D200 "Lady if you so spite me"/Aria
    † Primary: **6** (IX)
    Consort: **43** (XIX)

D201 "In darkness let me dwell"
    † Primary: **6** (X)

D202 "Adieu, sweet Amaryllis"* (lost and doubtful)
    Lute: **216**

D203 "An heart that's broken and contrite" (Psalm 51)
    † Primary: **8** (9)
    Song: **94** (f. 14r), **112** (f. 4v)

D204 "I shame at mine unworthiness"
    † Primary: **8** (19)
    Song: **112** (f. 28v)

D205 "Put me not to rebuke, O Lord" (Psalm 38). Other psalm titles in same volume using the same tune: "Before the Lord with my voice"/"The foolish man in that which he"/"Have mercy upon me O God"/"Have mercy upon me I pray"/"How long wilt thou forget me Lord"/"How pleasant is thy dwelling place"/"I mercy will and judgments sing"/"In speechless silence do not hold"/"In trouble and adversity"/"Lord be my judge and thou shalt see"/"The Lord be thanked for his gifts"/"Lord bow thine ear to my request"/"Lord plead my cause against my foes"/"The man is blessed whose wickedness"/"My Lord my God in all distress"/"O come let us lift up our voice"/"O give ye thanks unto the Lord"/"O Lord give ear to thy just cause"/"O Lord thou didst us clean forsake"/"O Lord unto my voice give ear"/"O sing ye now unto the Lord"/"Praise ye the Lord, for he is good"/"A Thanksgiving"/"Thee will I praise with my whole heart"/"Thou art O Lord, my strength and stay"/"Thou hast been merciful in deed"/"Thou heard that Israel dost keep"/"To these my words and plaint"/"Unto God we will give thanks"/"What is the cause that thou O Lord"/"When Israel by God's address"/"Why did the Gentiles tumults raise"/"Ye people all with one accord"
    † Primary: **10** (used in twenty-two settings in 1592, thirty-two settings in later
       volumes)
    Song: **44** (Psalm 5)

D206 "All people that on earth do dwell"/"Behold now give heed"/"Praise the Lord all ye Gentiles all"/Psalm 100 (harmonization i)
    † Primary: **10** (pp. 172–3, 260–1)
    Lute: **206** (f. 95r)

D207 "My soul praise the Lord" (Psalm 104)
    † Primary: **10** (pp. 180–3)

D208 "Lord to thee I make my moan" (Psalm 103) [i]
   † Primary: **10** (pp. 228–31)

D209 "Behold and have regard"/Psalm 134
   † Primary: **10** (pp. 234–5)

D210 "O God of power omnipotent"/"A prayer for the Queen's most excellent Majesty"
   † Primary: **10** (pp. 274–5)

D211 "All people that on earth do dwell"/Psalm 100 (harmonization ii)
   † Primary: **9** (pp. 172–3)
   Song: **91** (no. 11)

D212 *Lamentatio Henrici Noel*/"O Lord turn not away thy face"/"The Lamentation of a Sinner"
   † Primary: **123** (f. 2r)

D213 "Lord in thy wrath reprove me not" (Psalm 6)/"Domine ne in Furore"
   † Primary: **123** (f. 2v)

D214 "O Lord consider my distress" (Psalm 51)/"Miserere mei Deus"
   † Primary: **123** (f. 3r)

D215 "O Lord of whom I do depend"/"Humble suit of a sinner"
   † Primary: **123** (f. 3v)

D216 "Where righteousness doth say"/"Humble complaint of a sinner"
   † Primary: **123** (f. 4r)

D217 "Lord to thee I make my moan" (Psalm 103) [ii]/"De profundis"
   † Primary: **123** (f. 4v)

D218 "Lord hear my prayer, hark the plaint" (Psalm 143)/"Domine Exaudi"
   † Primary: **123** (f. 5r)

ALPHABETICAL WORKS LIST

"Adieu, sweet Amaryllis" **D202**

"All people that on earth do dwell" (harmonization i) **D206**

"All people that on earth do dwell" (harmonization ii) **D211**

"All ye whom love or fortune hath betrayed" **D134**

almain **D49, D51, D54, D96**

Aloe **D68**

Aria **D200**

"Awake sweet love, thou art returned" **D24**

"Away with these self-loving lads" **D139**

Battle Galliard **D40**

"Before the Lord with my voice" (Psalm 142) **D205**

"Behold a wonder here" **D162**

"Behold and have regard" (Psalm 134) **D209**

"Behold now give heed" **D206**

"Burst forth my tears" **D128**

"By a fountain where I lay" **D171**

"Can she excuse my wrongs" **D42**

Captain Candish, his Gallard **D21**

Captain Digorie Piper's Galliard **D19**

Captain Piper, his Galliard **D19**

Captain Piper's Pavan **D8**

"Cease these false sports" **D198**

"Clear or cloudy, sweet as April showering" **D158**

"Come again, sweet love doth now invite" **D60**

Come away (lute solo) **D60**

"Come away, come sweet love" **D131**

"Come heavy sleep" **D138**

"Come when I call or tarry till I come" **D180**

"Come ye heavy states of night" **D151**

Complaint **D63**

Coranto **D100**

courante **D55**

A Coy Toy **D80**

"Daphne was not so chaste as she was changing" **D163**

"De Profundus" (Psalm 130) **D217**

"Dear if you change I'll never choose again" **D127**

"Die not before thy day" **D143**

"Disdain me still that I may ever love" **D181**

Do. Re. Ha. Galliard **D41**

"Domine exaudi" **D218**

"Domine ne in furore" (Psalm 6) **D213**

Dowland's Adieu for Master Oliver Cromwell **D13**

Dowland's Allmaine **D109**

Dowland's Bells **D43**

Dr. Case's Pavan **D12**

A Dream **D75**

Earl of Derby's Galliard **D44**

Earl of Essex Galliard **D42**

"Faction that ever dwells in court" **D155**

fantasia **D1, D2, D3, D4, D5, D6, D7, D71, D72, D73, D74, D101**

"Far from triumphing court" **D199**

Farewell (fantasia) **D3**

Farewell (fantasia) **D4**

"Farewell too fair" **D160**

"Farewell unkind, farewell" **D173**

"Fie on this feigning, is love without desire" **D175**

"Fine knacks for ladies" **D149**

"Flow my tears, fall from your springs" **D15**

"Flow not so fast ye fountains" **D167**

"The foolish man in that which he" (Psalm 53) **D205**

Forlorn Hope (fantasia) **D2**

Fortune my foe **D62**

Fr. Cutting galliard **D24**

Frog Galliard **D23**

"From silent night, true register of moans" **D189**

Fuga **D124**

galliard **D20, D21, D22, D24, D27, D28, D30, D31, D35, D38, D76, D82, D85, D87, D103, D104, D105**

Galliard Can She Excuse **D42**

Galliard for Two to Play Upon One Lute **D37**

Galliard on a Galliard by Daniel Bacheler **D28**

Galliard on Gregory Huet's Galliard **D108**

Galliard to Captain Piper's Pavan **D19**

Galliard to Lachrimae **D46**

Giles Hoby's Galliard **D29**

"Go crystal tears" **D129**

Go from my Window **D64**

"Go nightly cares, the enemy to rest" **D188**

Hasellwood's Galliard **D84**

"Have mercy upon me God" (Psalm 51) **D205**

"Have mercy upon me I pray" (Psalm 56) **D205**

"An heart that's broken and contrite" (Psalm 51) **D203**

"His golden locks Time hath to silver turned" **D137**

"How long wilt thou forget me Lord" (Psalm 13) **D205**

"How pleasant is thy dwelling place" (Psalm 84) **D205**

"The humble complaint of a sinner" **D216**

"The humble suit of a sinner" **D215**

"Humor say what mak'st thou here" **D159**

"I mercy will and judgments sing" (Psalm 101) **D205**

"I must complain, yet do enjoy my love" **D176**

"I saw my lady weep" **D141**

"I shame at mine unworthiness" **D204**

"If floods of tears could cleanse my follies past" **D148**

"If my complaints could passions move" **D19**

"If that a sinner's sighs be angel's food" **D192**

"In darkness let me dwell" **D201**

"In speechless silence do not hold" (Psalm 109) **D205**

"In this trembling shadow cast" **D191**

"In trouble and adversity" (Psalm 20) **D205**

"It [/There] was a time when silly bees could speak" **D178**

jig **D78**

K. Darcy's Galliard **D41**

K. Darcy's Spirit **D45**

King of Denmark's Galliard **D40**

La mia Barbara (pavan) **D95**

Lachrimae **D15**

Lachrimae amantis **D118**

Lachrimae antiquae **D15**

Lachrimae antiquae novae **D114**

Lachrimae coactae **D117**

Lachrimae gementes **D115**

Lachrimae pavan **D15**

Lachrimae tristes **D116**

Lachrimae verae **D119**

Lady Hunsdon's Almain **D54**

Lady Hunsdon's Puffe **D54**

"Lady if you so spite me" **D200**

Lady Laiton's Almain **D48**

Lady Rich's Galliard **D43**

Lady Russell's Pavan **D17**

Lamentatio Henrici Noel **D212**

"The Lamentation of a Sinner" **D212**

"Lasso vita mia, mi fa morire" **D190**

"Lend your ears to my sorrow, good people" **D170**

"Lord be my judge and thou shalt see" (Psalm 26) **D205**

"The Lord be thanked for his gifts" **D205**

"Lord bow thine ear to my request" (Psalm 86) **D205**

"Lord hear my prayer, hark the plaint" (Psalm 143) **D218**

"Lord in thy wrath reprove me not" (Psalm 6) **D213**

"Lord plead my cause against my foes" (Psalm 35) **D205**

Lord Strang's March **D65**

"Lord to thee I make my moan" (Psalm 103) [i] **D208**

"Lord to thee I make my moan" (Psalm 103) [ii] **D217**

Loth to Depart **D69**

"Love stood amazed at sweet Beauty's pain" **D169**

"Love those beams that breed" **D184**

"The lowest trees have tops" **D178**

"The man is blessed whose wickedness" (Psalm 32) **D205**

"Me, me, and none but me" **D164**

Melancholy Galliard **D25**

Mignarda **D34**

"Miserere mei Deus" (Psalm 51) **D214**

Mistress Nichols Almand **D52**

Monsieur's Almain **D113**

The Most High and Mighty Christianus the Fourth, King of Denmark, his Galliard **D40**

The Most Sacred Queen Elizabeth, her Galliard **D41**

"Mourn, mourn, day is with darkness fled" **D144**

Mr. Bucton's Galliard **D38**

Mr. Dowland's Midnight **D99**

Mr. George Whitehead, his Almand **D123**

Mr. Giles Hobies Galliard **D29**

Mr. Henry Noel, his Galliard **D34**

Mr. John Langton's Pavan **D14**

Mr. Knight's Galliard **D36**

Mr. Langton's Galliard **D33**

Mr. Nicholas Gryffith, his Galliard **D121**

Mr. Thomas Collier, his Galliard **D122**

Mrs. Brigide Fleetwood's Pavan **D11**

Mrs. Clifton's Almain **D53**

Mrs. Jane Leighton's Choice **D112**

Mrs. Nichols Almain **D52**

Mrs. Norrish's Delight **D77**

Mrs. Vaux's Galliard **D32**

Mrs. Vaux's Jig **D57**

Mrs. White's Choice **D50**

Mrs. White's Nothing **D56**

Mrs. White's Thing **D50**

Mrs. Winter's Jump **D55**

"My heart and tongue were twins" **D195**

My Lady Mildmay's Delight **D83**

My Lord Chamberlain, his Galliard **D37**

"My Lord my God in all distress" (Psalm 71) **D205**

My Lord Willoughby's Welcome Home **D66**

"My soul praise the Lord" (Psalm 104) **D207**

"My thoughts are winged with hopes" **D26**

"Now cease my wandering eyes" **D150**

"Now O now I needs must part" **D23**

"O come let us lift up our voice" (Psalm 95) **D205**

"O give ye thanks unto the Lord" (Psalm 118) **D205**

"O God of power omnipotent" **D210**

"O Lord consider my distress" (Psalm 51) **D214**

"O Lord give ear to thy just cause" (Psalm 17) **D205**

"O Lord of whom I do depend" **D215**

"O Lord thou didst us clean forsake" (Psalm 60) **D205**

"O Lord turn not away thy face" **D212**

"O Lord unto my voice give ear" (Psalm 64) **D205**

"O sing ye now unto the Lord" (Psalm 98) **D205**

"O sweet woods, the delight of solitariness" **D147**

"O what hath overwrought my all amazed thought" **D172**

Orlando Sleepeth **D61**

pavan **D16**, **D18**, **D86**, **D94**, **D106**, **D107**

Piper's Pavan **D8**

"Praise blindness eyes, for seeing is deceit" **D146**

"Praise God Upon the Lute and Viol"/Psalm 150 (3-voice canon) **D140**

"Praise the Lord all ye Gentiles all" **D206**

"Praise ye the Lord, for he is good" (Psalm 106) **D205**

"A prayer before evening prayer" **D206**

"A prayer before morning prayer" **D206**

"A prayer for the Queen's most excellent Majesty" **D210**

prelude **D102**

preludium **D98**

Psalm 100 **D206**, **D211**

psalms **D140**, **D203**, **D205**, **D206**, **D207**, **D208**, **D209**, **D210**, **D211**, **D212**, **D213**, **D214**, **D215**, **D216**, **D217**, **D218**

"Put me not to rebuke, O Lord" (Psalm 38) **D205**

Queen Elizabeth's Galliard **D41**

Queen's Galliard **D97**

Resolution **D13**

"Rest awhile you cruel cares" **D132**

The Right Honorable Ferdinand Earl of Darby, his Galliard **D44**

The Right Honorable Robert, Earl of Essex, his Galliard **D42**

The Right Honorable the Lady Clifton's Spirit **D45**

The Right Honorable the Lord Viscount Lisle, his Galliard **D38**

Robin **D70**

Round Battle Galliard **D39**

"Say Love, if ever thou didst find" **D166**

Semper Dowland, semper dolens **D9**

"Shall I strive with words to move" **D34**

"Shall I sue, shall I seek for grace" **D156**

"A shepherd in a shade" **D154**

The Shoemaker's Wife, a Toy **D58**

Sir Henry Guilford, his Almain **D111**

Sir Henry Umpton's Funeral **D120**

Sir John Langton, his Pavan **D14**

Sir John Smith, his Almain **D47**

Sir John Souch, his Galliard **D26**

Sir Robert Sidney, his Galliard **D38**

"Sleep wayward thoughts" **D133**

Solus cum sola (pavan) **D10**

"Sorrow stay, lend true repentant tears" **D142**

"Stay Time, awhile thy flying" **D186**

Suzanna Galliard **D38**

"Sweet stay awhile, why will you rise" **D182**

Tarleton's Jig **D81**

Tarleton's Resurrection **D59**

"Tell me true Love" **D187**

"A Thanksgiving" **D205**

"Thee will I praise with my whole heart" (Psalm 138) **D205**

"Then sit thee down" **D145**

"Think'st thou then by thy feigning" **D130**

"Thou art O Lord, my strength and stay" (Psalm 28) **D205**

"Thou hast been merciful in deed" (Psalm 85) **D205**

"Thou heard that Israel dost keep" (Psalm 80) **D205**

"Thou mighty God" **D193**

"Time's eldest son, old age" **D145**

"Time stands still" **D161**

"To ask for all thy love" **D183**

"To these my words and plaint" (Psalm 5) **D205**

"Toss not my soul" **D157**

Une jeune filette **D93**

"Unquiet thoughts" **D125**

"Unto God we will give thanks" (Psalm 75) **D205**

"Up merry mates, to Neptune's praise" **D196**

volta **D110**

Walsingham **D67**

"Weep you no more, sad fountains" **D174**

"Welcome black night, Hymen's fair day" **D197**

"Were every thought an eye" **D185**

"What if a day" **D79**

"What if I never speed" **D168**

"What is the cause that thou O Lord" (Psalm 10) **D205**

"What poor astronomers are they" **D179**

"When David's life" **D193**

"When Israel by God's address" (Psalm 114) **D205**

"When others sing" **D145**

"When Phoebus first did Daphne love" **D165**

"When the poor cripple" **D193**

"Where righteousness doth say" **D216**

"Where sin sore-wounding" **D194**

"White as lilies was her face" **D152**

"Whoever thinks or hopes of love for love" **D126**

"Why did the Gentiles tumults raise" (Psalm 2) **D205**

"Wilt thou unkind thus reave me of my heart" **D135**

"Woeful heart with grief oppressed" **D153**

"Would my conceit that first enforced my woe" **D136**

"Ye people all with one accord" (Psalm 47) **D205**

3

Primary Sources

Music

PRINT SOURCES INITIATED BY DOWLAND, OR LIKELY PRODUCED WITH HIS KNOWLEDGE

1   Dowland, John. *The First Booke of Songes or Ayres of fowre partes with Tableture for the Lute: So made that all the partes together, or either of them seuerally may be Song to the Lute, Orpherian or Viol de gambo.* London: Peter Short, 1597. Reprinted in 1600, 1603, 1606, 1613.

Includes: (four voice parts, lute with cantus)

      I. Unquiet thoughts (D125)
     II. Who euer thinks or hopes of loue for loue (D126)
    III. My thoughts are wingd with hopes (D26)
    IV. If my complaints could passions moue (D19)
     V. Can she excuse my wrongs with vertues cloake (D42)
    VI. Now, O now *I* needs must part (D23)
   VII. Deare if you change ile neuer chuse againe (D127)
  VIII. Burst forth my teares (D128)
    IX. Go Cristal teares (D129)
     X. Thinkst thou then by thy faining (D130)
    XI. Come away come sweet loue (D131)
   XII. Rest a while you cruell cares (D132)
  XIII. Sleepe wayward thoughts (D133)
  XIV. All ye whom loue or fortune hath betraide (D134)
   XV. *Wilt* thou vnkind thus reaue me of my hart (D135)
  XVI. Would my conceit that first enforst my woe (D136)
 XVII. Come againe; sweet loue doth now enuite (D60)

XVIII. His goulden locks time hath to siluer turnd (D137)
  XIX. Awake sweet loue thou art returnd (D24)
   XX. Come heauy sleepe (D138)
  XXI. Awaie with these selfe louing lads (D139)

A Galliard for two to plaie vpon one Lute at the end of the booke (D37)

Facsimiles: *The First Booke of Songes or Ayres 1597.* Edited by Diana Poulton. London: Scolar, 1968. 53 p. (English Lute Songs, 1597–1632 14.) M2 .E64 no. 14; *The First Booke of Songs or Ayres of Foure Parts, with Tableture for the Lute* (1597). New York: Performers' Facsimiles, 1994. 50 p. (Performers' Facsimiles 127.) M1623.5 .D7 S61; *The First Booke of Songs 1613.* Edited by Diana Poulton. London: Scolar, 1968. 50 p. (English Lute Songs, 1597–1632 15.) ISBN 0859677036. Reprinted 1985. M2 .E64 no. 15. Digital images: (1597, Boston Public Library) https://archive.org/details/firstbookeofsong00dowl; (1600, Oxford, Bodleian Library) https://digital.bodleian.ox.ac.uk/inquire/p/03876a3a-5ea3-4b17-84c0-94d2e306e642; (1613, Oxford, Bodleian Library) https://digital.bodleian.ox.ac.uk/inquire/p/2eb397ec-ef9d-4e71-88ce-83121f5ec766.

2 Dowland, John. *The Second Booke of Songs or Ayres, of 2. 4. and 5. parts: With Tableture for the Lute or Orpherian, with the Violl de Gamba.* London: Thomas Este, 1600.

Includes: (canon)

Praise God vpon the Lute and Violl (D140)

(two voices, lute)

    I. I saw my Lady weepe (D141)
   II. Flow my teares fall from your springs (D15)
  III. Sorow sorow stay, lend true repentant teares (D142)
  IV. Dye not before thy day (D143)
   V. Mourne, mourne, day is with darknesse fled (D144)
VI.–VIII. Tymes eldest sonne, old age the heire of ease (D145)

(four voices, lute)

   IX. Praise blindnesse eies, for seeing is deceipt (D146)
    X. O sweet woods, the delight of solitarienesse (D147)
   XI. If fluds of teares could clense my follies past (D148)
  XII. Fine knacks for Ladies, cheap, choise, braue and new (D149)
 XIII. Now cease, my wandring eyes (D150)
 XIV. Come ye heauie states of night (D151)
  XV. White as Lillies was hir face (D152)
 XVI. Wofull heart with griefe oppressed (D153)
XVII. A Shepheard in a shade his plaining made (D154)
XVIII. Faction that euer dwells in court (D155)
 XIX. Shall I sue, shall I seeke for grace (D156)
  XX. Tosse not my soule (D157)

(five voices, lute, and treble viol)

    XXI. Clear or Cloudie sweet as *Aprill* showring (added treble viol part) (D158)

    XXII. Humor say what makst thou heere (dialogue: 2vv, four viols, four-part chorus, lute) (D159)

(lute and bass viol)

    Dowland's adew for Master Oliuer Cromwell (D13)

Facsimiles: *The Second Booke of Songs or Ayres 1600.* Edited by Diana Poulton. London: Scolar, 1970. 54 p. (English Lute Songs, 1597–1632 16.) ISBN 0859677044. M2 .E64 no. 16. Reprinted 1985; *The Second Booke of Songs or Ayres of Foure Parts, with Tableture for the Lute.* New York: Performers' Facsimiles, 1994. 50 p. (Performers' Facsimiles 128.) M1623.5 .D7 S62. Digital images: (Bodleian Library) https://digital. bodleian.ox.ac.uk/inquire/p/03876a3a-5ea3-4b17-84c0-94d2e306e642; (Boston Public Library) https://archive.org/details/secondbookeofson00dowl.

3   Dowland, John. *The Third and Last Booke of Songs or Aires Newly composed to sing to the Lute, Orpharion, or viols, and a dialogue for a base and meane Lute with fiue voices to sing thereto.* London: Peter Short, 1603.

Includes: (one voice, lute, bass viol)

    I. Farewell, too faire (D160)

    II. Time stands still (D161)

    III. Behold a wonder heere (D162)

    IV. Daphne was not so chaste as she was changing (D163)

(four voices, lute)

    V. Me me and none but me (D164)

    VI. When Phoebus first did Daphne loue (D165)

    VII. Say loue if euer thou didst finde (D166)

    VIII. Flow not so fast ye fountaines (D167)

    IX. What if I neuer speede (D168)

    X. Loue stood amaz'd at sweet beauties paine (D169)

    XI. Lend your eares to my sorrow good people (D170)

    XII. By a fountaine where I lay (D171)

    XIII. Oh what hath ouerwrought my all amazed thought (D172)

    XIV. Farewell vnkind farewell (D173)

    XV. Weepe you no more sad fountaines (D174)

    XVI. Fie on this faining, is loue without desire (D175)

    XVII. I must complaine, yet doe enjoy (D176)

    XVIII. It was a time when silly Bees could speake (D177)

    XIX. The lowest trees haue tops (D178)

    XX. What poore Astronomers are they (D179)

(dialogue—two voices, three viols, five-part chorus, two lutes)

    XXI. Come when I call, or tarrie till I come (D180)

Facsimiles: *The Third and Last Booke of Songs or Ayres 1603.* Edited by Diana Poulton. London: Scolar, 1970. 50 p. (English Lute Songs, 1597–1632 17.) Reprinted 1985. M2 .E64 no. 17; *The Third and Last Booke of Songs or Aires.* New York: Performers' Facsimiles, 1994. 49 p. (Performers' Facsimiles 129.) M1623.5 .D7 S63. Digital images: (Bodleian Library) https://digital.bodleian.ox.ac.uk/inquire/p/03876a3a-5ea3-4b17-84c0-94d2e306e642.

4 Dowland, John. *Lachrimae, or Seauen Teares Figured in Seauen Passionate Pauans, with diuers other Pauans, Galiards, and Almands, set forth for the Lute, Viols, or Violons, in fiue parts.* London: John Windet, 1604.

Includes: (five viols or violins and lute)

1. Lachrimæ Antiquæ (D15)
2. Lachrimæ Antiquæ novæ (D114)
3. Lachrimæ Gementes (D115)
4. Lachrimæ Tristes (D116)
5. Lachrimæ Coactæ (D117)
6. Lachrimæ Amantis (D118)
7. Lachrimæ Veræ (D119)
8. Semper Dowland semper Dolens (D9)
9. Sir Henry Vmptons Funerall (D120)
10. M. Iohn Langtons Pauan (D14)
11. The King of Denmarks Galiard (D40)
12. The Earle of Essex Galiard (D42)
13. Sir Iohn Souch his Galiard (D26)
14. M. Henry Noell his Galiard (D34)
15. M. Giles Hobies Galiard (D29)
16. M. Nicho. Gryffith his Galiard (D121)
17. M. Thomas Collier his Galiard with two trebles (D122)
18. Captaine Piper his Galiard (D19)
19. M. Bucton his Galiard (D38)
20. Mrs. Nichols Almand (D52)
21. M. George Whitehead his Almand (D123)

Facsimiles: *Lachrimae.* Edited by Warwick Edwards. Leeds: Boethius, 1974. 60 p. (Early Music Reprinted 1.) ISBN 0904263045. M672 .D68; *Lachrimae (1604).* Edited by Warwick Edwards, Stewart McCoy, and Robert Spencer. Newbury: Severinus, 1992. 56 p. (Musical Sources 5.) ISBN 086314229X. M990 .D685 L2; *Lachrimæ or, Seauen teares figured in seauen passionate pavans, with divers other pavans, galiards, and almands, set forth for the lute, viols, or violons, in five parts.* New York: Performers' Facsimiles, 1998. 49 p. (Performers' Facsimiles 209.) M990 .D68 L23. Digital images: (Bodleian Library) https://digital.bodleian.ox.ac.uk/inquire/p/03876a3a-5ea3-4b17-84c0-94d2e306e642.

5 Dowland, John. *A Pilgrimes Solace Wherein is contained Musicall Harmonie of 3. 4. and 5. parts, to be sung and plaid with the Lute and Viols.* London: Thomas Snodham, 1612.

Includes: (four voices, lute)

     I. Disdaine me still, that I may euer love (D181)
    II. Sweete stay a while, why will you? (D182)
   III. To aske for all thy loue (D183)
   IV. Loue those beames that breede (D184)
    V. Shall I striue with wordes to moue (D34)
   VI. Were euery thought an eye (D185)
  VII. Stay time a while thy flying (D186)
 VIII. Tell me true Loue (D187)

(voice, lute, two viols)

   IX. Goe nightly, cares the enemy to rest (D188)
    X. From silent night, true register of moanes (D189)
   XI. *Lasso vita mia, mi fa morire* (D190)

(four voices, lute)

    XII. In this trembling shadow cast (D191)
   XIII. If that a Sinners sighes be Angels food (D192)
XIV.–XVI. Thou mighty God (D193)
   XVII. Where Sinne sore-wounding (D194)
 XVIII. My heart and tongue were twinnes (D195)
   XIX. Vp merry Mates, to *Neptunes* praise (D196)

(voice, lute, four chorus parts)

   XX. Welcome, blacke night (D197)
  XXI. Cease these false sports (D198)

(lute)

 XXII. A Galliard to *Lachrimæ* (D46)

Facsimiles: *A Pilgrimes Solace 1612*. Edited by Diana Poulton. London: Scolar, 1970. 52 p. (English Lute Songs, 1597–1632 18.) Reprinted 1977. M2 .E64 no. 18; *A Pilgrimes Solace. Wherein is Contained Musicall Harmonie of 3. 4. and 5. Parts, to be Sung and Plaid with the Lute and Viols*. New York: Performers' Facsimiles, 1996. 50 p. (Performers' Facsimiles 195.) M1528 .D694 P5.

6   Dowland, Robert. *A Mvsicall Banqvet Furnished with varietie of delicious Ayres, Collected out of the best Authors in English, French, Spanish and Italian*. London: Thomas Adams, 1610.

Voice, lute, and bass viol. Includes **D38** (f. B1r), **D199** (VIII), **D200** (IX), **D201** (X). Facsimiles: *A Musicall Banquet*. New York: Performers' Facsimiles, 1990. 46 p. (Performers' Facsimiles 59.) M1611 .M96; *A Musicall Banquet 1610*. Edited by Diana Poulton. Menston, UK: Scolar, 1969. 49 p. (English Lute Songs, 1597–1632 19.) ISBN 0854171436, 9780854171439. Reprinted 1977. M2 .E64 no. 19.

Digital images: (University of Chicago) https://hdl.handle.net/2027/chi.16982982; (Library of Congress) https://loc.gov/item/ihas.200215646.

7   Dowland, Robert. *Varietie of Lute-lessons Viz. Fantasies, Pauins, Galliards, Almaines, Corantoes, and Volts: Selected out of the best approued Authors, as well beyond the Seas as of our owne Country*. London: Thomas Snodham, 1610.

Lute. Includes **D1** (ff. H1r–2r), **D14** (ff. K1v–2v), **D40** (ff. L2v–M1r), **D41** (f. M1v), **D42** (f. M2r), **D43** (f. N1r), **D44** (f. M2v), **D45** (ff. N1v–2r), **D47** (ff. P2v–Q1r), **D111** (f. P1r). Facsimiles: *Varietie of Lute-Lessons*. Edited by Edgar Hunt. London: Schott, 1958. vii, 72 p. MT640 .D7; *Varietie of Lvte-Lessons*. New York: Performers' Facsimiles, 1997. 72 p. (Performers' Facsimiles 159.) M140 .V35; *Varietie of Lute Lessons, London 1610*. Lübeck: Tree, 2005. 70 p. MT640 .D7 V3.

8   Leighton, William. *The Teares or Lamentacions of a Sorrowfvll Sovle: Composed with Musicall Ayres and Songs, both for Voyces and diuers Instruments*. London: William Stansby, 1614.

Consort songs. Includes **D203** (9), **D204** (19). Modern edition: *Sir William Leighton: The Tears or Lamentations of a Sorrowful Soul*. Edited by Cecil Hill. London: Stainer and Bell, 1970. 218 p. (Early English Church Music 11.) ISBN 9780852495391. M2 .E12 v. 11.

9   Ravenscroft, Thomas. *The Whole Booke of Psalmes: With the Hymnes Evangelicall, And Songs Spiritvall*. London: Thomas Snodham, 1621. Reprinted 1633.

Psalm harmonization. Includes **D211** (pp. 172–3). Facsimile and edition: *Ravenscroft's Revision of Est's Psalter*. 2 vols. Edited by Robert Schilling. Adelaide: Schilling, 1985. 118 p., 120 p. ISBN 0949302171, 094930218X. M2136 .W61 R4. Digital images: (Yale University) https://brbl-dl.library.yale.edu/vufind/Record/3445869.

10   Sternhold, Thomas, and John Hopkins. *The Whole Booke of Psalmes with their Wonted Tunes, as they are sung in Churches, composed into foure parts*. London: Thomas Est, 1592. Reprinted 1594, 1604, 1611.

Psalm settings. Includes **D205** (used in twenty-two settings in 1592, thirty-two settings in later volumes), **D206** (pp. 172–3, 260–1), **D207** (pp. 180–3), **D208** (pp. 228–31), **D209** (pp. 234–5), **D210** (pp. 274–5).

OTHER SIXTEENTH- AND SEVENTEENTH-CENTURY PRINT SOURCES

11   Allison, Richard. *An Howres Recreation in Musicke apt for Instrumentes and Voyces*. London, 1606.

Vocal a5. Includes **D79** (XVII).

12 Barley, William. *A New Booke of Tabliture*. London, 1596. Lute and orpharion.

Lute and orpharion. Includes **D8** (ff. E3r–F1r), **D10** (ff. B3v–4r), **D15** (ff. E1r–2v), **D42** (f. B4v), **D55** (f. D1r), **D62** (f. F3r–v), **D64** (ff. C2v–4r). Digital images: http://purl.org/rism/BI/1596/20/1.

13 Besard, Jean-Baptiste. *Novvs Partvs, fiue Concertationes Mvsicae, Dvodena Trivm, Ac Totidem binarum Testudinum (quibus & notæ Musicae adduntur) singulari ordine modulamina continentes*. Augsburg, 1617.

Three lutes, treble and bass viol. Includes **D15** (ff. D4v–E1r). Digital images: (Bayerische StaatsBibliothek) http://daten.digitale-sammlungen.de/bsb00085036/image_1; (Library of Congress) www.loc.gov/item/2011567025/; (University of California) https://hdl.handle.net/2027/uc1.l0069514446.

14 Besard, Jean-Baptiste. *Thesaurus Harmonicus*. Cologne, 1603.

Lute. Includes **D1** (ff. 170v–171v), **D15** (ff. 16v–17r; 30r, 30v–31r), **D19** (f. 107v), **D48** (f. 139v), **D66** (f. 134v). Facsimile: *Thesaurus Harmonicus: Avec un Index*. Geneva: Minkoff, 1975. Reprinted 1993. 172 p. ISBN 2826606018. M140 .B55 T44. Digital images: (Jagiellońska Biblioteka Cyfrowa) https://jbc.bj.uj.edu.pl/publication/294361.

15 Camphuysen, Dirck Raphaelsz. *Stichtelycke Rymen*. Amsterdam, 1647. Reprinted multiple times with additions and deletions.

Voice(s) with Dutch words. Includes **D8** (p. 110), **D15** (pp. 44–53), **D23** (pp. 24–6), **D42** (pp. 66–9), **D48** (pp. 197–203), **D79** (pp. 146–9). Digital images: (University of Illinois Urbana-Champaign) https://archive.org/details/stichtelyckeryme01camp.

16 Corkine, William. *Ayres, to Sing and Play to the Lvte and Basse Viol.* London, 1610.

Lyra viol. Includes **D62** (ff. F2v–G1r). Facsimile: *Ayres to Sing and Play to the Lute. 1610*. Edited by David Greer. Menston, UK: Scolar, 1970. Reprinted 1978. iii, 25 p. (English Lute Songs, 1597–1632 11.) ISBN 9780854172672. M2 .E64 v.11.

17 Corkine, William. *The Second Booke of Ayres*. London, 1612.

Lyra viol. Includes **D19** (f. G1v). Facsimile: *The Second Booke of Ayres: 1612*. Edited by David Greer. Menston, UK: Scolar, 1977. iii, 36 p. (English Lute Songs, 1597–1632 12.) ISBN 9780854173730. M2 .E64 v.12.

18 Forbes, John. *Songs and Fancies, To Thre Foure, or Five Partes, both apt for Voices and Viols*. Aberdeen, 1662. Revised 1666 and 1682.

Cantus voice. Includes **D15** (no. 61), **D23** (no. 47), **D24** (no. 23), **D60** (no. 60), **D79** (no. 17), **D133** (no. 20), **D148** (no. 13), **D152** (no. 40), **D154** (no. 56), **D162** (no. 46), **D177** (no. 54), **D178** (no. 27). Digital images: (Library of Congress, 1682 edition, page numbers vary) www.loc.gov/item/29006571/.

19   Francisque, Antoine. *Trésor d'Orphée.* Paris, 1600.

Lute. Includes **D19** (f. 13r, arr. Francisque). Facsimile: *Le trésor d'Orphée: livre de tablature de luth.* Geneva: Minkoff, 1973. Reprinted 1994. 32 p. ISBN 2826601369. M140 .F84 T7.

20   Fuhrmann, Georg Leopold. *Testudo Gallo-Germanica.* Nürnberg, 1615.

Lute. Includes **D3** (pp. 18–19), **D14** (pp. 53–5, 62, arr T. K.), **D15** (pp. 60–1, arr. Strobelius), **D28** (pp. 108–10), **D32** (p. 108), **D40** (pp. 112–13), **D42** (pp. 121, 122, var. Strobelius), **D48** (p. 80), **D61** (p. 47), **D70** (pp. 114–15). Digital images: (Bayerische StaatsBibliothek) http://daten.digitale-sammlungen.de/bsb00086008/image_1; (Jagiellońska Biblioteka Cyfrowa) https://jbc.bj.uj.edu.pl/publication/292215.

21   Füllsack, Zacharias, and Christian Hildebrand. *Ausserlesener Paduanen und Galliarden erster Theil.* Hamburg, 1607.

String consort. Includes **D38** (Galliard XVIII). Digital images: (Catholic University of Lublin, quinto) http://dlibra.kul.pl/dlibra/docmetadata?id=15499, (altus) http://dlibra.kul.pl/dlibra/doccontent?id=15466.

22   Gill, Alexander. *Logonomia Anglica.* London, 1619.

Single voice line in grammar text. Includes **D79** (p. 140). Credited to Campion.

23   Hagius, Conradus. *Newe Künstliche Musicalische Intraden, Pavanen, Galliarden, Passamezen, Courant unnd Uffzüg.* Nürnberg, 1616.

Consort. Includes **D8** (XXIV, a5), **D42** (f. 46, a4).

24   Haussmann, Valentin. *Rest von Polnischen und andern Tänzen.* Nürnberg, 1603.

Consort a5. Includes **D52** (LXXI).

25   Haussmann, Valentin. *Neue Intrade mit sechs und fünff Stimmen.* Nürnberg, 1604.

Consort a5. Includes **D42** (Galliarda II). Digital images: (Catholic University of Lublin, bass) http://dlibra.kul.pl/dlibra/docmetadata?id=15434.

26   Hove, Joachim van den. *Florida.* Utrecht, 1601.

Lute, arr. Includes **D15** (ff. 94r–95r), **D42** (f. 99r), **D61** (ff. 106r, 106v), **D62** (f. 106v), **D66** (f. 107v). Digital images: (Österreichische National-bibliothek) http://data.onb.ac.at/dtl/4096646; (Uniwersytet Wroclawski) www.bibliotekacyfrowa.pl/publication/5881.

27   Hove, Joachim van den. *Delitiae Musicae.* Utrecht, 1612.

Lute parts from **4**. Includes **D8** (f. 37v), **D9** (ff. 38v–39r), **D14** (f. 36v), **D15** (f. 2v), **D29** (f. 52v), **D48** (f. 59r), **D52** (f. 58r), **D121** (f. 51v), **D122** (f. 53v), **D123** (f. 57v). Digital images: (Bayerische StaatsBibliothek) http://daten.digitale-sammlungen.de/bsb00083380/image_1; (Uniwersytet Wroclawski) www.bibliotekacyfrowa.pl/publication/36939.

28 Matthysz, Paulus. *'T Uitnemend Kabinet*. Amsterdam, 1646.

Violin and bass. Includes **D15** (pp. 2, 7–8, arr. Schop).

29 Mertel, Elias. *Hortus Musicalis Novus*. Strasbourg, 1615.

Lute. Includes **D2** (pp. 210–11), **D6** (pp. 208–10), **D74** (pp. 226–8). Facsimile: *Hortus Musicalis Novus*. Geneva: Minkoff, 1983. xviii, 278 p. ISBN 2826607286. M140 .M447 H6.

30 Morley, Thomas. *The First Booke of Consort Lessons, made by diuers exquisite Authors, for six Instruments to play together, the Treble Lute, the Pandora, the Cittern, the Base-Violl, the Flute & Treble-Violl*. London: William Barley, 1599.

Consort music, arr. Includes **D8** (no. 4), **D15** (no. 7), **D19** (no. 5), **D23** (no. 10), **D42** (no. 6).

31 Mylius, Johann Daniel. *Thesaurus Gratiarum*. Frankfurt, 1622.

Lute. Includes **D2** (pp. 37–8), **D3** (pp. 1–2), **D6** (pp. 30–1), **D14** (pp. 48–9), **D71** (pp. 28–9), **D106** (pp. 52–3), **D107** (pp. 54–6).

32 Playford, John. *A Brief Introduction to the Skill of Musick*. London, 1660, 1662.

Voice and bass. Includes **D133** (p. 41).

33 Playford, John. *The Dancing Master, or Directions for dancing Country Dances, with the tunes to each Dance for the Treble-Violin*. London, 1686.

Violin. Includes **D42** (p. 188).

34 Praetorius, Michael. *Terpsichore, Musarum Aoniarum*. Wolfenbüttel, 1612.

Consort a4. Includes **D55** (CLVII, CCC).

35 Robinson, Thomas. *New Citharen Lessons*. London, 1609.

Cittern. Includes **D19** (f. D4v), **D23** (f. G1r), **D42** (ff. E2v, E3v), **D79** (f. K2r). Digital images: (University of California) https://hdl.handle.net/2027/ uc1.31210000842110.

36 Robinson, Thomas. *The Schoole of Musicke*. London, 1603.

Lute. Includes **D64** (f. H1r), **D66** (ff. K2v–L1v).

37 Rosseter, Philip. *A Booke of Ayres*. London, 1601.

Song. Includes **D54** (XI, opening melody only).

38 Rude, Johannes. *Flores Musicae*. Heidelberg, 1598.

Lute. Includes **D11** (II:110), **D15** (II:91).

39 Rude, Johannes. *Flores Musicae II*. Heidelberg, 1600.

Lute. Includes **D11** (f. III1r), **D15** (ff. GG5v–6r).

40   Scheidt, Samuel. *Ludi Musici: Paduana, Galliarda, Couranta, Alemande, Intrada, Canzonetto, ut vocant, quaternis & quinis vocibus.* Hamburg, 1621.

Instrumental ensemble. Includes **D66** (no. 28, arr. Strobelius).

41   Scheidt, Samuel. *Tabulatura Nova.* Hamburg, 1624.

Keyboard variations. Includes **D62** (II, pp. 143–56).

42   Simpson, Thomas. *Opusculum neuwer Pavanen.* Frankfurt, 1610.

Consort. Includes **D14** (XXI), **D95** (XI), **D114** (III).

43   Simpson, Thomas. *Taffel Consort erster Theil von allerhand neuen lustigen musicalischen Sachen mit vier Stimmen, neben einem General Bass.* Hamburg, 1621.

Consort a4 with continuo. Includes **D52** (IIX), **D94** (V), **D110** (XXXIX), **D185** (X), **D200** (XIX).

44   Slatyer, William. *The Psalmes of David in 4 Languages and in 4 Parts Set to ye Tunes of our Church by W.S.* London: Thomas Harper, 1643.

Psalms. Includes **D205** (Psalm 5).

45   Starter, Jan Janszoon. *Friesche Lust-hof.* Amsterdam, 1621.

Songbook. Includes **D79** (p. 77).

46   Swart, Willem. *Den Lust-Hoff der Nieuwe Musycke.* Amsterdam, 1603.

Songbook a5 (only cantus survives). Includes **D15** (f. 51r).

47   Valerius, Adriaen. *Neder-landtsche Gedenck-clanck.* Haarlem, 1626.

Voice, lute, and cittern with Dutch words. **D15** (pp. 116, 217–18), **D23** (pp. 54–5), **D60** (p. 167), **D62** (pp. 132–3), **D66** (p. 83), **D79** (p. 248). Facsimile: *Neder-landtsche Gedenck-clank.* New York: Broude Brothers, 1974. 295 p. (Monuments of Music and Music Literature in Facsimile 2s. 63.) ISBN 0845022636. M1754 .V25 N4.

48   Vallet, Nicolas. *Apollinis Süsse Leyr.* Amsterdam, 1642.

Violin and bass (only bass survives). Includes **D15** (III:17). Digital images: (Staatsbibliothek zu Berlin) http://resolver.staatsbibliothek-berlin.de/ SBB00014A3600000000.

49   Vallet, Nicolas. *Secretum Musarum/Het gheheymenisse der Zang-Godinnen.* Amsterdam, 1615.

Lute. Includes **D42** (pp. 36–40), **D66** (pp. 47–8).

50   Vallet, Nicolas. *Secretum Musarum/Het tweed Boeck van de Luyt-Tablatuer, ghenoemt het Gheheymenisse der Sangh-Godinnen.* Amsterdam, 1616.

Lute. Includes **D62** (p. 8).

51   Van Eyck, Jacob. *Euterpe oft Speel-Goddinne.* Part I. Amsterdam, 1644.

Recorder. Includes **D15** (ff. 11v–12v, 61v–63v), **D60** (ff. 36v–39r).

52   Van Eyck, Jacob. *Der Fluyten Lust-hof.* Part I. Amsterdam, 1649, 1656.

Recorder. Includes arrangements of **D15** (ff. 12r–13r, 62v–65r), **D60** (ff. 38v–41r). Digital images: (National Library of Scotland) https://digital.nls.uk/90251625.

53   Van Eyck, Jacob. *Der Fluyten Lust-hof.* Part II. Amsterdam, 1646, 1654.

Recorder. Includes **D42** (f. 30r–v).

SIXTEENTH- AND SEVENTEENTH-CENTURY MANUSCRIPT SOURCES

† Indicates manuscripts with works in Dowland's hand or signed by the composer

Great Britain and Ireland

54   Cambridge, Cambridge University Library (GB-Cu). Add. 2764(2). c. 1585–90.

Lute. **D15** (ff. 5v–6r), **D21** (f. 6v), **D47** (f. 10r), **D48** (f. 10v), **D50** (f. 6r), **D70** (f. 12r), **D85** (f. 7r), **D113** (f. 12v). Digital images: http://cudl.lib.cam.ac.uk/view/ MS-ADD-02764-00002/1.

55   Cambridge, Cambridge University Library (GB-Cu). Add. 3056. c. 1610.

"Cosens Lute Book." Includes **D1** (ff. 8v–9r), **D5** (ff. 17v–18r; 33v, incomplete), **D6** (ff. 7v–8r), **D8** (ff. 2v–3r), **D15** (ff. 4v–5r, 14v–15r; 36v–37r, arr. C.K.), **D17** (ff. 5v–6r), **D19** (ff. 3v–4r), **D23** (ff. 42v–43r), **D24** (f. 33v), **D42** (f. 48r), **D70** (f. 32v). Digital images: https://cudl.lib.cam.ac.uk/view/MS-ADD-03056/1.

56   Cambridge, Cambridge University Library (GB-Cu). Add. 8844. c. 1595.

"Trumbull Lute Book." Includes **D37** (f. 32v, variant), **D68** (f. 25r), **D79** (f. 2r). See **533**. Facsimile: *The Trumbull Lute Book c. 1595: Containing 26 Solos, 10 Duet Parts, and 2 Mixed Consort Parts, of which 36 are for 6-Course and 2 for 7-Course Renaissance Lute.* Edited by Robert Spencer. Clarabricken, Ireland: Boethius, 1980. v, 81 p. (Musical Sources 19.) M2 .M72 v.19. Digital images: http://cudl.lib. cam.ac.uk/view/MS-ADD-08844/1.

57   Cambridge, Cambridge University Library (GB-Cu). Dd.2.11. c. 1588–1595.

"Holmes Lutebook 1." Lute and bandora. Includes **D8** (ff. 46v–47r; 82r, bandora), **D10** (f. 58v), **D12** (f. 14v), **D15** (ff. 75v–77r, 81v; 84v, bandora), **D17** (f. 38v), **D19** (f. 53r), **D20** (f. 67v), **D21** (ff. 7v, 56r), **D22** (ff. 56r, 60r, 95r), **D23** (ff. 40v, 93r), **D24** (f. 58r), **D25** (f. 12r), **D31** (f. 82v), **D34** (f. 77r), **D38** (f. 52r, variant), **D41** (f. 59r), **D42** (ff. 40v, 62v), **D45** (f. 58r), **D48** (f. 48r), **D49** (ff. 38r, 47r), **D50** (f. 63v), **D52** (f. 100v), **D56** (f. 22r), **D61** (f. 55v), **D63** (f. 56r), **D65** (f. 58r), **D66** (ff. 14v, 58v), **D69** (f. 9r), **D70** (ff. 53r, 66r), **D75** (f. 48r), **D81** (f. 56r), **D85**

(f. 71v), **D97** (f. 62r), **D104** (ff. 41r; 44r, bandora). See **528**. Facsimile: *The Mathew Holmes Manuscripts I: Cambridge University Library MS Dd.2.11.* 3 vols. Edited by John H. Robinson and Steward McCoy. Guildford, UK: Lute Society, 2010. 70 p. (Lute Society Facsimiles 7.) ISBN 97809056551710. M2.8 .M34. Digital images: https://cudl.lib.cam.ac.uk/view/MS-DD-00002-00011/1.

58   Cambridge, Cambridge University Library (GB-Cu). Dd.3.18. c. 1590.

Cambridge Consort Lute Book. Includes **D15** (ff. 16v–17v), **D70** (f. 11r), **D81** (ff. 17r, cittern; 53r, lute), **D113** (f. 35v, first part of duet). See **528, 531**. Other associated consort books include **61, 62,** and **65**.

59   Cambridge, Cambridge University Library (GB-Cu). Dd.4.22. c. 1615.

Lute. Includes **D62** (f. 11v), **D113** (f. 12r). Digital images: http://cudl.lib.cam. ac.uk/view/MS-DD-00004-00022/1.

60   Cambridge, Cambridge University Library (GB-Cu). Dd.4.23. c. 1615.

Cittern. Includes **D8** (f. 27v), **D19** (f. 4v), **D22** (f. 28r), **D42** (f. 28r), **D50** (f. 31v), **D63** (f. 23r), **D79** (f. 32r), **D81** (f. 25r). See **528**.

61   Cambridge, Cambridge University Library (GB-Cu). Dd.5.20. 1590.

Cambridge Consort Bass Viol Book. Includes **D8** (f. 3v), **D15** (ff. 3v, 6v, 28v), **D22** (f. 5r), **D39** (f. 5r), **D41** (f. 5v), **D60** (ff. 26v, 28r), **D63** (f. 5r), **D81** (f. 5r). See **528, 531**. Other associated consort books include **58, 62,** and **65**.

62   Cambridge, Cambridge University Library (GB-Cu). Dd.5.21. c. 1590.

Cambridge Consort Recorder Book. Includes **D8** (f. 1v), **D15** (f. 3v), **D22** (f. 5r), **D39** (f. 5v), **D41** (f. 6r), **D62** (f. 1r), **D63** (f. 5r), **D81** (f. 5r). See **528, 531**. Other associated consort books include **58, 61,** and **65**.

†**63**   Cambridge University Library (GB-Cu). Dd.5.78.3. c. 1595–1600.

"Holmes Lutebook 2." Includes **D3** (ff. 43v–44r, signature and title in Dowland's hand), **D14** (ff. 2v–3r), **D15** (ff. 9v, 21r), **D16** (ff. 47v–48r), **D17** (ff. 64v–65r), **D18** (ff. 51v–52r), **D19** (ff. 21v, 10r), **D24** (f. 63r, arr. Cutting?), **D26** (f. 26r), **D27** (f. 49v), **D28** (ff. 35v–36r), **D29** (ff. 16v–17r), **D30** (ff. 25v–26r), **D31** (f. 37r), **D32** (ff. 18v–19r), **D34** (f. 31v), **D36** (f. 56r), **D43** (f. 9r), **D44** (f. 38r), **D51** (f. 32r), **D54** (f. 7r), **D58** (f. 6v), **D64** (ff. 39v–40r), **D66** (f. 28v), **D68** (ff. 38v–39r). See **528**. Digital images: http://cudl.lib.cam.ac.uk/view/MS-DD-00005-00078-00003/1.

64   Cambridge, Cambridge University Library (GB-Cu). Dd.9.33. c. 1600.

"Holmes Lutebook 3." Includes **D2** (ff. 16v–17r), **D4** (ff. 41v–42r, 50v–51r), **D6** (ff. 43v–44r), **D7** (ff. 6v–7v), **D11** (ff. 33v–34r), **D17** (ff. 5v–6r), **D18** (ff. 1v–2r), **D19** (f. 73v), **D32** (f. 20r), **D33** (ff. 17v–18r), **D34** (f. 29r), **D35** (f. 37v), **D36** (f. 19v), **D37** (f. 90r), **D40** (ff. 23r, 94v), **D43** (f. 91r), **D53** (f. 28v), **D54** (f. 38r), **D57** (f. 20v), **D58** (f. 21v), **D62** (f. 89r, duet part), **D67** (ff. 67v–68r, var.), **D69** (ff. 68v–69v), **D70** (ff. 29v–30r; 81v, bandora), **D73** (ff. 44v–45v), **D76** (f. 19v), **D79** (f. 62v), **D82** (f. 22r–v), **D84** (f. 17r, Holborne, arr. Dowland?), **D113** (ff. 53v–54r). See **528**. Digital images: http://cudl.lib.cam.ac.uk/view/MS-DD-00009-00033/1.

65   Cambridge, Cambridge University Library (GB-Cu). Dd.14.24. c. 1590.

Cambridge Consort Cittern Book. Includes **D8** (f. 31v), **D15** (f. 25r), **D22** (f. 33v), **D39** (f. 36v), **D41** (f. 20r), **D48** (f. 28v), **D61** (ff. 17v, 28v), **D62** (f. 21v), **D63** (f. 21v), **D75** (f. 26v). See **528, 531**. Other associated consort books include **58, 61**, and **62**.

66   Cambridge, Cambridge University Library (GB-Cu). Nn.6.36. c. 1610–1615.

"Holmes Lutebook 4." Includes **D6** (ff. 32v–33r), **D13** (ff. 17v–18r, 18r–v), **D42** (f. 37r, lute consort part), **D44** (ff. 1r, 2r), **D60** (f. 21v), **D62** (f. 15r), **D70** (ff. 19v–20r), **D83** (f. 11r). See **528**. Digital images: https://cudl.lib.cam.ac.uk/view/MS-NN-00006-00036/1.

67   Cambridge, Fitzwilliam Museum (GB-Cfm). Ms.Mus.168 (*olim* Mus. 32.g.29). c. 1609–1619.

"Fitzwilliam Virginal Book." Keyboard. Includes **D8** (pp. 298–9, arr. Peerson), **D15** (pp. 222–3, arr. Byrd; 406–8, arr. Farnaby), **D19** (pp. 299–303, arr./var. Bull), **D42** (p. 306), **D62** (pp. 123–5), **D66** (pp. 278–9, arr. Byrd).

68   Cambridge, Fitzwilliam Museum (GB-Cfm). Ms.Mus.689. c. 1624–c. 1640.

"Lord Herbert of Cherbury's Lute Book." Includes **D15** (ff. 8v–9r), **D28** (ff. 54v–55r), **D29** (f. 10r), **D42** (f. 55r).

69   Cambridge, Fitzwilliam Museum (GB-Cfm). Ms.Mus.782 (*olim* 52.d.25). c. 1600–c. 1620.

"Tisdale's Virginal Book"/"The John Bull Manuscript." Includes **D15** (ff. 75v–76r; 83r–84r, arr. Randall), **D19** (f. 62v), **D23** (f. 63v), **D42** (ff. 63r, 79v–80r), **D125** (f. 61v), **D126** (f. 61v), **D127** (f. 64r), **D128** (f. 64v), **D129** (f. 65r).

70   Cambridge, King's College (GB-Ckc). RW.MS.2A. c. 1610.

"Turpyn's Manuscript." Voice with lute tablature. Includes **D23** (f. 2v), **D42** (ff. 1v–2r), **D132** (ff. 3v–4r). See **532**.

71   Cambridge, Trinity College Library (GB-Ltc). Ms. O.16.2. 1620.

Lute. Includes **D34** (p. 123).

72   Dublin, Marsh's Library (IRL-Dm). Z.3.2.13. c. 1595.

"Marsh Lute Book." Includes **D43** (pp. 190, 381), **D47** (p. 384), **D77** (p. 382), **D85** (p. 386). See **539**. Facsimile: *The Marsh Lute Book c. 1595*. Edited by Robert Spencer. Kilkenny, Ireland: Boethius, 1981. xxii, 430 p. (Musical Sources 20.) ISBN 0863140149. M140 .M37.

73   Dublin, Marsh's Library (IRL-Dm). Z.4.3.1–5. c. 1610.

MS additions to the quinto and sesto volumes of Monte's *Il primo libro delli madrigali, a sei voce* (Venice, 1570). Superius and Quintus voices. Includes **D19** (S: f. R2v, Q: ff. O2v, O3r), **D23** (S: ff. O4r, Q4r, Q: f. N4r), **D60** (S: f. O3v, Q: f. N3v), **D132** (S: f. R3v, Q: ff. O3v, O4r), **D133** (S: f. R2r, Q: ff. O1v, O2r), **D136** (S: f. S3v, Q: f. P3v). See **524**.

74   Dublin, Trinity College Library (IRL-Dtc). MS 408 (*olim* II: Ms. D.1.21). c. 1590–1620.

Includes "Ballet Lute Book." Includes **D15** (pp. 42–3), **D42** (pp. 67–7, lyra viol), **D43** (p. 37), **D47** (p. 7, duet part), **D61** (p. 111), **D62** (pp. 14, 111), **D70** (p. 113). See **540**. Digital images: http://digitalcollections.tcd.ie/home/index.php?DRIS_ID=MS408_001.

75   Dublin, Trinity College Library (IRL-Dtc). MS 410/1 (*olim* MS. D.3.30/I). c. 1583.

"Thomas Dallis Lute Book." Melody line (no lyrics) with lute tablature. Includes **D62** (pp. 49–50). Digital images: https://digitalcollections.tcd.ie/home/index.php?DRIS_ID=MS410_001.

76   Dublin, Trinity College Library (IRL-Dtc). MS 412 (*olim* F.5.13). c. 1625.

MS additions, "Wode Partbook" (quintus). Includes **D15** (p. 34), **D60** (p. 53). For other partbooks, see **86** and **103**. Digital images: www.diamm.ac.uk/sources/2860/#/images.

77   Dublin, Trinity College Library (IRL-Dtc). OLS 192.n.40, no. 1 (*olim* B.1.32). Date unknown.

MS additions to *Cantiones* (1575) superius partbook. Voice. Includes **D15** (f. F4r).

78   Edinburgh, National Library of Scotland (GB-En). Acc.9769 84/1/6. c. 1701–1705.

"Balcarres Lute Book." Includes **D79** (p. 127). Facsimile and edition: *The Balcarres Lute Book*. 2 vols. Edited by Matthew Spring. Glasgow: Universities of Glasgow and Aberdeen, 2010. xxxiii, 271 p. ISBN 9780852618462, 9780852618974. ML96.4 .B174.

79   Edinburgh, National Library of Scotland (GB-En). Adv.MS.5.2.14. 1639.

"Stirling Cantus Book"/"Leyden Manuscript." Cantus voice only. Includes **D125** (f. 19r). Facsimile: *English Song 1600–1675: Facsimiles of Twenty-Six Manuscripts and an Edition of the Texts*. Vol. 11. Edited by Elise Bickford Jorgens. New York and London: Garland, 1986. M2 .E65 v.11.

80   Edinburgh, National Library of Scotland (GB-En). Adv.MS.5.2.15. c. 1625.

"The Skene Mandora Book." Includes **D23** (pp. 35–40), **D79** (pp. 113–14), **D133** (pp. 114–15, melody), **D148** (pp. 114–15, words).

81 Edinburgh, National Library of Scotland (GB-En). Advocates Library, K.33b. After 1615.

MS additions to *Archimedes* (Basel, 1544). Includes **D62** (pt. III, after p. 65).

82 Edinburgh, National Library of Scotland (GB-En). MS.5448. Date unknown.

"Lady Ann Ker's Book." Voice and bass. Includes **D15** (f. 1r–v).

83 Edinburgh, National Library of Scotland (GB-En). MS.9448 (*olim* Panmure 9). 1612.

"Clement Matchett Virginal Book." Includes **D23** (ff. 29v–32v, arr. Wilbye), **D62** (ff. 14v–20r).

84 Edinburgh, National Library of Scotland (GB-En). MS.9450 (*olim* Panmure 11). c. 1635–1670.

Commonplace book of Robert Edward. Untexted voice parts. Includes **D15** (f. 6v), **D19** (ff. 30v–31r), **D60** (ff. 9r, 23v–24r), **D127** (f. 7r), **D139** (f. 9r), **D149** (ff. 30v–31r).

85 Edinburgh, National Library of Scotland (GB-En). MS Dep. 314 no. 23. c. 1643–1644.

"Wemyss Manuscript." Lute. Includes **D133** (p. 6).

86 Edinburgh, University of Edinburgh Library (GB-Eu). MSS La.III.483.1, La. III.483.2, III.483.3. c. 1625.

MS additions, "Wode Partbooks." Includes **D15** (B: p. 202), **D60** (T: p. 183, B: p. 198), **D79** (C: p. 189, T: p. 178, B: p. 183), **D133** (C: p. 202, T: p. 184, B: p. 200), **D148** (C: p. 202, T: p. 184, B: p. 200). For other partbooks, see **76** and **103**. Digital images: www.wode.div.ed.ac.uk/resources.html.

87 Edinburgh, University of Edinburgh Library (GB-Eu). MS La.III.488. c. 1627–1637.

Sir William Mure of Rowallan's cantus partbook. Includes **D130** (p. 44), **D131** (p. 44), **D133** (p. 44), **D139** (p. 44), **D156** (p. 44).

88 Edinburgh, University of Edinburgh Library (GB-Eu). MS La.III.490. 1699–1701.

Voice. "John Squyer's Manuscript." Includes **D133** (p. 71).

89 Glasgow, University Library (GB-Ge). Euing 25 (*olim* Ms.R.d.43). c. 1595–1600.

"The Euing Lute Book." Includes **D1** (ff. 16v–17r), **D3** (ff. 41v–42r), **D7** (ff. 35r–36r), **D8** (f. 29v), **D9** (f. 25r), **D10** (ff. 27v–28r), **D15** (ff. 25v–26r), **D17** (ff. 37v–38r), **D19** (f. 28v), **D22** (f. 23r), **D23** (ff. 26v–27r), **D25** (f. 24v), **D28** (ff. 20v–21r), **D33** (f. 18v), **D42** (f. 24r), **D44** (f. 21r), **D52** (f. 24r), **D53** (f. 44r), **D55** (f. 24v), **D62** (f. 27r), **D64** (ff. 17v–18r), **D66** (f. 38r), **D68** (ff. 21v–22r), **D69** (f. 31r), **D70** (f. 31r), **D72** (ff. 42v–43r), **D76** (f. 42r), **D78** (f. 26r), **D85** (f. 29).

90 Haslemere, Dolmetsch Library (GB-HAdolmetsch). MS II.B.1. c. 1620–1660.

Lute. Includes **D15** (ff. 225v–227v), **D19** (ff. 92v–93r). See Poulton, Diana. "The Dolmetsch Library, Haslemere MS II. B. 1: A Preliminary Study." *Consort* 35 (1979): 327–41.

91 London, British Library (GB-Lbl). Add. MS 4429. Mid-17th century.

"Pell Papers." Four-part psalm score inserted into text collection. Includes **D211** (no. 11).

92 London, British Library (GB-Lbl). Add. MS 6402. c. 1600–1610.

Lute. Includes **D15** (f. 1r), **D54** (f. 2r).

93 London, British Library (GB-Lbl). Add. MS 10444. 17th century.

Two-part instrumental. Includes **D52** (ff. 9r, 64r), **D109** (ff. 6v, 61v).

94 London, British Library (GB-Lbl). Add. MS 15117. c. 1614–1616.

Voice and lute, keyboard. Includes **D19** (f. 15v), **D133** (ff. 7r; 22v, keyboard), **D159** (f. 12r), **D177** (f. 21r), **D203** (f. 14r). Facsimile: *English Song 1600–1675: Facsimiles of Twenty-six Manuscripts and an Edition of the Texts.* Vol. 1. Edited by Elise Bickford Jorgens. New York and London: Garland, 1986. M2 .E65 v.1.

95 London, British Library (GB-Lbl). Add. MS 15118. 17th century.

Untexted vocal. Includes **D43** (f. 30v), **D133** (f. 4v), **D135** (f. 6r).

96 London, British Library (GB-Lbl). Add. MS 17786–91. c. 1610.

Voice and viols. Includes **D15** (f. 14r), **D142** (f. 9r, arr. Wigthorpe).

97 London, British Library (GB-Lbl). Add. MS 24665. c. 1610–1626.

"Giles Earle Songbook." Includes **D15** (ff. 11v–12r), **D19** (ff. 12v–13r), **D42** (f. 42v), **D60** (ff. 26v–27r), **D79** (ff. 25v–26r, 69v–70r), **D133** (ff. 28v–29r), **D142** (ff. 31v–32r). Facsimile: *English Song 1600–1675: Facsimiles of Twenty-six Manuscripts and an Edition of the Texts.* Vol. 1 Edited by Elise Bickford Jorgens. New York and London: Garland, 1986. M2 .E65 v.1.

†98 London, British Library (GB-Lbl). Add. MS 27579. 1599–1606.

"Cellarius *Album amicorum.*" Two trebles. Includes **D124** (f. 88r, signed).

99 London, British Library (GB-Lbl). Add MS 29291. 17th century.

Four-part score. Includes **D23** (f. 22r–v), **D24** (f. 11r), **D60** (f. 11v), **D139** (f. 12r), **D140** (f. 25v).

100 London, British Library (GB-Lbl). Add. MS 29481. c. 1630.

Voice with bass. Includes **D19** (f. 14r), **D133** (f. 2r). Facsimile: *English Song 1600–1675: Facsimiles of Twenty-six Manuscripts and an Edition of the Texts.* Vol. 1. Edited by Elise Bickford Jorgens. New York and London: Garland, 1986. M2 .E65 v.1.

101   London, British Library (GB-Lbl). Add. MS 30485. c. 1600.

Keyboard. Possibly compiled by Thomas Weelkes. Includes **D15** (ff. 71r–72v), **D66** (ff. 115v, 116r–v). Facsimile: *Keyboard Music: In Facsimile from BL Add. MS 30485, NYPL Drexel Ms 5612, RCM (London) MS 2093.* Edited by Desmond Hunter. Clarabricken, Ireland: Boethius, 1985. x, 29 p. (Musical Sources 24.) ISBN 086314103X. M22 .W44.

102   London, British Library (GB-Lbl). Add. MS 31392. c. 1605.

Lute within volume of assorted instrumentation. Includes **D1** (ff. 13v–14v), **D8** (ff. 27v–28r), **D10** (ff. 14v–15r), **D15** (ff. 35v–36r), **D19** (ff. 28v–29r), **D55** (f. 23r), **D70** (f. 25r), **D74** (f. 24r), **D85** (f. 34).

103   London, British Library (GB-Lbl). Add. MS 33933. c. 1625.

MS additions, "Wode Partbook" (contratenor). Includes **D15** (f. 86r), **D60** (f. 85r), **D79** (ff. 81v–82r), **D133** (f. 85v, melody)/**D148** (f. 85v, words). Other partbooks, see **76** and **86**. Digital images: www.bl.uk/manuscripts/FullDisplay. aspx?ref=Add_MS_33933.

104   London, British Library (GB-Lbl). Add. MS 36484. After 1604.

"David Melvill's Bassus Book." Bass viol for songs and consort. Includes **D8** (f. 22v), **D15** (f. 22r), **D19** (f. 22v).

105   London, British Library (GB-Lbl). Add. MS 36526A. 1590–1620.

Untexted vocal or consort. Includes **D19** (ff. 2r, 7v, 8r), **D23** (ff. 2v, 7v, 8v), **D24** (ff. 3v, 9v), **D42** (ff. 2r, 7v, 8r), **D60** (ff. 3v, 9r), **D126** (ff. 2r, 8r), **D127** (ff. 3r, 9v), **D128** (ff. 2v, 8v), **D131** (ff. 2v, 8v), **D132** (ff. 3r, 8v), **D133** (ff. 3r, 9r), **D134** (ff. 3r, 9r), **D137** (f. 9r–v).

106   London, British Library (GB-Lbl). Add. MSS 37402–37406. After 1601.

Consort song partbooks. Includes **D142** (C: ff. 58v–59r, Q: ff. 57r–v, A: ff. 77v–78r, T: ff. 56v–57r, B: ff. 61r).

107   London, British Library (GB-Lbl). Add. MS 38539. c. 1612–1620.

"M. L. (*olim* John Sturt) Lute Book." Includes **D1** (ff. 14v–15r), **D15** (ff. 22v–23r), **D28** (ff. 15v–16r), **D40** (ff. 12v–13r), **D47** (f. 8v), **D50** (f. 2r), **D83** (f. 16v). Facsimile: *The M.L. Lute Book c. 1610–40: Containing 88 Solos and Duets for 6- to 10-Course Lute in Renaissance Tuning.* Edited by Robert Spencer. Clarabricken, Ireland: Boethius, 1985. xxxvi, 72 p. (Musical Sources 25.) ISBN 086314021. M140 .M2.

108   London, British Library (GB-Lbl). Add. MS 63852. 17th century.

"Griffith Boynton Lyra-Viol and Keyboard Manuscript." Includes **D133** (f. 91).

109   London, British Library (GB-Lbl). Egerton MS 2046. c. 1616–1650.

"Jane Pickeringe Lute Book." Includes **D1** (ff. 24v–25r), **D8** (ff. 19v–20r), **D9** (f. 31v), **D15** (ff. 16v–17r), **D40** (ff. 17v–18r), **D43** (f. 18r), **D50** (f. 19r), **D64**

(f. 29v), **D66** (ff. 25r; 33v, arr. of Byrd arr.?), **D69** (f. 33r), **D70** (ff. 22v, 35r), **D71** (ff. 23v–24r), **D79** (f. 19r). Facsimile: *Jane Pickeringe's Lute Book c. 1616–c. 1650 (London, British Library, MS Egerton 2046)*. Edited by Robert Spencer. Leeds: Boethius, 1985. xxxiv, 112 p. (Musical Sources 23.) ISBN 0863140165. M140 .J35.

110   London, British Library (GB-Lbl). Hirsch Ms. M.1353. c. 1595.

"Hirsch Lute Book." Includes **D15** (f. 11v), **D19** (f. 11r), **D21** (f. 11v), **D42** (f. 11v), **D75** (f. 3r), **D84** (f. 5r), **D104** (f. 7r). Facsimile: *The Hirsch Lute Book c. 1595 (London, British Library, MS Hirsch M 1353)*. Edited by Robert Spencer. Leeds: Boethius, 1982. xxiii, 26 p. (Musical Sources 21.) ISBN 0863140157. M140 .H5.

111   London, British Library (GB-Lbl). MS Mus. 1591. c. 1591.

"My Lady Nevell's Keyboard Book." Includes **D66** (ff. 146v–148v, arr. Byrd). Facsimile: *My Ladye Nevells Booke: Facsimile British Library MS Mus. 1591*. Edited by Oliver Neighbour. Kassel: Bärenreiter, 2012. 414 p. (Documenta musicologica 2.) ISBN 9783761822135. M2 .D62 v. 44. Digital images: www.bl.uk/manuscripts/FullDisplay.aspx?ref=MS_Mus._1591.

112   London, British Library (GB-Lbl). Royal MS Appendix 63. After 1614.

Cantus, lute, and treble viol. Sacred songs copied from **8**. Includes **D203** (f. 4v), **D204** (f. 28v).

113   London, British Library (GB-Lbl). Royal Music 23.l.4. c. 1600.

"Benjamin Cosyn Virginal Book." Includes **D15** (ff. 5v–7v), **D46** (ff. 7v–8v).

114   London, British Library (GB-Lbl). Royal Music 24.d.3. 1624.

"Will Forster's Virginal Book." Includes **D15** (ff. 167r–171r, arr. Byrd), **D19** (ff. 222v–224r), **D62** (ff. 127v–130r), **D66** (ff. 13v–14v, arr. Byrd).

115   London, British Library (GB-Lbl). Sloane MS 1021. c. 1635.

"Johann Stobaeus Lutebook." Includes **D15** (ff. 21v–22v), **D46** (ff. 44v–45r), **D62** (f. 79v).

116   London, Museum of London (GB-Lml). MS 46.78/748. c. 1638.

"Anne Cromwell Virginal Book." Includes **D23** (ff. 8r–9r), **D62** (f. 7r).

117   London, Royal Academy of Music Library (GB-Lam). MS 600. c. 1600.

"Browne [*olim* Braye] Bandora and Lyra Viol Manuscript." Includes **D8** (f. 89r), **D15** (ff. 17v, 92r), **D19** (f. 89r), **D20** (f. 10v), **D26** (f. 18v), **D48** (f. 11r).

118   London, Royal Academy of Music Library (GB-Lam). MS 601. c. 1597–1599.

"Mynshall Lute Book." Includes **D15** (f. 11r), **D21** (f. 1r), **D43** (f. 8r), **D48** (f. 10r), **D61** (f. 5v), **D62** (f. 9v), **D66** (f. 1r), **D70** (f. 8r), **D80** (f. 7r), **D83** (f. 12v), **D112** (f. 6v). See **533, 537**. Facsimile: *The Mynshall Lute Book*. Edited by Robert Spencer. Leeds: Boethius, 1975. 65 p. (Reproductions of Early Music 3.) ISBN 9780904263039. M140 .M2 M985.

119 London, Royal Academy of Music (GB-Lam). MS 602. c. 1609.

"Sampson (*olim* Tollemache) Lute Book." Includes **D20** (f. 6v), **D40** (f. 7v, misattrib. to Johnson), **D44** (f. 13v), **D50** (f. 7r), **D66** (f. 11v, duet part). See **533, 537, 538**. Facsimile: *The Sampson Lute Book (formerly known as the Tollemache Lute Manuscript).* Edited by Robert Spencer. Leeds: Boethius, 1974. 42 p. (Reproductions of Early Music 2.) M140 .S24.

†120 London, Royal Academy of Music Library (GB-Lam). MS 603. c. 1620–1630.

"Margaret Board Lute Book." Includes a fingering table, as well as least one non-John Dowland piece, possibly in Dowland's hand. Includes **D10** (ff. 10v–11r), **D15** (ff. 11v–12r), **D19** (f. 21v), **D22** (f. 22v), **D28** (ff. 16v–17r), **D40** (ff. 17v–18r), **D61** (f. 1r), **D69** (f. 7v), **D70** (f. 12v), **D96** (f. 13r), **D97** (f. 24r), **D98** (f. 29r), **D99** (f. 26v), **D100** (f. 30r). See **285, 533, 537**. Facsimile: *The Board Lute Book.* Edited by Robert Spencer. Leeds: Boethius, 1976. xii, 100 p. (Musical Sources 6.) M140 .B69.

121 London Royal College of Music (GB-Lcm). MS 2093. c. 1670.

Keyboard. Includes **D60** (ff. 16v–17r). Facsimile: *Keyboard Music: In Facsimile from BL Add. MS 30485, NYPL Drexel Ms 5612, RCM (London) MS 2093.* Edited by Desmond Hunter. Clarabricken, Ireland: Boethius, 1985. x, 29 p. (Musical Sources 24.) ISBN 086314103X. M22 .W44.

122 Manchester, Central Public Library, Henry Watson Music and Arts Library (GB-Mp). MS BRm 832 Vu 51. Mid-17th century.

"Manchester Lyra Viol Book." Arrangements by Sumarte. Includes **D10** (no. 11), **D15** (pp. 18–19), **D62** (p. 12), **D79** (p. 12). Facsimile: *Manchester Gamba Book.* Edited by Paul Furness. Hebden Bridge, UK: Peacock, 2003. xvii, 196 p., ISBN 0907908950. M59 .V54 M36.

†123 Nottingham, University of Nottingham (GB-NO). Pw V 77. c. 1597.

"Lamentatio Henrici Noel." 4 voices. Not in Dowland's hand, but possibly signed. Includes **D212** (f. 2r), **D213** (f. 2v), **D214** (f. 3r), **D215** (f. 3v), **D216** (f. 4r), **D217** (f. 4v), **D218** (f. 5r).

124 Oxford, Bodleian Library (GB-Ob). MSS. Mus. f. 7–10. c. 1630.

"Thomas Hamond Partbooks." 4 voices. Includes **D19** (f. 7r), **D23** (f. 5r), **D26** (f. 9r), **D42** (f. 8r), **D60** (f. 10v), **D125** (ff. 3v–4r), **D126** (ff. 2v–3r), **D127** (f. 9v), **D128** (f. 11v), **D129** (f. 10r), **D130** (f. 6r), **D131** (f. 6v), **D132** (f. 8v), **D133** (f. 7v), **D135** (f. 12r), **D137** (f. 11r), **D139** (f. 12v).

125 Oxford, Bodleian Library (GB-Ob). MS. Mus. Sch. d. 143. c. 1600.

Keyboard. Includes **D48** (ff. 6v, 5v–r).

126 Oxford, Bodleian Library (GB-Ob). MS. Mus. Sch. d. 247. 17th century.

Lyra viol. Includes **D15** (ff. 25v–26r).

127 Oxford, Bodleian Library (GB-Ob). MS. Rawl. poet. 148. 17th century.

"John Lilliat Commonplace Book." Poetry manuscript. Includes **D79** (f. 109v).

128 Oxford, Bodleian Library (GB-Ob). MS. Tenbury 1018. Early 17th century.

Voice with bass. Includes **D15** (f. 30v). Facsimile: *English Song 1600–1675: Facsimiles of Twenty-Six Manuscripts and an Edition of the Texts.* Vol. 6. Edited by Elise Bickford Jorgens. New York and London: Garland, 1986. M2 .E65 v.6.

129 Oxford, Christ Church Library (GB-Och). Mus. 431. c. 1625.

Keyboard. Includes **D19** (ff. 18v–19r, arr. Byrd), **D62** (ff. 20r–21v).

130 Oxford, Christ Church Library (GB-Och). Mus. 437. c. 1640.

Keyboard. Includes **D15** (f. 11r, incomplete), **D19** (f. 10v, incomplete).

131 Oxford, Christ Church Library (GB-Och). Mus. 439. c. 1620.

Voice with bass. Includes **D15** (pp. 6–7), **D19** (pp. 52–3), **D23** (p. 45), **D42** (p. 107, lyra viol), **D79** (p. 115), **D133** (p. 46), **D142** (p. 70), **D151** (p. 47). See **523**. Facsimile: *English Song 1600–1675: Facsimiles of Twenty-Six Manuscripts and an Edition of the Texts.* Vol. 6. Edited by Elise Bickford Jorgens. New York and London: Garland, 1986. M2 .E65 v.6.

132 Perth, AK Bell Library (GB-P). N.16. 1662.

Single voice. Includes **D15** (f. 51r–v), **D23** (ff. 38v–39r), **D24** (ff. 18v–19r), **D60** (ff. 49v–50v), **D133** (f. 16r), **D148** (f. 11r–v), **D152** (f. 33r–v), **D154** (ff. 45v–46v), **D162** (f. 38r), **D177** (f. 44r–v), **D178** (ff. 21v–22r).

133 Private Collection. Lancelyn Green Collection. c. 1645.

"Priscilla Bunbury's Virginal Book." Includes **D23** (ff. 28v–30r, arr. Hall).

134 Private collection. Willey Park, Shropshire. c. 1600.

"Welde Lute Book." Includes **D9** (f. 14v), **D15** (f. 4v), **D40** (f. 5v), **D43** (f. 5r), **D44** (f. 7r), **D48** (f. 5r), **D62** (f. 2r), **D83** (ff. 15v–16r). Facsimile: *The Welde Lute Book.* Edited by Ian Harwood. Albury, UK: Lute Society, 2004. xxix, 96 p. (Lute Society Facsimiles 4.) ISBN 9780905655390. M140 .W45.

Austria

135 Linz, Oberösterreichische Landesbibliothek (A-LIb). No shelfmark. c. 1610.

"Michael Eijsertt of Nürnberg Lute Book." Includes **D8** (f. 21r), **D15** (f. 11r), **D23** (ff. 94v, 100r; 102v, mandora), **D42** (f. 41r), **D48** (f. 28r), **D62** (ff. 34r, 38r).

136 Linz, Bibliothek der Oberösterreichischen Landesmuseen (A-LIn). 16, Mus. Hs. 512, Inv. 9467. c. 1611.

Keyboard. Includes **D47** (no. 11).

137 Vienna, Minoritenkonvent Musikarchiv (A-Wm). MS XIV.714 (*olim* 8). c. 1630.

Keyboard. Includes two versions of **D15** (ff. 60v–61r, arr. Scheidt; 224v–225r, arr. Scheidemann).

Belgium

138 Brussels, Bibliothèque Royale Albert 1er (B-Br). MS II.4109 (*olim* F.3095). c. 1612–1616.

Vocal a4, lower 2 voices untexted. Includes **D19** (pp. 2–3), **D23** (pp. 6–7), **D42** (pp. 4–5), **D60** (pp. 14–15), **D127** (pp. 18–19), **D128** (pp. 10–11), **D133** (pp. 12–13), **D137** (pp. 16–17), **D139** (pp. 8–9), **D146** (pp. 28–9), **D148** (pp. 24–5), **D154** (pp. 22–3), **D156** (pp. 30–1), **D157** (pp. 26–7), **D159** (pp. 20–1, a5).

139 Brussels, Library Conservatoire Royal de Bruxelles, Bibliothèque (B-Bc). MS. 26.369Z. c. 1620.

Keyboard. Multiple inclusions of **D15** (pp. 27, 28, 32).

Czech Republic

140 Prague, Narodni knihovna Ceske republiky, University Library (CZ-Pu). Ms. XXIII.F.174. c. 1608–1615.

"Nicolai Schmall von Lebendorf Lute Book." Includes **D61** (f. 22v), **D66** (f. 21v). Facsimile: *Loutnová Tablatura*. Edited by Jiří Tichota. Prague: Cimelia Bohemica, 1969. 72 p. (Editio Cimelia Bohemica 8.) M140 .M49 L70.

141 Prague, Narodni muzeum (CZ-Pdobrovského). Music Department. MS G IV 18. c. 1623–1627.

"Joannes Aegidius Rettenwert Lute Book." Includes **D9** (ff. 40v).

142 Prague, Narodni muzeum (CZ-Pdobrovského). Music Department, MS XIII B 237. Early 17th century.

"Jacobides Tablature." Lute. Includes **D66** (no. 8).

Denmark

143 Copenhagen, Det Kongelige Bibliotek (DK-Kmk). Box A 31.2001, mu 6610.2631, mu 6806.2031, U204. After 1642.

MS additions to Voigtländer's *Erster Teil allerhand Oden und Lieder*. Keyboard. Includes **D15** (ff. 2r–3v, arr. Schildt). Digital images: http://img.kb.dk/ma/vgtl/vgtl-add.pdf.

144 Copenhagen, Det Kongelige Bibliotek (DK-Kmk). Clausholm manuscript, fragment no. 1. 1634.

Keyboard. Includes **D15** (ff. 1r–4v, arr. Schildt, incomplete).

145 Copenhagen, Det Kongelige Bibliotek (DK-Kmk). Ms. Thott 841.4°. c. 1604–1608.

> "Peetrus Fabritius Lute Book." Includes D15 (ff. 109v–110r), D42 (nos. 131, 152, melody only), D50 (ff. 10v, 11r–v), D66 (f. 12v). Facsimile and Edition: *Lauten- und Liederbuch: Faksimile und Transkription der Handscrift in der Königlichen Bibliothek Kopenhagen, Signatur: Thott. 4° 841*. 2 vols. Edited by Ralf Jarchow. Glinde: Jarchow, 2013. 408, 346 p. M140 .K66. Digital images: www.kb.dk/da/nb/materialer/haandskrifter/HA/e-mss/thott-4_841.html.

France

146 Paris, Bibliothèque Nationale (F-Pn). Rés. 1122. 1654.

> Keyboard. Includes arrangement and fragment of D62 (pp. 174–81, 185). Facsimile: *Pièces pour Virginal 1646–1654: Facsimilé du Manuscrit de la Bibliothèque Nationale, Paris, Rés. 1122*. Edited by François Lesure. Geneva: Minkoff, 1982. 191 p. ISBN 2826606557. M21 .F81.

147 Paris Bibliothèque Nationale (F-Pn). Rés. 1185 (*olim* 18548). c. 1652.

> Keyboard. Includes arrangement of D15 (pp. 322–7).

148 Paris, Bibliothèque Nationale (F-Pn). Rés. 1186 (*olim* 18546). c. 1630–1640.

> Keyboard. Includes arrangements of D15 (ff. 115v–116r), D19 (f. 7v), D26 (f. 7r), D42 (ff. 8r, 117v), D48 (ff. 120v–121r), D62 (f. 24r), D79 (f. 15r–v), D125 (f. 6r), D126 (f. 6v), D127 (f. 8v), D129 (f. 9r), D130 (f. 13v), D131 (f. 13v), D132 (f. 9v), D133 (f. 10v), D134 (f. 10r), D135 (f. 13r), D137 (f. 11r), D138 (f. 11v), D139 (f. 13r), D142 (ff. 77r–78r), D146 (f. 58v), D150 (ff. 58v–59r), D152 (f. 59r), D155 (ff. 59r–60v), D156 (f. 77r). Digital images: https://gallica.bnf.fr/ark:/12148/btv1b531553751.

Germany

149 Arnsberg-Herdringen, Jagdschloss Herdringen, Bibliotheca Fürstenbergiana (D-HRD). Mus. Ms. Fü 3590a (*olim* Paderborn, Erzbischöfliche Akademische Bibliothek, Bib. 3590a). 1622.

> "Henricus Beginiker's Organ Book." Keyboard. Includes arrangement of D15 (ff. 2v–3r).

150 Bautzen, Stadt- und Kreisbibliothek (D-BAUk). Druck 13.4°.85. 1603–c. 1620.

> MS additions to Jean-Baptiste Besard's *Thesaurus Harmonicus*. Lute. Includes arrangements of D42 (p. 31), D61 (p. 50), D67 (p. 35).

151 Berlin, Staatsbibliothek zu Berlin (D-B) (*olim* Breslau Stadtbibliothek). Bohn Mus. Ms. 114.

> Keyboard. Includes arrangement of D10 (f. 76r, incomplete).

152 Berlin, Staatsbibliothek zu Berlin (D-B). Gkl Fol. 191 (*olim* HB 103, *olim* Gkl F 234, *olim* MS 52). c. 1630.

Keyboard. Includes arrangements of **D62** (ff. 27v–28v), **D79** (f. 42r).

153 Berlin, Staatsbibliothek zu Berlin, Preussischer Kulturbesitz (D-B) (*olim* Danzig/ Gdansk). Ms. Danzig 4022. c. 1621.

Lute. Includes **D47** (f. 43v), **D54** (ff. 44v–45r), **D62** (ff. 11v–12r), **D66** (f. 49v). See Tomsińska, Magdalena. "Gdańska Tablutura Lutniowa D-B Danzig 4022." *Polski Rocznik Muzykologiczny* 10 (2012): 45–102. Facsimile: *The Danzig Lutebook: D-B Danzig 4022 Staatsbibliothek zu Berlin PK.* Edited by Magdalena Tomsińska. Lübeck: Tree, 2013. M2.8 .D269. Digital images: http://resolver.staatsbibliothek-berlin.de/SBB0000148200000000.

154 Berlin, Staatsbibliothek zu Berlin, Preussischer Kulturbesitz (D-B). Ms. Lynar A1. c. 1637.

"Count zu Lynar Manuscript." Keyboard. Includes arrangement of **D66** (pp. 280–2).

155 Berlin, Staatsbibliothek zu Berlin, Preussischer Kulturbesitz (D-B). Mus. ms. 40141. c. 1607–1620.

"Johannes Nauclerus Lute Book." Includes **D15** (ff. 36v–38r), **D40** (f. 239r), **D42** (ff. 30r, 114r, 124v, 239r, 247v), **D47** (f. 43r), **D52** (f. 46v), **D79** (f. 186r). Facsimile: *Johannes Nauclerus Lautenbuch: Renaissance Laute.* Edited by Ralf Jarchow. Glinde: Jarchow, 2010. 205 p. M140 .L3773 2010.

156 Berlin, Staatsbibliothek zu Berlin, Preussischer Kulturbesitz (D-B). Mus. ms. 40377. Before 1606.

Consort. Includes **D15** (12).

157 Berlin, Staatsbibliothek zu Berlin, Preussischer Kulturbesitz (D-B). Mus. ms. autogr. Hove 1. c. 1615.

Lute. Includes multiple arrangements of **D62** (ff. 158v, 159r, 159v, 160r–159v). Facsimile: *Lautenbuch: Leiden 1615: Faksimile nach der Lautenhandschrift in der Staatsbibiothek zu Berlin-Preussischer Kulturbesitz, Signatur: Mus. ms. autogr. Hove 1.* Edited by Ralf Jarchow. Hamburg: Jarchow, 2006. Reprinted 2011. 98 p. M140 .L39.

158 Berlin, Staatsbibliothek zu Berlin, Preussischer Kulturbesitz, Musikabteilung mit Mendelssohn-Archiv (D-B). N. Mus. ms. 479.

"Grünbühel Lute Book." c. 1619. Includes **D15** (ff. 72v–74r), **D23** (ff. 60v–62r). See **534**.

159 Cologne, Staatliche Hochschule für Musik (D-KNh). Ms. R. 242. Late 16th/17th century.

"Elÿsabeth Romers Lute Book." Includes **D15** (ff. 103v–104r), **D42** (ff. 136v–137r).

160   Dresden, Sächsische Landesbibliothek (D-Dl). Handschriftenabteilung, Mscr.
      Dresd.M.297. 1603.

      "Jena Student B.K.K.S. Lute Book." Includes **D23** (p. 134), **D43** (p. 88). Digital
      images: http://digital.slub-dresden.de/id399601554.

161   Hamburg, Staats- und Universitätbibliothek (D-Hs). ND VI 3238 (*olim* Hs Ms.
      M B/2768). 1613–1619.

      "Schele Lute Manuscript." Includes **D15** (pp. 17–19, arr. van den Hove), **D23**
      (pp. 144–5), **D43** (pp. 146–7), **D44** (p. 142), **D47** (p. 148), **D48** (pp. 145–6), **D62**
      (pp. 20–4), **D93** (pp. 25–8), **D94** (pp. 28–31), **D95** (pp. 49–51), **D113** (pp. 147–8).
      Facsimile: *Tabulatur Buch: Musica et vinum lætificant cor hominis Anno 1619.*
      Edited by Ralf Jarchow. Glinde: Jarchow, 2004. 154 p. M140 .T332 2004.

162   Herdringen, Fürstlich Öttingen-Wallerstein'sche Bibliothek, Schloss Harburg.
      Mus. Ms. Fü 9829. c. 1600–1620.

      Lute. Includes **D62** (ff. 8v–9r).

163   Karlsruhe, Badische Landesbibliothek (D-KA). Mus. A 678. c. 1600–1625.

      MS bound with a copy of S. Ochsenkun, *Tabularturbuch auff die Lauten*
      (Heidelberg, 1558). Lute. Includes **D47** (f. 21r). Digital images: http://digital.
      blb-karlsruhe.de/id/3741403.

164   Kassel, Landesbibliothek und Murhardsche Bibliothek der Stadt Kassel (D-Kl).
      MS 4° mus. 108.1. c. 1609–1611.

      "Elisabeth's Lute Book"/"Victor de Montbuysson's Lute Book." Includes mul-
      tiple versions of **D8** (ff. 70v–71r), **D15** (ff. 5r–v, 55v–56r), **D19** (f. 92v), **D28**
      (ff. 94v–95r), **D42** (ff. 2r, 2v, 56v–57r), **D60** (ff. 32v, song; 1v, 64v, lute), **D61** (ff.
      23v, 38r), **D70** (f. 3v). See **404**. Facsimile: *Lautenbuch der Elisabeth von Hessen:
      Facsimile 4° Ms. Mus. 108.1, Universitätbibliothek Kassel.* Edited by Axel Halle.
      Kassel: Bärenreiter, 2005. ISBN 9783761817780. M140 .L375. Digital images:
      https://orka.bibliothek.uni-kassel.de/viewer/image/1484138262748/1/LOG_0000/.

165   Kassel, Landesbibliothek und Murhardsche Bibliothek der Stadt Kassel (D-Kl).
      MS 4° mus. 125/1–5. c. 1590–1600.

      Instrumental consort a5. Includes **D8** (no. 49), **D15** (no. 42).

166   Leipzig, Musikbibliothek der Stadt (D-LEm). II.6.15. 1619.

      "Dlugoraj Lute Book." Includes **D10** (pp. 104–5), **D15** (pp. 78–9, 122–3, duet or
      consort part), **D23** (pp. 198, 230), **D40** (pp. 198, 202, 518), **D43** (p. 147), **D48**
      (pp. 347, 367, 491, 498), **D49** (p. 479), **D52** (pp. 296, 448), **D54** (pp. 454, 499), **D55**
      (p. 241), **D60** (pp. 472, 502), **D62** (p. 412), **D66** (p. 372), **D85** (pp. 218, 234), **D86**
      (p. 114), **D87** (p. 195). Facsimile: *Sogenanntes Lautenbuch des Albert Dlugorai
      1619: Handschrift, Signature II. 6.15, Musikbibliothek der Stadt Leipzig.* Edited
      by Herbert Speck and John H. Robinson. Lübeck: Tree, 2001. M140 .S43 2004.

167 Leipzig, Musikbibliothek der Stadt (D-LEm). Ms. II.6.23. Early 17th century.

"Johannes Friedericus Lute Book." Includes **D62** (f. 45r–v).

168 Leipzig, Musikbibliothek der Stadt (D-LEm). Ms. III.11.26. c. 1625–1630.

Lute. Includes **D48** (p. 2). Facsimile: *15 Stücke für Renaissance-Laute: Reproduktion nach der Handschrift im Besitz der Stadt Leipzig Städtische Bibliotheken Musikbibliothek (Signatur III. 11.26), ca 1620 (15 Pieces)*. Munich: Tree, 1998. 32 p. M140 .F933.

169 Lüneburg, Ratsbücherei und Stadtarchiv (D-Lr). Mus.ant.pract. 2000. First half 17th century.

"Wolf Christian von Harling Lute Book." Includes **D23** (pp. 4–5), **D55** (pp. 12–13), **D62** (p. 13). Facsimile: *Lautenbuch des Wolff Christian von Harling.* Edited by Joachim Lüdtke. Lübeck: Tree, 2005. 117 p. M2.8 .H37 L83.

170 Lüneburg, Ratsbücherei und Stadtarchiv, Musikabteilung (D-Lr). Mus.ant.pract. K.N. 146. c. 1650.

Keyboard. Includes **D15** (ff. 154v–157r), **D19** (ff. 173v–175r), **D42** (no. 71).

171 Lüneburg, Ratsbücherei und Stadtarchiv (D-Lr). Mus.ant.pract. K.N.148. 1655–1659.

"Franciscus Witzendorff Keyboard Book." Includes **D62** (no. 47).

172 Nürnberg, Germanisches Nationalmuseum (D-Ngm). Ms. 33748.I. c. 1615–1620.

Lute. Includes multiple versions of **D23** (ff. 9v–10r, duet; 13v), **D42** (ff. 6v, 7r–v, 7v–8r, 65v, 66r), **D43** (f. 3r), **D48** (f. 36v), **D105** (f. 4v). Digital images: http://dlib.gnm.de/item/Hs33748-1.

173 Themar, Evangelisch-Lutherisches Pfarramt, Pfarrarchiv (D-TH). No shelfmark. 1600–1649.

Keyboard. Includes **D15** (ff. 11v–12r, 12v–13r).

174 Ulm, Stadtbibliothek (D-Us). MS Smr Misc 130. 1620.

Violin and bass. Includes **D15** (no. 8, arr. Schermer). Facsimile: *Tänze für 2 Violen. Schermar-Bibliothek, Stadtbibliothek, Ulm, Sign. misc 130.* Stuttgart: Cornetto, 1997. (Faksimile-Edition Schermar-Bibliothek Ulm 13.) M990 .T123 C8.

175 Weimar, Hochschule für Musik Franz Liszt, Hochschularchiv (D-WRha). Udestedt 38 a, Teilband 9. c. 1650.

Consort a5 plus bass. Includes **D15** (f. 8v, arr. Hausmann).

176 Wolfenbüttel, Herzog August Bibliothek (D-W). Cod. Guelf. 18.7 and 18.8 Aug. 2°. 1603.

"Philipp Hainhofer Lute Books." **D42** (f. 22v), **D66** (f. 36r), **D101** (f. 17r), **D102** (f. 17r), **D103** (f. 6v). Digital images: http://diglib.hab.de/mss/18-8-aug-2f/start.htm.

Hungary

177 Budapest, Országos Széchényi Könyvtár (H-Bn). Mus.ms. Bártfa 27. c. 1660.

Keyboard. Includes arrangements of **D15** (ff. 34v–36r, arr. Sweelinck), **D40** (ff. 50v–52r, arr. Scheidt).

Italy

178 Florence, Biblioteca Nazionale Centrale (I-Fn). Dipartimento Musica, MS Magl. XIX, 115. c. 1600–1620.

Keyboard. Includes an arrangement of **D54** (f. 5r–v).

179 Genoa, Biblioteca Universitaria (I-Gu). M. VIII.24. c. 1603.

Lute. MS additions to *Thesaurus Harmonicus* (1603). Includes **D113** (ff. 140r–139v).

180 Turin, Biblioteca Nazionale Universitaria (I-Tn). MS Foà 7. Early 17th century.

Keyboard. Includes arrangements of **D15** (ff. 56v–57v), **D60** (ff. 54v–55v, 56r–57r).

181 Turin, Biblioteca Nazionale Universitaria (I-Tn). Ms. Fondo Mauro, Foà MS 8. 17th century.

Keyboard. Includes an arrangement of **D62** (ff. 132r–134r).

Lithuania

182 Vilnius, Central Library of the Lithuanian Academy of Science (LT-Vu). Manuscript 285-MF-LXXIX (*olim* Preußisches Staatsarchiv, Königsberg, Msc. A 116.fol.). c. 1605–1625.

"The Königsberg Manuscript." Lute. **D15** (ff. 24v, lute; 38v–41r, consort bandora), **D23** (ff. 5v, consort lute; 21r, 22v, lute; 40v, consort bandora), **D40** (ff. 22v; 22v–23r, var.), **D42** (ff. 22v–23r, 58v), **D43** (ff. 21r, 21v, 56v), **D48** (f. 66v), **D61** (f. 1r, treble lute and bandora consort parts), **D62** (ff. 7v, 20v, 27v, 60r), **D66** (ff. 14v, 41r, 57r), **D67** (f. 24r), **D70** (f. 6v), **D108** (f. 66r), **D113** (f. 1r). Facsimile: *The Königsberg Manuscript: A Facsimile of Manuscript 285-MF-LXXIX (olim Preussisches Staatsarchiv, Königsberg, Msc. A 116. fol.), Central Library of the Lithuanian Academy of Science, Vilnius.* Edited by Arthur J. Ness and John M. Ward. Columbus: Editions Orphée, 1989. ISBN 0936186313. M140 .K65.

Netherlands

183 The Hague, Nederlands Muziek Instituut (NL-DHnmi). Ms. 20.860 (*olim* Gemeentemuseum MS 28 B 39). c. 1560–1570.

"Siena Lute Book." Includes **D54** (f. 113v).

184 The Hague, Nederlands Muziek Instituut (NL-DHnmi). NMI kluis A 16 (*olim* Gemeentemeseum Den Haag MS 21 E 47). 1609.

Keyboard. Includes an arrangement of **D15** (f. 19v, arr. Schmidt).

185 Leiden, Bibliotheca Thysiana (NL-Lt). Ms. 1666. c. 1610–1620.

"The Thysius Lute Book." **D15** (ff. 388v; 389v, duet or consort part), **D20** (f. 22r), **D23** (f. 28v), **D35** (f. 26v), **D42** (f. 22v, duet), **D43** (ff. 21v, 392v), **D47** (f. 503r), **D48** (ff. 492r–493r), **D61** (f. 399r), **D62** (ff. 387r, 387v, 388r, 477r), **D66** (f. 389r), **D85** (f. 33r).

186 Utrecht, Instituut voor Muziekwetenschap der Rijkuninversiteit (NL-Uim). Mso-2 Hans Brandts Buys, 1.B.37. Mid-17th century.

Keyboard. Includes an arrangement of **D62** (ff. 34v–35r). Digital images: http://objects.library.uu.nl/reader/resolver.php?obj=002311150.

Poland

187 Kraków, Biblioteka Jagiellońska (PL-Kj) (*olim* Staatsbibliothek zu Berlin). Mus. ant. pract. H 540. 1590s.

MS additions to *Neue Teutsche Weltliche Lieder*. 3 voice partbooks. Includes **D15** (f. 1r). See **525**. Digital images: https://jbc.bj.uj.edu.pl/publication/302664.

188 Kraków, Biblioteka Jagiellońska (PL-Kj). Mus.ms.40089. 1598.

"August Nörmiger's Tablature." Keyboard. Includes an arrangement of **D43** (pt. 2, no. 43). Digital images: https://jbc.bj.uj.edu.pl/publication/294021.

189 Kraków, Biblioteka Jagiellońska (PL-Kj). Mus. ms. 40143. 1594/1601.

"Richard Manuscript." Lute. Includes **D48** (ff. 59v–60r), **D52** (f. 60v), **D62** (f. 62r), **D66** (f. 24r).

190 Kraków, Biblioteka Jagiellońska (PL-Kj). Berol. Mus. ms. 40153. c. 1620.

"Casimir Rudomina Dusiacki Lute Book." Includes **D54** (ff. 59v–60r). Digital images: https://jbc.bj.uj.edu.pl/publication/330386.

191 Kraków, Biblioteka Jagiellońska (PL-Kj). Mus. ms. 40159. c. 1635–1640.

Lute. Includes **D62** (f. 16r).

192 Kraków, Biblioteka Jagiellońska (PL-Kj). Mus.ms.40316. Before 1626.

Keyboard. Includes two arrangements of **D19** (ff. 8v–9r, 30v–31r, arr. Philips).

Sweden

193 Skokloster, Slottsbiblioteket (S-B). Carl Gustaf Wrangels Bibliotek, MS 2245. 1615–1622.

"Lucas Beckman Lute Book." Includes arrangements of **D23** (ff. 15v–16r), **D62** (ff. 13r–13v, 13v).

194   Skokloster, Slottsbiblioteket (S-B). PB.fil.172. c. 1610–1620.

"Per Brahe Lutebook." Includes **D1** (ff. 27v–31r), **D23** (ff. 15v–16r), **D40** (f. 33r), **D43** (ff. 25v–26r), **D47** (ff. 16v–17r), **D62** (f. 14r), **D74** (ff. 27v–31r). See **535**.

195   Stockholm, Musik- och teaterbiblioteket (S-SKma). Tablature no. 1. c. 1600.

"Elisabeth Eysbock's Keyboard Book." Includes **D8** (f. 57r), **D15** (ff. 24v–25v), **D42** (ff. 62v–63r), **D48** (f. 10v), **D62** (f. 34r), **D66** (f. 2r).

196   Uppsala, Universitetsbibliotek (S-Uu). Instr. mus. i. hs. 408. 1637–1653.

"Gustav Düben's Keyboard Book"/ "The Anders von Duben Tablature." Includes **D15** (ff. 28v–29r, arr. Schildt, incomplete; 34v–35r, arr. Schildt), **D95** (ff. 1v–3r, arr. Siefert). Digital images: http://www2.musik.uu.se/duben/presentationSource1.php?Select_Dnr=2835.

Switzerland

197   Basel, Öffentliche Bibliothek der Universität Musiksammlung (CH-Bu). Ms. F IX.53. c. 1620–1645.

Lute. Includes **D79** (f. 19r). Digital images: http://doi.org/10.7891/e-manuscripta-15690.

198   Basel, Öffentliche Bibliothek der Universität Musiksammlung (CH-Bu). Ms. F IX.70. c. 1591–1594.

"Emanuel Wurstisen Lute Book." Includes **D66** (pp. 331–2). Digital images: http://doi.org/10.7891/e-manuscripta-13217.

Ukraine

199   Lviv, Ivan Franco National University Library (UA-LVu). Ms 1400/1. Date uncertain.

"Crakow Lute MS." Lute. Includes **D2** (ff. 54v–56r), **D3** (ff. 41v–43r), **D6** (ff. 39v–41r). See **536**.

United States

200   Berkeley, University of California Music Library (US-BEb). Ms. 757. c. 1615–1630.

Lute. Includes **D54** (f. 1v).

201   Berkeley, University of California Music Library (US-BEb). Ms. 760. c. 1615–1630.

Lute. Includes **D54** (f. 17r).

202 Cambridge, MA, Harvard University, Houghton Library (US-CAh). MS Mus 181. c. 1600/after 1650.

"Matthew Otley Cittern Book." Includes **D19** (f. 14r), **D48** (ff. 13v–14r), **D60** (f. 11r), **D104** (f. 10v, arr. Springell). Digital images: http://nrs.harvard.edu/ urn-3:FHCL.HOUGH:4686836.

203 Los Angeles, University of California, William Andrews Clark Memorial Library (US-LAuc). MS.1959.003. c. 1676–1689.

"Robert Taitt Musical Commonplace Book." Vocal a4. Includes **D60** (ff. 75v, 86v), **D79** (f. 34v), **D125** (f. 149r), **D133** (f. 67r), **D148** (f. 74v), **D156** (f. 64r), **D168** (f. 66v).

204 New Haven, Yale University Music Library (US-NH). Misc. MS 170 (*olim* Beinecke MS 469). 1588–1603.

3 voice partbooks. Includes **D134** (ff. 12v, 12v, 28v).

205 New Haven, Yale University Music Library (US-NH). Music Deposit 1 (*olim* Rare Ma21 W632). c. 1595.

"Wickhambrook Lute Book." Includes **D48** (f. 17r), **D50** (f. 15r), **D59** (f. 11r), **D66** (f. 12r), **D67** (f. 17r). Facsimile: *The 'Wickhambrook Lute Manuscript': US-NH, New Haven (CT) Yale University Irving S. Gilmore Music Library Music Deposit 1 (formerly Rare Ma21 W632).* Edited by Ian Harwood. Inventory, Notes, and Bibliography by John H. Robinson. Guildford, UK: Lute Society, 2008. 56 p. (Lute Society Facsimiles 6.) ISBN 97809056553659. ML96.4 .W637.

206 New Haven, Yale University Music Library (US-NH). Osborn fb7.

Lute. Includes **D206** (f. 95r). See **502**. Facsimile: *Osborn fb7: The James Marshall and Marie-Louise Osborn Marshall Collection Beinecke Rare Book and Manuscript Library, Yale University.* Edited by Stewart McCoy. Albury, UK: Lute Society, 2007. xxxvii, 78 p. (Lute Society Facsimiles 5.) ISBN 0905655508. M140 .O81. Digital images: https://brbl-dl.library.yale.edu/vufind/Record/3524653.

207 New York Public Library (US-NYpl). Drexel 4175. Before 1630.

"Anne Twice her booke." Includes **D132** (f. 8r). Voice with bass. Facsimile: *English Song 1600–1675: Facsimiles of Twenty-Six Manuscripts and an Edition of the Texts.* v. 11. Edited by Elise Bickford Jorgens. New York and London: Garland, 1986. M2 .E65 v.11. Digital images: https://digitalcollections.nypl.org/items/ c7e43b20-9257-0134-1943-00505686a51c.

208 New York Public Library (US-NYpl). Drexel 5612. c. 1620–1660.

Keyboard. Includes **D8** (p. 4), **D10** (p. 4), **D15** (pp. 186–7), **D19** (p. 4), **D79** (pp. 70–1). Facsimile: *Keyboard Music: In Facsimile from BL Add. MS 30485, NYPL Drexel Ms 5612, RCM (London) MS 2093.* Edited by Desmond Hunter. Clarabricken, Ireland: Boethius, 1985. x, 29 p. (Musical Sources 24.) ISBN 086314103X. M22 .W44.

209   New York Public Library (US-NYpl). Mus. Res. MN T131. c. 1635.

Keyboard. Includes **D15** (f. 14r), **D60** (f. 14r).

210   Private collection. MS additions to *Parthenia*. c. 1640–1650.

Keyboard. Includes an arrangement of **D15** (ff. 2v–4v, arr. Cussen).

211   San Francisco, California State University and Colleges, Frank V. De Bellis Collection (US-SFsc). M2.1 M3. 1615.

Lute. Includes two versions of **D54** (pp. 26–7, 79). Digital images: http://digital-collections.library.sfsu.edu/cdm/ref/collection/p16737coll4/id/1154.

†**212**   Washington, Folger Shakespeare Library (US-Ws). Ms. V.b.280 (*olim* MS 1610.1). c. 1590s.

"Folger-Dowland Lutebook." Lute. Includes **D15** (ff. 18v–19r), **D23** (f. 12v, signed), **D39** (f. 6r, possible consort part), **D40** (ff. 10v–11r), **D42** (f. 16r, signed), **D47** (ff. 13v–14r, signed), **D48** (f. 11v, signed), **D53** (f. 23v, in Dowland's hand), **D54** (f. 22v, in Dowland's hand and signed), **D55** (f. 5v), **D62** (f. 57r), **D66** (f. 9v, first part of duet, signed), **D70** (f. 16v), **D79** (ff. 23r, in Dowland's hand; 87r), **D83** (f. 22r), **D113** (f. 13r). See **285**, **527**, **541**. Facsimile: *The Folger 'Dowland' Manuscript*. Introduction and notes by Christopher Goodwin and Ian Harwood. Concordances by John H. Robinson. Guildford, UK: Lute Society, 2003. xxxi, 82 p. (Lute Society Facsimiles 3.) ISBN 0905655281. ML96.4 .D747. Digital images: http://luna.folger.edu/luna/servlet/s/22omo6.

Sources Lost or Based on Lost Sources

213   Destroyed. *Olim* Bassano, Private Library, Oscar Chilesotti.

Copied from "Dusiacki Lute Book." Included **D54** (p. 78). c. 1590s.

214   Location unknown. Private collection. "Herhold Lute Book." 1602.

Copied in Padua. Included **D15** (ff. 24r–27r), **D44** (ff. 39v–40v), **D46** (ff. 27r–28r), **D62** (ff. 18v–21r).

215   Lost. "Robert Gordon of Straloch Lute Book." 1627–1629.

Copied in Edinburgh, National Library of Scotland (GB-En). Adv.MS.5.2.18, 1847. Included **D23** (13), **D133** (f. 6v, index only).

216   Lost. Previously UK private collection. c. 1600.

Song. Included **D202**. See **396**. Served as basis for Hamilton Harty's *Adieu, sweet Amaryllis*, manuscript housed at Belfast, Queen's University, MS 14/1/59. Whereabouts of original unknown.

4

Editions

LUTE SONG-AIRS

217   Dart, Thurston, and Edmund Horace Fellowes, eds. *The English Lute Songs, Series 1*. London: Stainer and Bell. M2 .F4213.

Updated versions of Fellowes's collection of the 1920s (**220**), with improvements and corrections. The volumes include only voice and lute (in tablature and modern staff notation), without any additional voice parts. This series is superseded by **219**, which provides the best, most complete modern edition of Dowland's lute song-airs.

v. 1–2 *The First Book of Ayres (1597, 1600, 1603, 1606, 1613)*. 1965. Reprinted 1998. iv, 44 p.

v. 5–6 *The Second Book of Songs (1600)*. 1969. Reprinted 1998. 55 p.

v. 10–11 *The Third Booke of Songs (1603)*. 1970. Reprinted 1996. vi, 45 p.

v. 12, 14 *A Pilgrimes Solace (1612). Three Songs from a Musicall Banquet (1610)*. 1969. Reprinted 1995. v, 86 p.

v. 20 *A Musicall Banquet (1610)*. Edited by Peter Stroud. 1968. vii, 66 p. Reprinted 1977.

218   Dowland, John. *Ayres for Four Voices*. Edited by Thurston Dart and Nigel Fortune. London: Stainer and Bell, 1953. xv, 115 p. (Musica Britannica 6.) M2 .M638 v.6.

Supplements Fellowes's original series (**220**) to offer versions of Dowland's lute song-airs with all four voice parts represented, but lacks lute tablature. Revised and reissued in 1963 and 1970. Superseded by **219.**

219   Dowland, John. *Ayres for Four Voices.* 2nd ed. Edited by David Greer. London: Stainer and Bell, 2000. xxxv, 215 p. (Musica Britannica 6). ISBN 0852498586. M2 .M638 v.6.

Critical edition of Dowland's four songbooks (1597, 1600, 1603, and 1612). Features transcription of all voice parts and lute in tablature and modern notation. Textual spellings are modernized. Also includes facsimiles of a title page and dedicatory material, a lute tablature manuscript with Dowland's signature, and pages from a seventeenth-century collection of Dutch prints. Other material encompasses a list of sources, textual commentary with notes, variant readings of four *First Booke* editions, and an index of poets. This edition is an update of Edmund Fellowes's solo voice with accompaniment lute song series (**220**) that was edited and updated by Nigel Fortune and Thurston Dart in 1953 to include all voice parts (**218**). Presented as part of the Musica Britannica series. Highly recommended for any research related to Dowland's songs.

220   Fellowes, Edmund Horace, ed. *English School of Lutenist Song Writers.* London: Stainer and Bell. M2 .F42.

Dowland volumes in this series present two versions of each included song: voice with transcribed tablature notation with original tablature below; and voice with edited piano accompaniment, sometimes transposed to another key "to align [them] with a medium voice part." Each Dowland collection is issued in two volumes. Parts for violin and cello (or viols) are included, as needed. English text is modernized. A short preface opens each, and some volumes have selected facsimile pages and transcriptions of prefatory material. No individual song commentary is provided. Many biographical facts referenced in the introduction have come into question in more recent years. Superseded by **217**, which was further updated and revised to meet higher editorial standards in **219**. Use only for historical purposes.

v. 1–2 *John Dowland: First Book of Airs. 1597.* 1920, 1921.

v. 5–6 *John Dowland: Second Book of Airs. 1600.* 1922, 1925.

v. 10–11 *John Dowland: Third Book of Airs. 1603.* Parts I and II. 1923.

v. 12, 14 *John Dowland: A Pilgrimes Solace (Fourth Book of Airs) 1612 and Three Songs included in Musicall Banqvet. 1610.* Parts I and II. 1924, 1925. 124 p.

LUTE SOLOS AND DUOS

221   Poulton, Diana, and Basil Lam, eds. *The Collected Lute Music of John Dowland.* 3rd ed. Kassel, Germany: Faber Music, 1995. xvi, 343 p. ISBN 0571100392. M140 .D69 P7.

An esteemed musical anthology attempting comprehensive presentation of Dowland's solo lute music, though other works have been discovered since publication. In addition to musical transcriptions (in both modern staff notation and tablature), the volume features a Dowland timeline, commentary on selected persons for whom works were named, and textual notes providing concordances, information on sources, keys, and variants. First edition printed in 1974.

CONSORT MUSIC

222 Dowland, John. *Complete Consort Music for Viols or Recorders*. Edited by Edgar Hunt. London: Schott, 1985. ix, 96 p. M990 .D68 C53.

Score includes five instrumental parts in modern notation, but no lute tablature. Intended as a performance edition, there are separate partbooks for each instrumentalist, and the lute partbook features tablature. Contains items from *Lachrimae* (1604), as well as pieces from other consort sources such as Füllsack and Hildebrand's *Ausserlesener Paduanen und Galliarden*, Simpson's *Opusculum* and *Taffel Consort*, Cellarius's *Album amicorum*, and British Library, Add. MS 10444. Features an introduction in English and German, but no critical commentary.

223 Dowland, John. *Lachrimae or Seaven Teares*. Edited by Linda Sayce and David Pinto, London: Fretwork Editions, 2004. xxxi, 56 p. ISBN 1898131600. M990 .D68 L33.

A performance edition produced with extremely high editorial standards and scholarly intentions. Includes all the original viol parts, as well as a lute transcription. Original tablature is omitted. Textual notes, commentary on variants, and introductory material are impressive.

PSALMS

224 Dowland, John. *Complete Psalms for SATB*. Edited by Diana Poulton. London: Stainer & Bell, 1973. 28 p. ISBN 0852491689. M2082.4 .D73 P8.

Anthologizes Dowland's psalm settings, including those found in Sternhold and Hopkins's *Whole Booke of Psalmes* (1592), Ravenscroft's *Whole Booke of Psalmes* (1621), and *Lamentatio Henrici Noel*, the manuscript set of psalms composed upon the death of Dowland's patron Sir Henry Noel.

KEYBOARD ARRANGEMENTS

225 Dowland, John. *John Dowland: Keyboard Music*. Edited by Christopher Hogwood. Launton, UK: Edition HH, 2005. xii, 84 p. ISBN 1904229573. M32.8 .D68 K4.

Includes contemporaneous keyboard arrangements of Dowland's works, some by named arrangers and some anonymous. Contains just thirty compositions, so this volume is not a complete representation of all keyboard works inspired by

Dowland, but the anthology includes many of the most important, including versions of *Lachrimae Pavan, Piper's Galliard, Frog Galliard, Lady Laiton's Almain,* and others, arranged by composers such as Byrd, Peerson, Sweelinck, and others.

MISCELLANEOUS

226   Musica Britannica series. London: Stainer and Bell. M2 .M638.

Though scattered throughout the enormous Musica Britannica series, the following volumes include Dowland-inspired pieces arranged by English composers or found in English manuscripts. See also **219**.

v. 9 *Jacobean Consort Music.* Edited by William Coates and Thurston Dart. 1971. Revised from original 1955 print. Reprinted 1977. ISBN 9780852494097.

Includes Corkine's arrangement of "If my complaints" and a Dowland pavan.

v. 19 Bull, John. *Keyboard Music II.* 3rd ed. Edited by Alan Brown. 2016. Revision of 1963 edition, edited by Thurston Dart. ISBN 0852499507.

Includes Dowland-inspired pieces from manuscripts including Cambridge, Fitzwilliam Mus. MS 168 (Fitzwilliam Virginal Book).

v. 22 *Consort Songs.* Edited by Philip Brett. 1974. ISBN 9780852494219.

Includes "Sorrow come" for voice and viols, transcribed from British Library, Add. MSS 17786–91.

v. 24 Farnaby, Giles, and Richard Farnaby. *Keyboard Music.* Edited by Richard Marlow. 1974. Revision of 1965 edition. ISBN 9780852494233.

Includes Farnaby's arrangement of *Lachrimae Pavan.*

v. 40 *Music for Mixed Consort.* Edited by Warwick Edwards. 1977. Reprinted with corrections 1985. ISBN 9780852494363.

Includes "Fortune my Foe" (lute part only).

v. 55 *Elizabethan Keyboard Music.* Edited by Alan Brown. 1989. ISBN 0852497652.

Includes Dowland-inspired pieces from British Library, Add. MS 30485 and Royal Music 24.d.3, New York Public Library, Drexel 5612, and Bodleian Library, MS. Mus. Sch. d. 143.

v. 75 Philips, Peter. *Complete Keyboard Music.* Edited by David J. Smith. 1999. ISBN 0852498519.

Includes Dowland-inspired pieces from Kraków, Biblioteka Jagiellońska, Mus. MS 40316

v. 96 *English Keyboard Music c. 1600–1625.* Edited by Alan Brown. 2014. ISBN 9780852499375.

Includes Dowland-inspired pieces from Oxford, Christ Church Library, Mus. 431, New York Public Library, Drexel 5612, and National Library of Scotland, MS.9448.

v. 102 *Keyboard Music from Fitzwilliam Manuscripts*. Edited by Christopher Hogwood and Alan Brown. 2017. ISBN 9780852499528.

Includes Dowland-inspired pieces from the *Fitzwilliam Virginal Book* (**67**) and *Tisdale's Virginal Book* (**69**).

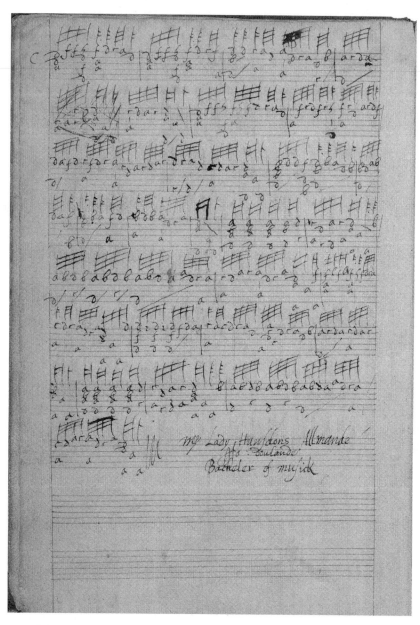

Figure 2 "My Lady Hunsdons Allmande," in the hand of the composer. US-Ws, V.b.280, 22v. By permission of the Folger Shakespeare Library.

Source: By permission of the Folger Shakespeare Library.

5

Primary Source Bibliography
Documents and Literature

For primary source musical prints and manuscripts, and facsimiles of musical volumes, see Chapter 3.

DOWLAND'S WRITINGS

Letters

227 Letter, John Dowland to Robert Cecil. Nüremberg. November 10, 1595. Hatfield, UK, Hatfield House Archives. Cecil Papers, 172: 91–3, 94.

The famous "Cecil letter" from which more Dowland commentary is derived than any other primary source. Followed by Dowland's inclusion of an introductory letter from the priest John Scudamore to Nicholas Fitzherbert, written the previous July. Catalogued and transcribed in the *Calendar of the Manuscripts of the Most Hon. the Marquis of Salisbury, K. G., preserved at Hatfield House, Hertfordshire: Part 5*, ed. R. A. Roberts (London: Her Majesty's Stationery Office, 1894), 269, 445–7. For an online transcription, see **302** or *British History Online*, www.british-history.ac.uk/cal-cecil-papers/vol5/pp437-458. Facsimile in **264**.

Material in Printed Volumes

228 Dowland, John. *Andreas Ornithoparcus his Micrologus, or Introduction: Containing the art of singing Digested into foure bookes. Not onely profitable, but also necessary for all that are studious of musicke. Also the dimension and perfect vse of the monochord, according to Guido Aretinus.* London: Thomas Snodham, 1609.

Dowland's 1609 translation of Orinthoparcus's 1517 theoretical treatise. For a facsimile and commentary, see *A Compendium of Musical Practice*, Gustave Reese and Steven Ledbetter, eds. New York: Dover, 1973. xxx, 212 p. ISBN 9780486209128. MT6 .Q7.

229 Dowland, John. *The First Booke of Songes or Ayres of fowre partes with Tableture for the Lute: So made that all the partes together, or either of them seuerally may be song to the Lute, Orpherian or Viol de gambo.* London: Peter Short, 1597. Reprinted in 1600, 1603, 1606, 1613.

Prefatory material written by the composer includes a dedicatory epistle to Sir George Carey, Baron Hunsdon and instructions "To the courteous reader," which hints at some biographical information. Musical portions are detailed in **1**.

230 Dowland, John. *Lachrimae, or Seauen Teares Figured in Seauen Passionate Pauans, with diuers other Pauans, Galiards, and Almands, set forth for the Lute, Viols, or Violons, in fiue parts.* London: John Windet, 1604.

Non-musical inclusions written by Dowland consist of an epigram and dedication to Queen Anne, and a letter "To the Reader." Musical portions are detailed in **4**.

231 Dowland, John. "Other Necessary Obseruations belonging to the Lute." In **252**.

Includes commentary on the best types of strings for the lute, as well as fretting and tuning (ff. D1r–E2r), which should be of special interest to those involved in lute organology and historical performance practice.

232 Dowland, John. *A Pilgrimes Solace Wherein is contained Musicall Harmonie of 3. 4. and 5. parts, to be sung and plaid with the Lute and Viols.* London: Thomas Snodham, 1612.

A dedication to Lord Walden and extended introduction "To the reader" open Dowland's 1612 songbook. Musical portions are detailed in **5**.

233 Dowland, John. *The Second Booke of Songs or Ayres, of 2. 4. and 5. parts: With Tableture for the Lute or Orpherian, with the Violl de Gamba.* London: Thomas Este, 1600.

Dowland wrote less in the prefatory sections of his second lute song-air book than in his other anthologies, but does include a short dedication to Lady Lucy Russell, Countess of Bedford. The letter to the reader and an acrostic poem on Russell's name titled "To I. Dowlands Lute" are provided by publisher George Eastland. For musical portions of volume, see **2**.

234 Dowland, John. *The Third and Last Booke of Songs or Aires Newly Composed to sing to the Lute, Orpharion, or viols, and a dialogue for a base and meane Lute with fiue voices to sing thereto.* London: Peter Short, 1603.

Opens with a dedicatory epistle to John Souch and a comparatively brief "epistle to the reader." Musical portions are detailed in **3**.

Dedicatory Poems

235 Dowland, John. "Figurate Musicke doth in each Degree." In Thomas Ravenscroft, *A Briefe Discourse Of the true (but neglected) vse of Charact'ring the Degrees, by their Perfection, Imperfection, and Diminution in Measurable Musicke, against the Common Practise and Custome of these Times*. London: Edward Allde, 1614.

Prefatory material includes a verse tribute to Ravenscroft from "Iohn Dowland Bachelar of Musicke, and Lutenist to the Kings Sacred Maiestie, in Commendation of this Worke" (no Sig). Ward suggests that this stanza was perhaps a paid commission (**265**, p. 24, n73).

236 Dowland, John. "If Musicks art by Sacred and Divine." In Richard Alison, *The Psalmes of Dauid in Meter, The plaine Song beeing the common tunne to be sung and plaide vpon the Lute, Orpharyon, Citterne or Base Violl, seuerally or altogether, the singing part to be either Tenor or Treble to the Instrument, according to the nature of the voyce, or for foure voyces*. London: William Barley, 1599.

Dowland is featured as the first contributor of commendatory verse in this psalm collection with his sonnet "If Musicks arte by Sacred and Divine" (f. A3r).

237 Dowland, John. "If that be true the Poet doth auerre." In William Leighton, *The Teares or Lamentacions of a Sorrowfvll Sovle: Composed with Musicall Ayres and Songs, both for Voyces and diuers Instruments*. London: William Stansby, 1614.

Dowland provides a commendatory verse (f. a2r), labeled "Vpon this Excellent and diuine Worke." As with **235**, Ward suggests the poem was solicited and paid for (**265**, p. 24, n73).

238 Dowland, John. "Thou only shalt have Phyllis." In Giles Farnaby, *Canzonets to Fowre Voyces, With a Song of eight parts*. London: Peter Short, 1598.

Dowland contributes one of three prefatory verse commendations to Farnaby's song collection.

OTHER IMPORTANT PRIMARY SOURCE DOCUMENTS

Letters to Dowland

239 Letter, Stephen Lesieur to John Dowland. December 9, 1602. Copenhagen, Det Kongelige Bibliotek, NKS 1305 2°, læg 5.

A letter from Stephen Lesieur, an agent for the English court, asking for Dowland's assistance acquiring information related to ongoing maritime issues between England and Denmark. May or may not have been received by Dowland. Facsimile in **288**. See also **287**, **288**, **289**, and **290**.

240 Letters, Henry Noel, and Moritz, Landgrave of Hesse, to John Dowland. 1596, 1598. Washington, Folger Shakespeare Library, V.a.321.

Includes early seventeenth-century copies of two letters written to Dowland, one from Noel, written in 1596 to reassure the musician of the queen's favor while he was still at the Landgrave of Hesse's court (ff. 52v–53r), and the second from the Landgrave himself, written in 1598, offering understanding for Dowland's departure and assuring continued esteem (f. 53r). For facsimiles and transcriptions, see **281**. Digital images: http://luna.folger.edu/luna/servlet/s/w6fvn1.

Other Selected Manuscript Documents

241   Berkeley, UK, Berkeley Castle Archives (GB-BER). Berkeley Family Muniments, General series Bound Book 108, f. 196.

Records a January 1598/9 payment to "Dowland and his Consorte." See **279** for image.

242   Copenhagen, Rigarkivet (Danish National Archives). Rentemesterregnskaber, 1599–1600, ff. 474v, 476r–v; 1600–1601, ff. 529v, 530r, 532v; 1601–1602, f. 711; 1602–1603, ff. 978v–979r, 982v; 1603–1604, "Instrumentister" (no f.); 1604–1605, ff. 590v, 593r, 595r; 1605–1606, ff. 532v, 535r, 536v–537r; Bilag til Rentemesterregnskaber (Udg. konto no. 7 [C.d.]), 1600–1601, 1601–1602; D. Kanc. Sjaell. Tegn. no. 19, 1596–1604, f. 326v, f. 379r; no. 15, 1605–1612, ff. 65v–66r.

Payment records related to Dowland's salary and service while the musician was employed by Christian IV of Denmark from 1598 to 1606. For transcriptions, see **265** (pp. 100–7).

243   Kew, National Archives. Assorted records.

AO 389/49, specifies appointment to the King's Lutes; AO 392/65, records final payment to Dowland and indicates his son Robert has replaced him in the King's Lutes; E179/70/34a, taxation records; E351/543/254–71, records appointment of Dowland to James I's musicians; E351/544 (1612–1625), details payments from the Treasurer to Dowland throughout James I's reign; LC2/6 f. 45v, listed as part of "The Consorte" for James I's funeral; SO 3/5, grants position to Dowland as one of the King's lutenists; SO 3/8, warrant to pay Robert for services since John's death; SP 78/12/142, a 1584 petition to Sir Edward Stafford identifying Dowland as a messenger for the new French ambassador. See **278.**

244   London, Lincoln's Inn Archives. Black Book VI, f. 527.

Records payments to Cutting, Dowland, and Rosseter, among others, for playing the lute for a masque celebrating the nuptials of Princess Elizabeth and Frederick of Palatine, presented at Whitehall in 1613. Transcribed in *Records of the Honourable Society of Lincoln's Inn: The Black Books*. Vol. II. London: Lincoln's Inn, 1898 (pp. 155–6). See **321**.

245   London, Metropolitan Archives. P69/ANN.

St. Ann, Blackfriars parish record. Records Dowland's February 1626 burial. Described in **304**.

246   London, Middle Temple Archives. MT.7/GDE/3.

Receipt with Dowland's signature, for payment to the lutenist and others for participation in Candlemas Day festivities in 1612. For more details, see **283** and **284.**

247   Oxford, Bodleian Library. MS Douce 280.

Describes Dowland as "an excellent Musitian" and advocates for Dowland's teaching and songwriting. Quoted in **264** and other sources.

Contemporaneous Printed Material with Dowland Allusions

248   Barnfield, Richard. *Poems: In diuers humors.* London: G. S., 1598.

Dowland and Spencer are heralded in "If Musique and sweet Poetrie agree," the first sonnet of this poetic anthology (f. E2r).

249   Campion, Thomas. *Poemata.* London: Richard Field, 1595.

Includes a substantial Latin epigram praising Dowland's playing and comparing him to Orpheus, labeled "Ad. Io. Dolandum" (f. G3r–v).

250   Campion, Thomas. "Tho. Campiani Epigramma de instituto Authoris." In **229.**

Thomas Campion provided a Latin commendatory verse presented in the prefatory pages of Dowland's first songbook (f. A1r). Campion's poem is much shorter than the one he included in **249** two years earlier.

251   Case, John. *Apologia musices tam vocalis quam instrumentalis et mixtae.* Oxford, 1588.

Includes Dowland in a Latin list of contemporaneous English musicians of note (p. 44).

252   Dowland, Robert. *Varietie of Lute-lessons Viz. Fantasies, Pauins, Galliards, Almaines, Corantoes, and Volts: Selected out of the best approued Authors, as well beyond the Seas as of our owne Country.* London: Thomas Snodham, 1610.

Features a pavane ascribed to Moritz, Landgrave of Hesse that heralds the dedication "fecit in honorem Ioanni Doulandi Anglorum Orphei," dubbing Dowland an "English Orpheus" (f. H2v). For musical portions, see **7.**

253   Lodge, Thomas. *A Learned Summary Upon the famous Poeme of William of Saluste Lord of Bartas.* London: John Grismand, 1621.

Concluding this voluminous treatise is a statement on the affects of music that expresses the author's admiration for "Doctor Dowland, an ornament of Oxford" (p. 264/f. Eeee4v).

254   Marenzio, Luca. "Molto Magnifico Signior mio offeruandissimo." In **229.**

Dowland contemporary Luca Marenzio contributed a Latin commendatory statement to Dowland's first songbook (f. Title2v).

255   Meres, Francis. *Palladis Tamia. Wits Treasvry Being the Second part of Wits Commonwealth*. London: Peter Short, 1598.

In a section titled "Musicke," the author lists great musicians from ancient Greece and comparable ones from England, including "Maister Dowland" (f. 288v).

256   Mertel, Elias. *Hortus Musicalis Novus*. Strasbourg: Anthony Bertram, 1615.

Includes a Latin poem of commendation, written by Johannes-Philippus Medelius, describing Dowland as England's foremost musician (Poem XI). See also **29**.

257   Peacham, Henry. *The Compleat Gentleman Fashioning him absolute in the most necessary & Commendable Qualities concerning Minde or Bodie that may be required in a Noble Gentleman*. London: Francis Constable, 1622.

Features an anagram of Dowland's Latin name and a statement of esteem, which describes the musician, in part, as "a rare Lutenist as any of our Nation, beside one of our greatest Masters of Musicke for composing" (p. 198).

258   Peacham, Henry. *Minerua Britanna or A Garden of Heroical Deuises, furnished, and adorned with Emblemes and Impresas of sundry natures*. London: Walter Dight, 1612.

Includes the emblem labeled, "Ad amicum suum Iohannem Doulandum Musices peritissimum," with title, image, sonnet, and an anagram based on Dowland's Latin name (p. 74).

259   Peacham, Henry. *Thalia's Banqvet*. London: Nicholas Okes, 1620.

In the first printed mention of Dowland as a Doctor, Epigram 99 is dedicated "To Maister Doctor *Dowland*." The two-line verse mentions both *Lachrimae* and a venetian lute (f. C8v).

260   Pilkington, Francis. *The Second Set of Madrigals and Pastorals, of 3. 4. 5. and 6. Parts*. London: Thomas Snodham, 1624.

William Webbe's commendatory poem preceding Pilkington's songs lists Dowland, alongside Byrd, Bull, and Morley, as holding "Matchlesse Excellencies" (f. A2v).

261   *The Retvrne from Pernassvs: Or the Scourge of Simony*. London: G. Eld, 1606.

In Act 5, Scene 2 of this anonymous theatrical comedy, Sir Raderick's page asks "Have you never a song of Master Dowland's making?" (f. H2r). The line acknowledges Dowland's reputation, as disseminated through popular culture. The single allusion, however, pales when compared to the extensive number of times that Shakespeare is mentioned.

262   Sylvester, Joshua, trans. *Bartas His Diuine Weekes & Werkes*. London: Humfrey Lownes, 1605.

In the chapter, "The Imposture. The Second Part of the First Day of the II. Week," the author proclaims, in verse, Dowland's musical superiority to the younger generation (p. 308).

263 Tompkins, Thomas. *Songs of 3. 4. 5. and 6. parts.* London: Matthew Lownes, John Browne, and Thomas Snodham, 1622.

The four-voice madrigal "O let me live" is dedicated to "Doctor *Douland*" (cantus, B2r).

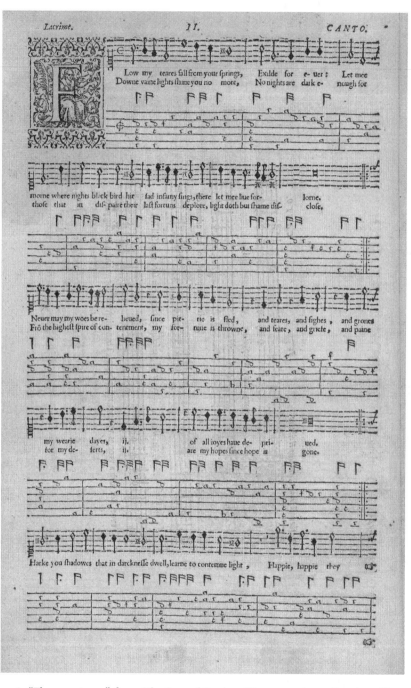

Figure 3 "Flow my tears," from *The Second Booke of Songes or Ayres*. London: Thomas Este, 1600, ff. B2v–C1r. RB 59101. The Huntington Library, San Marino, CA.

Source: The Huntington Library, San Marino, California.

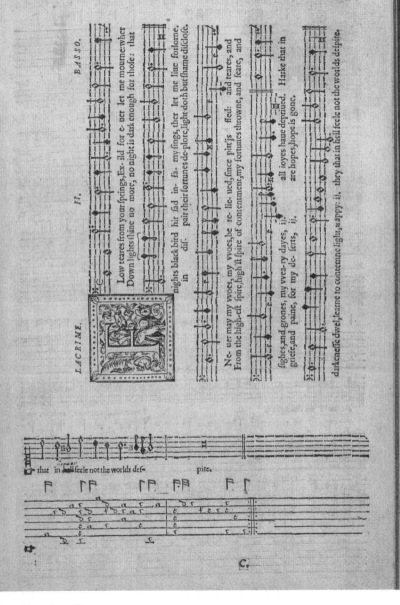

Figure 3 (Continued)

6

Secondary Source Bibliography
Overviews, Reference, and Biography

GENERAL SURVEYS OF LIFE AND WORKS

Comprehensive Surveys

264 Poulton, Diana. *John Dowland*. 2nd revised ed. Berkeley: University of California Press, 1982. 528 p. ISBN 0520046870. ML410 .D808 P7.

The only comprehensive, full-length published monograph on Dowland's life and works. As such, it serves as the foundational secondary source consulted for much subsequent Dowland research. The volume consists of eight chapters devoted to biography, works by genre, Dowland's treatises, contemporaries associated with Dowland, and reception history, as well as an appendix listing Dowland lute manuscripts and a "Fretting and Tuning the Lute" essay by David Mitchell that adds an element of performance practice for lute players (see **580**). An impressive bibliography of primary and secondary sources is limited only by the volume's date of publication. Poulton's strengths lie in her overview of Dowland's music, though the book is also an especially rich source of primary source data. The number of included musical examples is commendable. The footnote style, however, is odd and can be confusing. The book was originally released in 1972 by Faber and Faber with much excitement, as it filled a long-held lacuna. The author, a lutenist who devoted her life's work to Dowland scholarship, was especially qualified to take on the task. In spite of, or perhaps because of, the completeness with which the author presented her research, reviews were mixed. The volume has been criticized for Poulton's bias on certain topics, misrepresentation of certain works, and for difficulties in distinguishing truly important research finds from more subjective assertions. A second, revised edition was published in 1982, in order to amend incorrect and out-of-date information and to add new discoveries. Poulton gave due credit to scholar John M. Ward for much of the additional information included in the update (see **265**). The monograph remains essential to Dowland scholarship, both for its historical role, and for its presentation and analysis of Dowland's musical works. Although researchers might start with this book, they should also supplement their study with more current scholarship.

265   Ward, John. "A Dowland Miscellany." *Journal of the Lute Society of America* 10 (1977): 5–153. ISSN 0076–1524. ML1 .L75.

Written by a respected scholar, this full journal issue is a sort of addenda to **264**, with additional insights, clarifications, and corrections to biographical and musical studies, supplementing manuscript source lists with newly discovered (to that time) and unmentioned primary sources of music. Poulton took to heart much of Ward's work, incorporating it into her updated 1982 version. An errata list for Ward's offering is included in the next journal issue in "Communications," *Journal of the Lute Society of America* 11 (1978): 101–5.

Other General Surveys

266   Caldwell, John. *The Oxford History of English Music. Volume 1: Beginnings to c. 1715*. Oxford: Clarendon, 1991. Reprinted 2002. 691 p. ISBN 0198161298. ML286 .C28 1991 v.1.

This impressive history includes general study of Dowland and his works, featured most predominantly within sections devoted to English lute song, consort music, and lute solo repertoire. Most relevant are chapters 7 and 8 ("Secular Vocal Music, 1575–1625" and "Instrumental Music, 1575–1625: Musical Life and Thought").

267   Greer, David. "John Dowland (1563?–1626)." *Oxford Dictionary of National Biography*. doi:10.1093/ref:odnb/7962.

A concise, well-written, general chronological overview of John Dowland's biography, followed by brief commentary on the musician's works and compositional style.

268   Holman, Peter, and Paul O'Dette. "John Dowland." In *Grove Music Online*. Oxford University Press. Updated 2009. www.oxfordmusiconline.com/public/article/grove/music/08103.

This extended encyclopedia article includes a well-balanced and impartial biography, concise descriptions of categories of Dowland's diverse musical output, a roster of editions, works list by composition type, a list of works with uncertain authorship, and a significant unannotated bibliography. The "gold standard" of encyclopedia articles. Subscription required.

269 Kelnberger, Christian. *Text und Musik bei John Dowland.* 3rd ed. Passau: Verlag Karl Stutz, 2010. 461 p. ISBN 3888492076. ML410 .D718 K45. In German.

The only monograph about Dowland's life and his music produced since Poulton's foundational tome (**264**). Works covered are limited primarily to the lute song-airs. The first part focuses on Dowland's life and individual works, with separate chapters for biography, history of the lute song, Dowland's texts, Elizabethan music, comparisons with other composers, analyses of selected songs, and reception history. The second half of the book provides German translations for lyrics of songs printed in Dowland's four songbooks and *Musicall Banquet.* Facsimiles and transcriptions are provided for selected songs, and the author includes a discography and non-annotated bibliographies.

270 Kenny, Elizabeth, ed. *Early Music* 41, no. 2 (May 2013). ISSN 0306–1078. ML5 .E18.

A special edition of the academic journal *Early Music*, published by Oxford University Press, to coincide with the 450th anniversary of Dowland's birth. Featured articles in this issue cover a wide span of topics, from biographical and analytical essays to philosophical, linguistic, and performance-related articles. Collectively, they provide a well-rounded presentation of recent Dowland scholarship from viewpoints of both scholars and performers. Annotations for individual articles are included in later topical sections. See **285, 287, 300, 313, 364, 374, 445, 488, 503, 570, 592.**

271 Riley, Paul. "John Dowland: The Master of Gloom." *BBC Music Magazine* 21, no. 13 (2013): 62–6. ISSN 0966–7180. ML5 .B349.

A well-written, lovely biographical-musical introduction to Dowland and his works intended for a general audience. This brief, accessible article relies on the standard melancholic stereotype of the composer and his compositions. Includes a basic timeline of significant dates in Dowland's life, listed side-by-side with contemporaneous historical events.

272 Robins, Brian. "John Dowland." *Goldberg: Early Music Magazine/Revista de Musica Antigua* 37 (December 2005): 16–27. ISSN 1138–1531. ML5 .G55.

A review of Dowland's biography and works, intended for a general audience. The author does not add any new information to previously published material, but provides a well-written essay for those who need an introduction to the composer. The *Grove* "Dowland" article, however, is probably a better starting choice for those doing academic research (**268**).

273 Van Tassel, Eric. "Dowland and O'Dette." *Early Music America* 3 (Fall 1997): 20–5. ISSN 1083–3633. ML1 .E15.

Introduces the lute, John Dowland, their places in Elizabethan-Jacobean society, and early musical improvisation to a general audience. Includes a discography of recordings made by modern lutenist Paul O'Dette and others.

ANNOTATED BIBLIOGRAPHIES OF LITERATURE

274   Grapes, K. Dawn. "John Dowland." *Oxford Bibliographies.* www. oxfordbibliographies.com/view/document/obo-9780199757824/ obo-9780199757824-0081.xml. doi:10.1093/OBO/9780199757824-0081.

Limited to approximately 150 secondary and tertiary sources, this annotated bibliography provides an overview of John Dowland scholarship and aids researchers by selecting specific starting points for exploring topics related to the composer. Subscription only, though the introduction and general overviews sections are available for public viewing.

275   Turbet, Richard. *Tudor Music: A Research and Information Guide.* New York: Routledge, 1994. xiii, 247 p. ISBN 0824042964. ML114 .T887.

Some two-dozen descriptions of books and articles directly related to Dowland (published prior to this volume) are included among 700-plus annotated entries of secondary sources related to Elizabethan-Jacobean music. Perhaps of greater value, this guide is useful to those looking for resources to better understand the composer-musician in a wider, late sixteenth-century historical-musical-social context. A 2007 update containing another ten Dowland-specific items is provided by the author in Richard Turbet, "A Selective Bibliography of Writings about Tudor Music 1992–2007: For John Harley on his Eightieth Birthday," *Fontes Artis Musicae* 55, no. 2 (April–June 2008): 340–62. ISSN 0015-6191. ML5 .F66.

BIOGRAPHY

see also all items in the section **General Surveys of Life and Works,** *especially* **264, 265, 268, 269,** *and* **511, 545**

276   Alexander, Gavin. "The Elizabethan Lyric as Contrafactum: Robert Sidney's 'French Tune' Identified." *Music & Letters* 84, no. 3 (August 2003): 378–402. ISSN 0027-4224. ML5 .M64.

This article does not focus on Dowland or his music, though the composer is referenced multiple times throughout due to his relationship with Robert Sidney. The author suggests Dowland as the source from which Sidney may have become acquainted with the music of Charles Tessier. Speaks to Dowland's influence on others of his era, even those outside the musical community.

277   Alexander, Gavin. "The Musical Sidneys." *John Donne Journal* 25 (2006): 65–105. ISSN 0738-9655. PR2248 .A2.

An overview of the Sidney family's connections to the Elizabethan-Jacobean professional music community, particularly those of Robert Sidney (as the author points out, an exact contemporary of Dowland's). Devotes several pages to *Sir Robert Sidney's Galliard* (D38), also known as *Mr. Bucton's Galliard*. Also explores

Dowland's potential knowledge of Philip Sidney's poetry, John and Robert Dowland's associations with courtly society, and in one instance, suggests that Robert Sidney may have connected with Dowland at Christ Church, Oxford.

278 Ashbee, Andrew, ed. *Records of English Court Music*. Vols. 3 and 4. Aldershot, UK: Scolar, 1991, 1998. xix, 258 p., xvii, 285 p. ISBN 0950720755, 0950720747. ML286 .A8.

Transcribed within this volume are multiple state payment records and warrants related to Dowland's employment during James I's reign. See **243**.

279 Ashley, Michael J. "Who Sent Dowland to Coventry in 1598?" *Lute News: The Lute Society Magazine* 82 (July 2007): 17–20. ML5 .L885.

Introduces an account book entry from Gloucestershire's Berkeley Castle, which records a payment to "Dowland and his Consorte" in January 1598/9 (**241**). The author then considers the implications of this record: that Dowland may have been back in England from Denmark at this time; that Dowland had a regular group of musicians with whom he performed; and, because Dowland is listed as part of a consort, the composer may have been responsible for some of the manuscript consort arrangements of his music. Highly speculative, but compelling nonetheless in its questioning format.

280 Boyd, Morrison Comegys. *Elizabethan Music and Musical Criticism*. 2nd ed. Westport, CT: Greenwood, 1962. xi, 363 p. ISBN 0837168058. ML286.2 .B59 E48.

First published in 1940, the author pens quite a charming description of Dowland, with quotes from his book introductions and those of contemporaneous musicians in commendation of Dowland (pp. 135–42). The musician is also mentioned throughout the rest of the book, as a central figure in Elizabethan music. Readers should keep in mind the early creation date of the original volume. E-book: Philadelphia: University of Pennsylvania Press, 2016.

281 Braunmuller, A. R. *A Seventeenth-Century Letter-Book: A Facsimile Edition of Folger MS. v.a.321*. Newark: University of Delaware Press, 1983. 463 p. ISBN 0874132010. PR1344 .F64.

Includes facsimiles and transcriptions of Henry Noel's letter to Dowland, which suggests the composer return to England, and a 1598 letter from Moritz, Landgrave of Hesse, implying the possibility of future patronage (**240**).

282 Dobbins, Frank. "The Lute Tunes of Charles Tessier, Lutenist and Composer in England at the Time of Dowland." In *Luths et luthistes en Occident: actes du colloque organisé par la Cité de la musique, 13–15 mai 1998*, 169–83. Paris: Cité de la musique, 1999. ISBN 2906460982. ML1010 .L877.

Focuses primarily on the music of Dowland's contemporary, French composer Charles Tessier, but opens by considering parallels in the two composers' lives and careers, imagining what overlaps there may have been in their travels.

283 Elliott, Jr., John R. "Invisible Evidence: Finding Musicians in the Archives of the Inns of Court, 1446–1642." *Royal Musical Association Research Chronicle* 26 (1993): 45–57. ISSN 1472–3808. ML5 .R14.

Includes mention of Dowland primary source information first revealed in Priska's 1983 article (**284**) to advocate for Inns of Court archives as valuable sources for researching Elizabethan artists.

284 Frank, Priska. "A New Dowland Document." *The Musical Times* 124, no. 1679 (January 1983): 15–16. ISSN 0027–4666. ML5 .M85.

Details a Middle Temple Library receipt (signed by Dowland) for musical services related to a Candlemas Day 1612 performance (**246**) and comments on the other musicians, William Corkine and William Goosey, who are also listed on the receipt.

285 Gale, Michael. "John Dowland, Celebrity Lute Teacher." In **270**: 205–18.

Notes the "Folger-Dowland Lutebook" (**212**) and the "Margaret Board Lutebook" (**120**) as two manuscript sources that speak to Dowland's pedagogical activities, an aspect of Dowland's career that, due to a relative lack of evidence, has often been overlooked. The context and locations of Dowland's teaching activities are also probed. One helpful table lists Dowland's contributions to the Folger manuscript.

286 Harwood, Ian. "So Who's Really a 'Lutenist' Then?" *The Lute: Journal of the Lute Society* 37 (1997): 1–4. ISSN 0952–0759. ML5 .L89.

Considers Dowland's self-description as "Lutenist, Lute-player, and Bachelor of Musicke," illuminating the early meaning of "lutenist" as one who composes for the instrument, as opposed to lute players, who simply gave voice to others' compositions.

287 Hauge, Peter. "Dowland and His Time in Copenhagen, 1598–1606." In **270**: 189–203. ISSN 0306–1078. ML5 .E18.

This primary source-based article, with information collated from several of the author's previous publications, presents perhaps the most well-rounded description of Dowland's employment in the court of Christian IV of Denmark. An especially important resource for researchers interested in Dowland's international career.

288 Hauge, Peter. "Dowland in Denmark 1598–1606: A Rediscovered Document." *The Lute: The Journal of the Lute Society* 41 (2001): 1–27. ISSN 0952–0759. ML5 .L89.

Details a letter (**239**) sent from English diplomat Stephen Lesieur to Dowland during the musician's years of service to Christian IV that suggests the English court hoped Dowland would provide intelligence on Danish affairs in aid of his home country. No response from Dowland has been documented, so the musician's stance remains uncertain. Includes both a transcription and images of the document. The letter is now housed in Copenhagen's Royal Library.

289   Hauge, Peter. "John Dowland's Employment at the Royal Danish Court: Musician, Agent—and Spy?" Chapter 10 in *Double Agents: Cultural and Political Brokerage in Early Modern Europe*. Edited by Marika Keblusek and Badeloch Vera Noldus, 193–212. Leiden: Brill, 2011. ISBN 9789004202696. D247 .D68.

This article succinctly collates much of the information put forth in the author's earlier articles and positions Dowland as both an agent for Christian IV, securing music, musicians, and other items for the Danish court, and possibly as an informant for the English court. Much of the author's assertions are deduced from primary sources found in Copenhagen. Also positions *Lachrimae* (1604) as a tribute to Queen Elizabeth.

290   Hauge, Peter. "Was Dowland a Spy?" *Early Music Performer* 6 (2000): 10–13. ISSN 1477–478X.

Outlines English-Danish political tensions surrounding coastline properties and maritime activities during Dowland's years in Christian IV's court, as a means to contextualize the Lesieur letter transcribed in **288**. Also presents evidence that William Leighton (of *Teares or Lamencations of a Sorrowfull Soul*) was once in Denmark, at the same time as Dowland. Much of the same information is repeated in the Danish article, Peter Hauge, "Et brev fra diplomaten Stephen Lesieur til Christian IV's lutenist John Dowland," *Magasin fra Det Kongelige Bibliotek* 15, no. 2 (March 2002): 3–13.

291   Henriksen, Olav Chris. "A Possible Likeness of John Dowland." *Journal of the Lute Society of America* 30 (1997): 1–6. ISSN 0076–1524. ML1 .L75.

This conjectural article suggests that three adult musicians depicted in the title page border of Melchior Borchgrevink's 1605 *Giardino novo bellissimo* were perhaps members of the Danish court and, if so, that the tenor lute player may be John Dowland. There is, however, no way to ascertain if these musicians' images were based on living musicians, or if they were simply drawn from the artist's imagination. If the image was indeed inspired by specific employees of Christian IV, as suggested by the author, this would be the only portrait we have of Dowland. Lack of supporting evidence means that, for the time being, this possibility remains purely speculative.

292   Hill, Cecil. "John Dowland: Some New Facts and a Quartercentenary Tribute." *The Musical Times* 104, no. 1449 (November 1963): 785–7. ISSN 0027–4666. ML5 .M85.

A short article re-examining what was known and not known about facts related to Dowland's birth and death at the time of publication. Also includes a commendation of the composer's lute songs. A response in Diana Poulton, "John Dowland: Diana Poulton Replies," *The Musical Times* 105, no. 1451 (January 1964): 25–7, questions some of Hill's statements, outlining information on possible Dowland connections in London and Westminster parish records, considering Dowland's death date, and stressing the difficulties of categorizing Dowland's songs.

The discussion is continued in letters to the editor, in **402** and **348**. On subsequent findings related to Dowland's burial, see **304**.

293 Keller, Arne. "Dowland on the Rocks, or, Dowland and the Ship's Cat." *Lute News: The Lute Society Magazine* 62 (June 2002): 20. ML5 .L885.

More of an essay than an article, in which the author asserts that Dowland was likely included as part of a naval voyage taken by Christian IV to visit his northern lands. This idea, however, has not been substantiated in any state records. In spite of this article's title, the main focus of the essay is not Dowland, but an animal brought onboard by another musician and taken into the custody of the king—a fun, but inconsequential story.

294 Keller, Arne. "Where Was John Dowland in 1593?" *Lute News: The Lute Society Magazine* 70 (July 2004): 13–14. ML5 .L885.

Asks for reader thoughts on a theory that Dowland may have traveled to Wolfenbüttel in 1593, rather than the traditionally quoted 1594, based on a reference in a play penned by the Duke of Brunswick that includes a non-speaking part for a lutenist named Johan. No follow-up providing responses or answers follows.

295 Kelnberger, Christian. "Einige Anmerkungen zum Aktuellen Forschungstand und zur Biographie John Dowlands: Ein Euszugweiser Voradruck aus der im Herbst dieses Jahres Erscheinenden Publikation Text und Musik bei John Dowland." *Gitarre & Laute* 21, no. 6 (1999): 59–63. ISSN 0172–9683. In German.

Written as a preview to the author's 1999 monograph (**269**), this article provides a useful biographical overview of Dowland for those who prefer German text.

296 Klessmann, Eckart. "Die Deutschlandreisen John Dowlands." *Musica* 11 (1957): 13–15. ISSN 0027–4518. ML5 .M71357. In German.

Like all of the author's works listed here, this piece is more essay than article. Quite readable and enticing, it outlines Dowland's German travels, drawing upon primary source quotes from Dowland's musical collection prefaces and letters. Also comments upon the musician's enduring legacy in Germany. Readers should be cautioned, however, as some erroneous information is included. For example, Dowland is purported to have returned to Germany in the 1620s, which repeats an earlier misidentification of Fellowes's, confusing Robert's travels with John's.

297 Klessmann, Eckart. "Die Italienreise John Dowlands." *Musica* 11 (1957): 320–2. ISSN 0027–4518. ML5 .M71357. In German.

Despite its title, this article does not so much describe Dowland's Italian travels, as it collates the composer's writings related to Italy, most specifically his statements in the Cecil letter and in the preface of the 1597 *First Booke*. Tries to convince the reader of the Italian influence Dowland's travels had on his musical philosophy. Like all older articles, researchers should verify information in more recent, reliable sources.

298 Klessmann, Eckart. "Die Letzten Jahre John Dowlands." *Musica* 12 (1958): 390–4. ISSN 0027–4518. ML5 .M71357. In German.

Considers Dowland's last fifteen years, opening with statements taken from the preface of *A Pilgrimes Solace*, which the author believes is Dowland's finest work. Presents the composer as an unhappy, unfulfilled man who lived out his final days unappreciated in England, even as his works were still being published in the German lands. This article serves as a parallel to some of Dowland's melancholic lyrics with its tendency to wallow in a perceived Dowland self-pity. Some biographical information is erroneous, so readers should also consult more recent scholarship.

299 Knispel, Claudia. "The International Character of the Lute Music at the Court of Moritz, Landgrave of Hesse." *The Lute: The Journal of the Lute Society* 36 (1996): 1–16. ISSN 0952–0759. ML5 .L89.

Describes Dowland's continental patron Moritz (also known as Maurice) and the diverse musicians of the Hesse court. Devotes a short section to Dowland pieces surviving in Princess Elisabeth's (daughter of the Landgrave) manuscript, Kassel, Landesbibliothek und Murhard'sche Bibliothek der Stadt Kassel, 4° MS mus. 108.1 (**164**).

300 Lindberg, Jakob. "Touch and Passion: Unlocking the Power of the Lute." In **270**: 298–300.

Contemporaneous primary sources are examined to comment upon reasons why virtuoso lutenists were so highly valued during Dowland's lifetime.

301 Pinto, David. "Dowland's True Tears." *The Lute: Journal of the Lute Society* 42 (2002): 1–26. ISSN 0952–0759. ML5 .L89.

Expands on ideas presented in the author's 2000 article (**303**), providing a careful line-by-line analysis of the Cecil letter to support the contention that Dowland was a life-long, if not outwardly practicing, Catholic. Explores issues of equivocation advocated by the contemporaneous Catholic Church. Goes on to comment on Dowland's training (e.g. he had genius, but little early music education), and to evaluate Dowland's 1604 collection *Lachrimae*, which Pinto reinterprets as a recusant-themed, textless work, the seven pavans fashioned in the manner one might if treating the seven penitential psalms. (The author presents this theory in more detail in **498**.) Includes a full transcription of the Cecil letter and an epilogue-like appendix that compares scripture from the book of *Job* directly with the lyrics of "In darkness let me dwell."

302 Pinto, David. "John Dowland, Letter to Robert Cecil (1595): A Critical Hypertext Edition." *The Philological Museum*. www.philological.bham.ac.uk/dowland/text. html.

Transcription of the Cecil letter (**227**) and its accompanying Scudamore letter with linked commentary.

303 Pinto, David. "John Dowland: Tears and Equivocations." *Lute News: The Lute Society Magazine* 56 (December 2000): 8–10. ML5 .L885.

Muses on the Cecil letter and Dowland's possible practice of equivocation, in which a writer deliberately misleads for a final purpose. Places Dowland as a life-long Catholic, a view not accepted by all scholars. Serves as a sort of introduction to the author's 2002 entry (**301**), which is better supported and more complete.

304 Poulton, Diana. "The Burial of John Dowland." *The Lute Society Journal* 4 (1962): 32. ISSN 0460–007X. ML5 .L89.

The first announcement of the discovery of Dowland's burial record in the register of St. Anne, Blackfriars (**245**), which records a date of February 20, 1625/1626.

305 Poulton, Diana. "Dowland Rehabilitated." *The Musical Times* 118, no. 1607 (January 1977): 25–8. ISSN 0027–4666. ML5 .M85.

A short overview of Dowland's life and works, printed in honor of the 350th anniversary of the musician's death. Also includes a brief review of Dowland scholarship through the 1920s.

306 Poulton, Diana. "Dowland's Darkness." *Early Music* 11, no. 4 (October 1983): 517–19. ISSN 0306–1078. ML5 .E18.

A response to **314**, in which Poulton insists that Dowland was "a man embittered by long failure to achieve ambition," discounting Rooley's portrayal of the musician's melancholic aura as a self-created public persona.

307 Poulton, Diana. "John Dowland, Doctor of Musick." *Consort* 20 (1963): 189–97. ISSN 0268–9111. ML5 .C664.

Focuses on known (to the date of publication) biographical details of Dowland's life. Like so many of the author's articles, this information is later included in her 1972/1982 monograph (**264**).

308 Poulton, Diana. "John Dowland's Patrons and Friends." *The Lute Society Journal* 5 (1963): 7–17. ISSN 0460–007X. ML5 .L89.

Considers known patrons and friends of Dowland, as well as those named in his composition titles, noting that many of the composer's associations were with those of the most elite social classes of the time.

309 Poulton, Diana. "Some Corrections to the Three Spanish Songs in 'A Musicall Banquet.'" *The Lute Society Journal* 2 (1961): 22–6. ISSN 0460–007X. ML5 .L89.

Contends that language errors in "Passava amor suarco desarmado," "Sta note mien yaua," and "Vestros oios tienen d'Amor no se que," found in *A Musicall Banquet*, demonstrate that neither John nor Robert Dowland were well versed in Italian or Spanish. In "Notes and Information" of a later issue of the same journal, the author corrects a date, clarifying that if a Bataille anthology was printed in 1608, then that collection is the likely source of "Passava amor" and "Vuestros oios": *The Lute Society Journal* 7 (1965): 45.

310 Poulton, Diana. "Was John Dowland a Singer?" *The Lute Society Journal* 7 (1965): 32–7. ISSN 0460–007X. ML5 .L89.

Disputes the idea, put forth in several earlier articles and originating from Fuller's unreliable statements (see **324**), that Dowland was a singer as well as a lutenist. The author's contention is based primarily on lacking evidentiary primary sources indicating the composer was a singer. For example, in many state records, Dowland is listed only with instrumentalists and never included in lists of singers.

311 Price, David C. *Patrons and Musicians of the English Renaissance.* Cambridge: Cambridge University Press, 1981. xix, 250 p. ISBN 0521228069. ML286.2 .P7.

Valuable for contextualization of Dowland's life and career, this volume discusses the types of patrons who supported Dowland and others like him, acknowledging that he attracted both Catholic and Protestant sponsors. Outlines some of the manuscripts and libraries in which Dowland's music was collected, and contains an appendix that transcribes excerpts from some of Dowland's dedicatory epistles.

312 Reischert, Alexander. "Unheilbar melancholisch: John Dowland und John Bull zum 450. Geburtstag." *Concerto: das Magazin für alte Musik* 249 (2013): 8–9. ISSN 0177–5944. ML169.8 .C66. In German.

A very brief overview of Dowland's life, presented side-by-side with a biography of English composer and musician John Bull, who was born around the same time and who arranged some of Dowland's works. Otherwise, the keyboardist has no known connections to the lutenist. Encyclopedic in nature. There are several unsupported assertions and, therefore, other biographical articles, such as **268**, are likely more useful.

313 Rooley, Anthony. "1612—John Dowland and the Emblem Tradition." In **270**: 273–80.

A study examining an emblem, dedicated to John Dowland, that appears in Henry Peacham the Younger's 1612 *Minerva Britanna*. Explores how other images within Peacham's volumes might illuminate Dowland's personality and the contemporaneous public perception of the artist. The author goes on to classify Dowland's *lachrimae* theme as a musical emblem, paralleling literary emblems of the time, and suggests other potential "emblems" created by Dowland in his music.

314 Rooley, Anthony. "New Light on John Dowland's Songs of Darkness." *Early Music* 11, no. 1 (January 1983): 6–21. ISSN 0306–1078. ML5 .E18.

As illustrated through selected Dowland works and primary source quotes, the author contends that the melancholic outlook portrayed in a small proportion of the composer's songs does not necessarily reflect Dowland's personality, but was, rather, a self-created artistic persona built upon a foundation of Hermetic philosophy that subsequently helped shape the era's cult of melancholy. Diana Poulton responds with skepticism in **306** and Robin Headlam Wells proposes an alternative view in **485**.

315 Rooley, Anthony. "On Patronage: 'Musicke, that Mind-Tempering Art': The Role of Patron and Artist as Revealed in the Dedicatory Material in the English Lute-Song Books." Chapter 11 in *Companion to Contemporary Musical Thought*. Vol. 1. Edited by John Paynter, Tim Howell, Richard Orton, and Peter Seymour, 226–47. London and New York: Routledge, 1992. ISBN 0415072247. ML55 .C74 1992.

Uses *Micrologus*'s dedication from Dowland to the Earl of Salisbury as the starting point from which to discuss conventions of printed dedicatory epistles and perceived social roles of artist and patron.

316 Rupp, Suzanne. "John Dowland's Strategic Melancholy and the Rise of the Composer in Early Modern England." *Shakespeare-Jahrbuch* 139 (2003): 116–29. ISSN 1430–2527. PR2889 .D43 S53.

Positions Dowland as an early example of the relatively new-to-his-time concept of "composer." The author believes Dowland's marketing of himself as such was not representative of his self-defined identity of musician (as exemplified by his lute virtuoso status), but a necessary means to seek a permanent court position. Further, using careful historical and social contextualization, Rupp presents Dowland's music printing as a means of authority over its presentation, used for authorial self-fashioning of a chosen artistic persona. In this case, that persona is linked to the *lachrimae* theme.

317 Sparr, Kenneth. "Some Unobserved Information about John Dowland, Thomas Campion, and Philip Rosseter." *The Lute: Journal of the Lute Society* 27 (1987): 35–7. ISSN 0952–0759. ML5 .L89.

Restates information from a 1929 German article regarding the contents of an early seventeenth-century *libri amicorum*, a diary kept by one Hans von Bodeck on his journeys. Apparently, during his visit to London, von Bodeck received autographs from several English composers, including Dowland. Von Bodeck's entry included a short lute piece with Dowland's signature, but the original has been lost, quite possibly in World War II destruction. The most important bit of information may be mined from the date, which, if accurate, shows that Dowland was still in England on May 9, 1604, rather than back in Denmark.

318 Spiessens, Godelieve. "Der Antwerpse Luitcomponist Gregorius Huet alias Gregory Howet." *Revue Belge de Musicologie/Belgisch Tijdschrift voor Muziekwetenschap* 57 (2003): 87–111. ML5 .R292. In Dutch.

Belgian lutenist Gregory Howet is the focus of this article, which in part recounts Howet and Dowland's time together in Kassel in 1594 and 1595. Presents primary source accounts comparing their playing and compositional acumen. Questions whether one's music influenced the other's, but does not provide an answer.

319 Spohr, Arne. *"How Chances it They Travel?": Englische Musiker in Dänemark und Norddeutschland, 1579–1630*. Wiesbaden: Harrassowitz Verlag, 2009. 435 p. ISBN 9783447060585. ML311.2 .S664. In German.

Information on Dowland is scattered throughout this published version of the author's PhD dissertation (Hochschule für Musik, Köln, 2006). The author relies primarily on secondary sources, such as **264**, **287**, and **493**, for biographical content. There is great value, however, in Spohr's contextualization of Dowland's place within Christian IV's Danish court (one of the most influential European centers for music of its time), the effects he had on shaping musical choices of his employer, and his role as a political, musical, artistic, and economic agent for both Denmark and England.

320   Staak, Robert. "John Dowland—450 Aastat Sünnist: Semper Dowland Semper Dolens." *Teater, Muusika, Kino* 4 (2013): 50–61. ISSN 0207–6535. PN2725 .E8 T42. In Estonian.

A basic overview of Dowland's life and works appearing in an Estonian magazine.

321   Stainer, J. F. R. "The Middle Temple Masque." *The Musical Times and Singing Class Circular* 47, no. 755 (January 1, 1906): 21–4. ML5 .M85.

Details information on a masque performed at Whitehall and presented by Middle Temple and Lincoln's Inn in February 1612/1613 for the marriage of Princess Elizabeth. Includes a transcript of a Lincoln's Inn expense account (**244**) including payments to both John and Robert Dowland, among others, for "playing of Lutes."

322   Wells, Robin Headlam. "The Orpharion: Symbol of a Humanist Ideal." *Early Music* 10, no. 4 (October 1982): 427–40. ISSN 0306–1078. ML5 .E18.

Though the main point of this article is to examine physical characteristics of the orpharion (an early plucked string instrument perceived as reflecting renaissance-embraced classical ideals), Dowland is portrayed as a self-fashioned Orpheus, with supporting primary source quotes.

323   Wilson, Richard. *Free Will: Art and Power on Shakespeare's Stage.* Manchester: Manchester University Press, 2013. 466 p. ISBN 9780719091780. PR3024 .W556.

Posits Dowland's Denmark experiences as a parallel to the absolutist monarchy portrayed in Shakespeare's *Hamlet*. While most of the information presented is accurate, some is portrayed in a fashion teetering on the edge of historical fiction (perhaps not surprising after Dowland is introduced through his portrayal in a novel). Includes some unproven assertions with no evidentiary documentation, including Dowland's birth into Roman Catholicism and the strong statement that "we know that Dowland spied for English intelligence." While enjoyably written, other sources are perhaps more appropriate for Dowland research projects.

Historical Texts in Chronological Order

The following items, published from the late seventeenth- through the early twentieth-centuries, are important in tracing the history of Dowland scholarship, and are included as samples of historical accounts of Dowland's life. Caution, however, is noted for those seeking credible biographical information, as erroneous or misguided assertions run rampant. Entries are ordered chronologically, providing a historiographical timeline.

324   Fuller, Thomas. *The History of the Worthies of England*. London, 1662.

A brief Dowland (spelled Douland) biography is included in the section on Westminster, under "Masters of Musick" (p. 244). It is here that the author places Dowland's birth in Westminster, and yet even he hedges with a statement in parentheses, "as I have most cause to believe." This account is full of erroneous information, including placement of the musician within Elizabeth's and James's chapels and suggestion that the composer died in Denmark. In spite of the misinformation, the source is important as one of the earliest biographies of Dowland, and because of its influence on later biographical sketches, including the one by Anthony à Wood (**326**).

325   Mace, Thomas. *Musick's Monument, or, A Remembrancer Of the Best Practical Musick, Both Divine and Civil, that has ever been known to have been in the World*. London: T. Ratcliffe, 1676.

The section titled "The Lute made Easie" includes dialogue from a character named "Lute," who states, "Despair I do: Old Dowland he is Dead; R. Johnson too; Two Famous Men; Great Masters in My Art" (p. 34).

326   Wood, Anthony à. *Athenae Oxonienses. An Exact History of all the Writers and Bishops who have had the Education in the most ancient and famous University of Oxford from the Fifteenth Year of King Henry the Seventh, Dom. 1500, to the End of the Year 1690*. Vol. 1. London: Thomas Bennett, 1691.

Includes a biography noting Dowland's 1588 BMus, but restates much misinformation from **324**, and adds even more, including a statement that *Pilgrimes Solace* was written by son Robert, rather than John (p. 760). Consider for historical purposes only.

327   Hawkins, John. *A General History of the Science and Practice of Music*. Vol. 1. London: T. Payne, 1776.

Though portrayed in a more positive light than by Burney (**328**), the author presents Dowland as a more accomplished lutenist than composer. Includes several examples of contemporaneous allusions to the musician, including ones by Shakespeare (err.), Peacham, and Marenzio (pp. 481–3). With the exception of Dowland's death date, biographical information is carefully considered and mostly accurate. The author takes Wood to task for his earlier biographical errors (**326**). Modern edition: *A General History of the Science and Practice of Music*. Vol. 1. Edited by Charles Cudworth. New York: Dover, 1963. xlii, 486 p. ML159 .H393.

328   Burney, Charles. *A General History of Music from the Earliest Ages to the Present Period*. Vol. 2. London: 1782.

Dowland receives sporadic mentions throughout Burney's original 1789 volume and is afforded a brief biography (pp. 115–17), which is overshadowed by the author's personal opinions that Dowland lacked ability in counterpoint, his works were of lesser quality than his contemporaries, and his reputation over-inflated. Includes a transcription of "An heart that's broken" (D203), from Leighton's *Lamentacions* (1614). Modern edition: *A General History of Music From the Earliest Ages to the Present Period (1789)*. Vol. 2. Edited by Frank Mercer. New York: Dover, 1935. Reprinted 1955. 1098 p. ML159 .B96.

329 Holmes, E. "English Glee and Madrigal Composers." *The Musical Times and Singing Class Circular* 4, no. 92 (January 1, 1852): 313–14, 319–20; 4, no. 93 (February 1, 1852): 329–36. ML5 .M85.

This serial article provides several brief, insightful glimpses of mid-nineteenth-century portrayals of Dowland. For example, part two declares: "Dowland also possessed fascinating personal talents and acquirements. He was an instrumental artist in an ungrateful time; he played exquisitely on the lute, but the patronage which he received did not enable him to support himself in the position to which his exertions and merit entitled him." Part three presents its own historiography, reaching back to Burney's comments on the composer (**328**). Includes some incorrect biographical information, indicative of its early date. Readers should use this article as a historical representation, and explore more recent biographies for established information.

330 Hammerich, Angul. *Musiken ved Christian den Fjerdes Hof*. Copenhagen: Wilhelm Hanson, 1892. 258 p. ML311.8 .K8. In Danish.

A history of the court of Christian IV with multiple mentions of Dowland and his duties while serving the Danish king. Also presents a number of English contemporaneous mentions of the court lutenist.

331 S[quire], W. B[arclay]. "John Dowland." *The Musical Times and Singing Class Circular* 37, no. 646 (December 1, 1896): 793–4; 38, no. 648 (February 1, 1897): 92–3. ML5 .M85.

A two-part article revealing details of Dowland's biography. The initial entry consists of the first reprint (outside the publication of the *Calendar of the Marquis of Salisbury Papers*) of the important Cecil letter that provides much of the information we know about Dowland's life. The second part provides information on those mentioned in or connected to the letter, and concludes with Dowland biographical information known to that time. Contains less inaccuracies than biographies that would soon follow, and is important in considering Dowland historiography.

332 Phillips, J. S. Ragland. "Why John Dowlande Went Over-Sea." *Cornhill Magazine* n.s. 3 (1897): 240–57. ISSN 0010–891X. AP4 .C8.

Contextually situates Dowland in his geographical place and time. Also offers the first analytic reading of the Cecil letter, quoting excerpted sections with inserted commentary. In charming late nineteenth-century anachronistic rhetoric, the author claims that "the rewards [Dowland] could claim [in his talents], though not equalling those of a Pederewski, were comparable with those of a Mendelssohn or Chopin."

333   Flood, Wm. H. Grattan. "Correspondence: New Facts About John Dowland." *The Gentleman's Magazine* 301 (1906): 287–91. AP4 .G3.

This is the article in which Flood first makes his claim that Dowland was born in Ireland, a statement that to date has not been substantiated, but which was repeated in many biographical sketches over the next half century. Poulton dismisses Flood's claims and offers up other possibilities for family ties in **264**. Flood also attempts to create a timeline for Dowland's early activities.

334   J. D. "On Lutenists and Lute Music in England." *Euterpe: A Collection of Madrigals and Other Music of the 16th and 17th Centuries* (1908): i–xi. ML5 .E93.

A very general, encyclopedic essay placing Dowland at the forefront of the late sixteenth- to early seventeenth-century English school of lutenists.

335   Hammerich, Angul. "Musical Relations between England and Denmark in the Seventeenth Century." *Sammelbände der Internationalen Musikgesellschaft* 13, no. 1 (1911): 114–19. ISSN 1612-0124. ML5 .I66.

Includes one of the earliest accounts of Dowland's time in Denmark, though citation of source material is missing.

336   Flood, Wm. H. Grattan. *A History of Irish Music.* 2nd ed. Dublin: Browne and Nolan, 1913. xiii, 356 p. (Reprint New York: Praeger, 1970 and Milton Keynes: Dodo, 2011). ML287 .F63.

Only briefly mentions Dowland, but claims he was an Irishman and that he was great friends with Shakespeare, likely providing the bard with much of his background information on Denmark for use in *Hamlet* and on Irish music (see pp. 177–9). None of these assertions have been substantiated and readers are advised to avoid this volume.

337   Fellowes, Edmund Horace. *The English Madrigal Composers.* Oxford: Clarendon, 1921. 364 p. ML2631 .F46.

Includes a biography (pp. 304–13) that repeats much of the questionable information produced by Flood (see **333**, **338**). More valuable is the way the author weaves information on Dowland's music throughout the book, providing a synthesis of Dowland's compositional philosophy with those of his contemporaries. Important for its historical standing as one of the first monographs to consider early modern English secular vocal music.

338   Flood, W. H. Grattan. "Irish Ancestry of Garland, Dowland, Campion, and Purcell." *Music & Letters* 3, no. 1 (1922): 59–65. ISSN 0027-4224. ML5 .M64.

Continues the author's claim of Dowland's Irish ancestry, noting a Dowland *Pilgrames Solace* song dedication "to my loving countryman, Mr. John Forester the younger, merchant of Dublin, in Ireland." He further grants Dowland an honorary degree from Trinity College, Dublin in 1604, which also has not been substantiated. Information provided must be approached with care.

339 Mark, Jeffrey. "Thomas Ravenscroft, B. Mus. (c. 1583-c. 1633)." *The Musical Times* 65, no. 980 (October 1, 1924): 881–4. ML5 .M85.

Quotes the commendatory verse by Dowland included at the beginning of Ravenscroft's 1614 *Brief Discourse*.

340 Warlock, Peter (Philip Heseltine). *The English Ayre*. London: Oxford University Press, 1926. Reprint: Westport, CT: Greenwood Press, 1970. ISBN 0837142377. ML2831 .W37.

The author honors Dowland by affording him the first regular chapter (chapter 2, pp. 21–51) in this collection that offers biographies and works overviews of some two-dozen English lute song-air composers. Presents a very even account of Dowland's life, questioning previous assertions by Flood (**333, 336**) and providing primary source transcriptions of the Cecil letter, contemporaneous mentions, as well as prefatory material from the composer's printed volumes. Illuminating, as the volume reveals how little new Dowland biographical information has been acquired in the last almost one hundred years.

341 Pulver, Jeffrey. "The English Abroad (Concluded)." *The Musical Times* 67, no. 1005 (November 1, 1926): 990–3. ML5 .M85.

This historical article on multiple composers includes a brief, early overview of Dowland's activities on the continent.

342 Flood, H. Grattan. "New Light on Late Tudor Composers: XXV. John Dowland." *The Musical Times* 68, no. 1012 (June 1, 1927): 504–5. ML5 .M85.

A biography of Dowland in which the author contends that Dowland was an Irishman and that he moved to London at age fifteen. As stated in other Flood article annotations, the author does not provide any surviving evidence for this claim, which has since been generally discounted. **343** should be read alongside this piece, as it directly refutes fourteen points made in the article.

343 Cooper, Gerald M. "John Dowland." *The Musical Times* (July 1, 1927): 642. ML5 .M85.

A letter challenging many of the "facts" presented in a biographical article by H. Grattan Flood, published in the same journal a month earlier (**342**). Flood responded the following month, insisting his information is correct, in H. Grattan Flood, "John Dowland," *The Musical Times* 68, no. 1014 (August 1, 1927): 741.

344 Kosack, Hans-Peter. *Geschichte der Laute und Lautenmusik in Preussen*. Kassel: Barenreiter, 1935. 137 p. ML1013 .K7. In German.

Contains only a brief section on Dowland, but positions him as the most important influence on lute culture in early seventeenth-century Prussia, especially in the 1620s and 1630s. Some biographical information is superseded by later Dowland scholarship.

7

Secondary Source Bibliography
Works Analysis and Criticism

see also items in Chapter 6, **General Surveys of Life and Works,** *especially* **264** *and* **265**

WRITINGS COVERING MULTIPLE GENRES

345 Gale, Michael, and Tim Crawford. "John Dowland's 'Lachrimae' at Home and Abroad." *The Lute: Journal of the Lute Society* 44 (2004): 1–34. ISSN 0952-0759. ML5 .L89.

A notable exploration of many extant manuscript and print renderings of *Lachrimae pavan/*"Flow my tears" (D15), both vocal and instrumental, disseminated during Dowland's lifetime. An impressive six-page appendix identifies almost one hundred fragments, complete versions, and arrangements in the forms of plucked string solos, vocal arrangements, instrumental consort music, and keyboard settings.

346 Haar, James, ed. *European Music 1520–1640.* Woodbridge, UK: Boydell, 2006. x, 576 p. ISBN 1843832003. ML172 .E88.

Dowland's music is mentioned many times throughout this volume of collected essays, especially in the section devoted to instrumental music after 1560. Though none of the information delves deeply into the composer's life or music, the book does a fine job situating Dowland's music within the Elizabethan-Jacobean music establishment.

347 Heseltine, Philip. "A Note on John Dowland (d. January 20–21, 1626)." *The Musical Times and Singing Class Circular* (March 1, 1926): 209–12. ML5 .M85.

A brief, early overview and assessment of Dowland's four songbooks and *Lachrimae* (1604). Provides titles of some items contained within each and excerpted musical examples. Readers should use caution, however, as there are some questionable assertions (representative of the date of this article), such as the claim that all the works in Dowland's first book were originally conceived as part songs.

348   Poulton, Diana. "John Dowland." *The Musical Times* 105, no. 1454 (April 1964): 275–6. ISSN 0027–4666. ML5 .M85.

A letter to the editor, answering Cecil Hill's response of the previous month (**402**). Maintains that many of Dowland's lute song-airs were likely first composed in versions different from the four-part vocal works found in Dowland prints, with logically argued counterpoints. See **292** and **402** to follow the entire discussion.

349   Poulton, Diana. "John Dowland (1563–1626) und Lachrimae." Translated by Irene Koch. *Gitarre & Laute* 18, no. 2 (March–April 1996): 18–24. ISSN 0172–9683. In German.

Contextualizes *lachrimae* renditions (D15) within the melancholic atmosphere of early modern England. Also attempts a chronological dating of Dowland's versions for solo lute, lute song-air, and consort, and provides a brief description of Dowland's 1604 viol consort plus lute version. A sidebar features a list of contemporaneous references to *Lachrimae*.

350   Schmees, Iwen. *John Dowland*. Munich, 2010. www.johndowland.de.

This German-English website consists of a works list with lyrics and selected video links, a selected unannotated bibliography, and a limited number of related English, German, French, and Spanish website links, some of which are now outdated.

351   Smith, Douglas Alton. *A History of the Lute from Antiquity to the Renaissance*. Lexington, VA: Lute Society of America, 2002. 389 p. ISBN 097140710X. ML1010 .S558.

Dowland's importance to the history of his musical instrument is demonstrated in this volume, exemplified through the number of instances in which his name is mentioned in relation to cultural trends, musical geographical centers, and composers of his time. Two brief sections are devoted solely to the composer's works, specifically his solo lute music and ayres (see pp. 274–83 and 284–9).

352   Spink, Ian, and Roger Bray, eds. *The Blackwell History of Music in Britain*. Vols. 2 and 3. Oxford: Blackwell, 1992, 1995. ISBN 0631179240, 0631165185. ML285 .B58.

Volumes two and three (*The Sixteenth Century* and *The Seventeenth Century*) each contain information related to Dowland, most specifically in sections allocated to "Secular Vocal Music" (2: Tim Carter, author); "Ensemble and Lute Music" (2: John Harper, author), which emphasizes dance forms as the basis of Dowland's music; "Vocal Music I" (3: David Greer, author), which includes a section titled "Dowland and the Lute Song" (pp. 153–61); "Consort Music I" (Christopher D. S. Field, author); and "Solo Music for Tablature Instruments" (Matthew Spring, author). There is little content here that is new or original, but the two volumes are valuable for their success in situating Dowland within the larger musical context of his time.

353   Ward, John M. "'Excuse Me': A Dance to a Tune of John Dowland's Making." In *Libraries, History, Diplomacy, and the Performing Arts: Essays in Honor of Carleton Sprague Smith*. Edited by Israel J. Katz, 379–88. Stuyvesant, NY: Pendragon, 1991. (Festschrift Series 9). ISBN 0945193130. ML55 .S673.

Considers the origins of a tune included in Playford's *Dancing Master* (1651) titled "Excuse me." Concludes that, although the original melody developed from Dowland's "Can she excuse" (D42, also known as the *Earl of Essex Galliard* in lute solo form), the Playford rendition was likely adapted from a version included in Thomas Robinson's *New Citharen Lessons* (1609), with no direct influence of Dowland. The Playford rendering was then printed or referenced in at least twenty later eighteenth-century musical or theatrical volumes.

LUTE SOLOS AND DUOS

see also **277, 348, 351, 352, 395, 446, 490, 496, 502, 517, 544**

354   Harper, Sally. "An Elizabethan Tune List from Lleweni Hall, North Wales." *Royal Musical Association Research Chronicle* 38 (2005): 45–98. ISSN 1472–3808. ML5 .R14.

Details a list of tune titles contained within a late sixteenth-century Welsh manuscript owned by an aristocratic family. A number of the titles have associations with Dowland lute solos, for which commentary and concordances are provided.

355   Heseltine, Philip. "More Light on John Dowland." *The Musical Times* 68, no. 1014 (August 1, 1927): 689–91. ML5 .M85.

An overview of Dowland's lute music, limited by the article's early date, which disallows examination of many later identified works.

356   Koltai, Katalin. "A Kaleidoscope of Motives or Conscious Unity? A Formal Analysis of Motivic Development in John Dowland's Chromatic Lute Fantasie 'Farewell.'" *Lute Society of America Quarterly* (Summer–Fall 2017): 19–26. ISSN 1547–982X. ML1 .L88.

A close analysis of one of Dowland's "Farewell" fantasies (D3), in which the author contends the opening motive and subsequent countermotives derive from the same material. Also links Dowland's *lachrimae* motive to melodic passages within the piece. Provides numerous musical examples and is followed by a full transcription of the lute tablature found in Cambridge University, Dd.5.78 (**63**).

357   Long, John H. "Sneak's 'Noyse' Heard Again?" *The Musical Quarterly* 44, no. 1 (January 1958): 76–81. ISSN 0027–4631. ML1 .M725.

Suggests a musical piece mentioned in a 1657 travel account may have been a Dowland galliard with direct ties to Shakespeare's *Henry IV, Part II*. Though the thesis is intriguing, much conjecture is necessary to make the argument work, as no musical link to the suggested lute solo is provided, and the music itself, found in the Folger Dowland manuscript (**212**), has not been definitively ascribed to Dowland. John Ward disputes the author's scholarship and assertions in "Music for *A Handefull of Pleasant Delites*," *Journal of the American Musicological Society* 10, no. 3 (Autumn 1957): 171 n71.

358   Lumsden, David. "The Sources of English Lute Music (1540–1620)." *The Galpin Society Journal* 6 (July 1953): 14–22. ISSN 0072–0127. ML5 .G26.

This rather surface-level article attempts to defend the place of lute music in the repertoire of early modern England. Dowland is mentioned more than any other composer. The reader is cautioned, as the essay positions Dowland's part songs as the model for his lute solos, which in some cases is likely reversed.

359   Marriott, Jr., David Franklin. "An Anonymous Lute Fancy Ascribed to John Dowland." *Soundboard* 6, no. 3 (1979): 89–95. ISSN 0145-6237.

Argues for Dowland authorship of an unattributed fancy (D103) found in Cambridge University Library manuscript Dd.9.33 (**64**). The attribution is based on concordant compositional traits demonstrated in other authenticated Dowland pieces. Reconstructs the piece in both lute tablature and modern treble-clef guitar notation.

360   McGrady, Richard. " 'Chromatique Tunes and Measur'd Accents': John Danyel's *Can Dolefull Notes*." *Music Review* 50, no. 2 (May 1989): 79–92. ISSN 0027–4445. ML5 .M657.

Dowland is not the focus of this article and is mentioned only sporadically. His music is, however, the standard by which the author analyzes Danyel's compositions, as an example of Dowland fantasia-inspired chromatic song.

361   Meadors, James. "Dowland's 'Walsingham'." *Journal of the Lute Society of America* 14 (1981): 59–68. ISSN 0076–1524. ML1 .L75.

Examines Dowland's set of variations on the popular folk tune *Walsingham*, as found in Cambridge University, Dd.9.33 (**64**). After a brief comparison of the work to variations on the tune by other composers, the author provides an analysis and reconstruction, necessitated by damage to the original manuscript. Challenges Poulton's assertion that the work is not one of Dowland's best (see **264**, pp. 171–2).

362   Mies, Otto. "Dowland's Lachrymae Tune." *Musica Disciplina* 4, no. 1 (1950): 59–64. ISSN 0077–2461. ML5 .M722.

A shallow exploration of pieces based on the *lachrimae* theme, using lute arrangements from the Ballet Lute Book (**74**), the Schele Lute Book (**161**), and Besard's 1603 print (**14**) as examples.

363 Nordstrom, Lyle. "A Lute Duet of John Dowland." *Journal of the Lute Society of America* 12 (1979): 43–7. ISSN 0076–1524. ML1 .L75.

Suggests that the lute piece titled *Complaint* (D63), found in the Matthew Holmes volume, Cambridge University Library Dd. 2.11 (**57**), is not a lute solo as previously identified, but the second part of a lute duet arrangement associated with *Fortune my Foe* (D62).

364 O'Dette, Paul. "Dowland's iPod: Some Possible Models for John Dowland's Lute Fantasias." In **270**: 306–16.

Noted performer-scholar O'Dette suggests possible musical works from which Dowland may have borrowed or that he adapted for his lute fantasias.

365 Poulton, Diana. "Captain Digory Piper of the 'Sweepstake.'" *The Lute Society Journal* 4 (1962): 17–22. ISSN 0460–007X. ML5 .L89.

Traces the biographical background and reputation (as pirate) of the colorful character who lent his name to a Dowland pavane and galliard. *Captain Digory Piper's Galliard* and "If my complaints could passions move" (both D19), from the *First Booke*, use the same musical material, which was then adapted as a consort setting in *Lachrimae* (1604).

366 Poulton, Diana. "Lady Hunsden's Puffe." *The Musical Times* 105, no. 1457 (July 1964): 518. ISSN 0027–4666. ML5 .M85.

A short notification of an incorrectly titled guitar publication. Though titled *Lady Hunsden's Puffe by Dowland*, the composition is actually a galliard ascribed in different sources, under different titles, to Cutting, Ferrabosco, and Dowland. Modern scholars have cast doubt on Dowland as the composer.

367 Poulton, Diana. "The Lute Music of John Dowland." *Consort* 8 (1951): 10–15. ISSN 0268–9111. ML5 .C664.

A general overview of Dowland lute solos recognized at the time this article was written. Superseded by subsequent scholarship from both the author and others, but provides some insight into the knowledge with which Poulton started, and the amount of additional discovery achieved by the time her tome on Dowland (**264**) and collection of lute music (**221**) were released in the 1970s.

368 Richardson, Brian. "New Light on Dowland's Continental Movements." *Monthly Musical Record* 90, no. 997 (1960): 3–9. ML5 .M6.

A largely conjectural article that attempts to trace several late sixteenth-century continental pieces, most especially *My Lady Hunsdon's Puffe* (D54), back to Dowland's travels in the Italian and German lands.

369   Shepherd, Martin. "How Much of Dowland's Lute Music Do We Actually Have?:
Problems of Authorship and Arrangement in English Lute Sources." *Lute Society
of America Quarterly* 51, no. 1 (Spring 2016): 27–31. ISSN 1547–982X. ML1 .L88.

Stresses that most music found in manuscripts, including the lute solos of John
Dowland, likely does not represent the compositional choices of the composer,
but instead are adaptations for purposes of the copyist or owner. Promotes the
idea that arrangements were often created either for pedagogical reasons, adaptation to particular instruments, or personal preference. This assertion, which
aligns with David Tayler's earlier thesis (**376**), is illustrated with Dowland examples, paying special attention to *Lady Russell's Pavan* (D17).

370   Sheptovitsky, Levi. "Mastery of Sorrow and Melancholy: Expressivity in Two
Chromatic Fantasias by John Dowland." *Lute News: The Lute Society Magazine*
(April 2007): 20–32. ML5 .L885.

Closely analyzes the fantasias *Farewell* (D3) and *Forlorn Hope* (D2) with careful consideration of musical-rhetorical figures such as the chromatic fourth and
Dowland's own tear motive, in order to depict Dowland as "one of the earliest
composers of the new instrumental style to have achieved a strong expression
of feelings in musical composition without a literal text." Also speculates that
perhaps these two pieces were written by the composer in 1594 (rather than later,
as has been proposed) as a response to the musician's unsuccessful application
for a position as English court lutenist. The author, however, acknowledges this
supplemental theory is purely conjectural.

371   Sheptovitsky, Levi. "Two Chromatic Fantasias by John Dowland: Were They
Composed as a Pair?" In *Across Centuries and Cultures: Musicological Studies in
Honor of Joachim Braun*. Edited by Kevin C. Karnes and Levi Shepovitsky, 291–
314. Frankfurt am Main and New York: Peter Lang, 2010. ML160 .A28 2010.

Hypothesizes that *Farewell* (D3) and *Forlorn Hope* (D2) were intended to be
performed as a set. Presents extensive theoretical analysis. The article concludes
with the author's own edition of the pieces, offered in both lute tablature and
modern staff notation.

372   Smith, David John. "The Instrumental Music of Peter Philips: Its Sources,
Dissemination, and Style." 3 vols. PhD Diss., Oxford, 1993.

Dowland and his works are mentioned sporadically throughout. A short section
in the second volume compares the composer's works with those of Peter Philips,
specifically Dowland's *Piper's Galliard* (D19) and *M. Collier his Galliard* (D122),
and Philips's *Paget Galliard*.

373   Smith, Hopkinson. "Francesco da Milano's Dance Music, and John Dowland's
Character Portraits, a Pre-Concert Talk by Hopkinson Smith." *Lute News: The
Lute Society Magazine* 89 (April 2009): 9–14. ML5 .L885.

Transcription of a pre-concert talk in which the author, an active lutenist,
describes the *Earl of Essex Galliard* (D42) as a musical depiction of Essex's

personality. He further speculates on the personality of Lady Clifton (of *Lady Clifton's Spirit*, D45) by applying the same principles. Finally, the author discusses his performance choices when altering traditional works. Tablature transcriptions are provided for compositions considered.

374 Smith, Hopkinson. "'Whose Heavenly Touch Doth Ravish Human Sense. . . .'." In **270**: 295–7.

Four musical lute lines by Dowland are examined to comment upon Richard Barnfield's and Thomas Campion's descriptions of Dowland's "divine" playing.

375 Spencer, Robert. "Dowland's Dance-Songs: Those of his Compositions which Exist in Two Versions, Songs and Instrumental Dances." In *Le concert des voix et des instruments a la Renaissance: Actes du XXXIVe Colloque International d'Etudes Humanistes, Tours, Centre d'Etudes Supérieures de la Renaissance, 1–11 Juillet 1991. Arts du Spectacle.* Edited by Jean-Michel Vaccaro, 587–99. Paris: CNRS, 1995. ISBN 2271050677. ML172 .C64.

Suggests that Dowland pieces written both in song and lute solo formats originated as instrumental pieces, and that words were added later in the manner of contrafactum associated with the French *voix de ville*. Uses *Lachrimae Pavan/* "Flow my tears" (D15) and *Earl of Essex Galliard/*"Can she excuse my wrongs" (D42) as examples.

376 Tayler, David Stanley. "The Solo Lute Music of John Dowland." PhD Diss., University of California, Berkeley, 1992. UMI 9330755.

Written by a practicing lutenist, this dissertation attempts to establish a canon of "authoritative" lute works, based on solos printed during the composer's lifetime or that survive in manuscripts in Dowland's own hand or feature his autograph. The author then attempts to define Dowland's style by analyzing these pieces. This selective view of declared authorized primary sources re-aligns the numerical proportion of lute solos to lute songs and consort music, reducing the extensive list of pieces extant in manuscript collections, which the author argues are more indebted to copyists and manuscript owners, and therefore cannot decidedly be counted as works approved by Dowland. Important as an alternative view to Poulton and Lam (**221**), the author also takes the stance that Poulton's scholarship (see **221** and **264**) requires re-evaluation due to many misconceptions concerning style and character. The author posits Dowland as a composer influenced as much by continental musical practice as English, one who forged new, individualistic paths with his music.

LUTE SONG-AIRS

General

see also **264**, **269**, **292**, **348**, **351**, **352**, **375**, **395**, **462**, **549**, **553** *and items in sub-sections* **Lute Song Airs: Lyrics** *and* **Music and Text**

377 Agrawal, Susan Rachel. "'Tune Thy Temper to These Sounds': Music and Medicine in the English Ayre." PhD Diss., Northwestern University, 2005. UMI 3177677.

Two sections of this 1,075-page thesis consider melancholy, prominently featuring Dowland's lute song-airs in a creative and compelling medical-musical analysis informed both by treatises of the time and modern secondary sources (see pp. 598–686 and 799–928).

378 Alcade, Antonio Corona. "*Tears of Joy or Tears of Woe?* El Emblema de la *Lachrima* en la Obra de John Dowland: Un Ensayo de Interpretación." *Revista del Instituto de Investigación Musicológica "Carlos Vega"* 24 (2010): 203–52. ISSN 1515-050X. ML5 .R213. In Spanish.

A unique and in-depth textual, numerological, and philosophical analysis of Dowland's tear motive, couched in the principles of neoplatonism, which are supported with primary source quotations. Special attention is given to the song "Come heavy sleep" (D138) as example of application of the author's theory. The author cites Anthony Rooley as inspiring his research (see **314**).

379 Arten, Samantha. "The Origin of Fixed-Scale Solmization in *The Whole Booke of Psalmes.*" *Early Music* 46, no. 1 (May 2018): 149–65. ISSN 0306-1078. ML5 .E18.

Argues that a fixed-solmization system was solidly established in England by the end of the sixteenth century through the use of sacred songbooks. A final section quotes the letter to the reader from Dowland's *Pilgrimes Solace* to support the claim that English practices were different from those on the continent. Uses the song "Lasso vita mia" (D190) as an example to demonstrate Dowland's knowledge of the hexachordal system still in use in Italy and other countries at the time, commenting on English musicians who were not educated beyond their own English experiences.

380 Brown, Patricia A. "Influences on the Early Lute Songs of John Dowland." *Musicology Australia* 3 (1968–9): 21–33. ISSN 0814-5857. ML5 .M897.

A thoughtful analysis of the works in Dowland's first songbook, with special attention to poetic and musical forms, as well as influences, both continental and English, on the development of the lute song-air. Dowland's volume is given credit for popularizing the song type with the English public.

381 Butler, Katherine. *Music in Elizabethan Court Politics.* Woodbridge, UK: Boydell, 2015. x, 260 p. (Studies in Medieval and Renaissance Music). ISBN 9781843839811. ML3917 .G7 B87.

Considering that Dowland never held an official post in Elizabeth I's court and was removed from England for long periods of time during her reign, the composer's music receives quite a few mentions within this monograph. Allusions are primarily related to songs perhaps performed during entertainments related to the queen's progresses, official celebrations such as Accession Day tilts, and those with possible connections to the Earl of Essex. Information is scattered throughout. Mostly synthesizes Dowland content mined from other sources, though the author adds some valuable analytic musical insight (see especially pp. 131–42).

382   Button, H. Eliot. "Music Printing in the Year 1603." *The Musical Times* 64, no. 965 (July 1, 1923): 472–3. ML5 .M85.

A brief, accessible article examining basic features of songs found in Dowland's *Third Booke*. Includes a facsimile and excerpted musical examples in modern notation. Might serve as a starting point for future research related to one of Dowland's lesser-studied anthologies.

383   Conner, Ted. "Structural Ornaments: Transcending Binaries in Elizabethan and Jacobean Music." *Journal of the Viola da Gamba Society of America* 42 (2005): 19–75. ISSN 0507–0252. ML1 .V295.

In this study of musical-textual relationships in multiple Dowland lute songs, the author seeks to determine if the composer's words embellish his music, or vice versa. He concludes that their co-existence is a specific convention of music of the time. The last portion of this article provides rather surface-level melodic analyses of voices within "Unquiet thoughts" (D125), "Burst forth my tears" (D128), "Go crystal tears" (D129), and "All ye whom love or fortune" (D134).

384   Cutts, John P. "Everie Woman in her Humor." *Renaissance News* 18, no. 3 (Autumn 1965): 209–13. ISSN 0277–903X. CB361 .R45.

Notes that "Sleep wayward thoughts" (D133) is used within the anonymous theatrical entertainment, *Everie Woman in her Humor*, printed in London in 1609.

385   Dart, Thurston. "Role de la danse dans L'Ayre' Anglais." In *Musique et poésie au XVIᵉ siècle: Paris, 30 juin–4 juillet 1953.* 203–9. Paris: Éditions Centre National de la Recherche Scientifique, 1954. ML3849 .F83. In French.

This short conference proceeding, in which Dowland's music assumes a significant role, considers use of instrumental dance forms in lute song-airs of the late sixteenth century.

386   Davidson, Audrey Ekdahl. "Five Settings of Songs Attributed to Sir Philip Sidney." In *Aspects of Early Music and Performance*. Edited by Audrey Ekdahl Davidson, 101–22. Brooklyn, NY: AMS, 2008. (AMS Studies in Music 1) ISBN 9780404646011. ML1400 .D38.

Briefly compares Dowland's setting of "O sweet woods" (D147) to one found in the "Henry Lawes autograph manuscript" (British Library, Add. MS 57723).

387   Davie, Cedric Thorpe. "A Lost Morley Song Rediscovered." *Early Music* 9, no. 3 (June 1981): 338–9. ISSN 0306–1078. ML5 .E18.

A side-by-side comparison of Dowland's "White as lilies" (D152), from the *Second Booke*, and a setting of the same text, attributed to Thomas Morley in a manuscript copied by Margaret Wemyss, dated 1643, later housed in the private collection of the Countess of Sutherland, and "discovered" by Davie as a lost selection from Morley's *First Booke of Ayres* (1600).

388   Doughtie, Edward. "John Dowland and the Air." Chapter 7 in *English Renaissance Song*. Edited by Edward Doughtie, 122–41. Boston, MA: Twayne, 1986. ISBN 0805769153. ML3849 .D7.

An excellent general overview of Dowland's lute song-airs, considering texts, form, and development of the genre. Especially notable are the insightful musico-textual analyses afforded a number of the composer's most famous works.

389   Duckles, Vincent. "English Song and the Challenge of Italian Monody." In *Words to Music: Papers on English Seventeenth-Century Song Read at a Clark Library Seminar, December 11, 1965*. Edited by Vincent Duckles and Franklin B. Zimmerman, 3–25. Los Angeles: University of California, Los Angeles William Andrews Clark Memorial Library, 1967. ML2831.2 .D83.

Transcription of a 1965 lecture given at UCLA that posits Dowland and his contemporaries as beginning a monodic trend in English music that carried forward into the music of Purcell. Key quote: "The work of these lutenist song composers, combined with a renewed strain of pure English lyric verse, produced one of the most perfect fusions of music and poetry that has ever been witnessed in English culture." Not really focused on Dowland, who only figures into the background of the topic presented, but his importance within the school of lute songwriters is clearly portrayed.

390   Fellowes, Edmund H. "The Songs of Dowland." *Proceedings of the Musical Association* 56 (1929–1930): 1–26. ISSN 0958-8442. ML5 .R888.

An early twentieth-century lecture transcript that introduces Dowland through his lute songs. Proclaims him to be the first, and perhaps greatest, English songwriter. In considering this article, Turbet (in **275**) insightfully notes that in spite of biographical inaccuracies, Fellowes's song analyses "are worthwhile as coming from one who not only edited them but who also performed them in public." Important for its historical place in Dowland studies, but the reader should critically evaluate assertions, as some have been disproved.

391   Fischer, Kurt. "Gabriel Voigtländer. Ein Dichter und Musiker des 17. Jahrhunderts." *Sammelbände der Internationalen Musikgesellschaft* 12, no. 1 (1910): 17–93. ISSN 1612-0124. ML5 .I66.

This article compares Dowland's "Can she excuse my wrongs" (D42) from the *First Booke* (1597) to a version included in a 1642 songbook by German composer Gabriel Voigtländer, as well as borrowings in other seventeenth- and eighteenth-century collections.

392   Foxe, Wilfred. "John Dowland and the *Soggetto Cavato*." *Lute News: The Lute Society Magazine* 66 (June 2003): 7–15. ML5 .L885.

Contends that while developing his own compositional style, Dowland was especially affected by Italian composers on his journeys, with influences manifested in his songs through the use of musical punning, adapted *soggetto cavato*, and formulaic affective compositional choices. Examines "Can she excuse my wrongs" (D42—the author asserts the b-natural/b-flat cross relation is intentional—see also **399**, **416**, and **425**), "Now cease my wandering eyes" (D150), "Sorrow stay" (D142), and "I saw my lady weep" (D141), for which the author includes a line-by-line musical-textual analysis and suggests that the work may be a tribute to Marenzio. The author also advocates for anachronistic Schenkerian analysis of Dowland's works, which undercuts consideration of other ideas.

393   Gibson, Kirsten Vanessa. "John Dowland's Printed Ayres: Texts, Contexts, Intertexts." PhD Diss., University of Newcastle upon Tyne, 2006. http://hdl.handle.net/10443/1636.

Explores Dowland's self-fashioned persona, as portrayed through the prefatory material, lyrics, and music presented in his printed songbooks. Alongside contextualization of contemporaneous rhetorical practices, social standards, and tropes such as solitude, exile, and melancholy, the author treats specific compositions as case studies to work toward her thesis. Includes facsimiles and transcriptions of selected songs. Material from this dissertation is developed more fully in the author's later articles (see especially **394** and **545**).

394   Gibson, Kirsten. "The Order of the Book: Materiality, Narrative, and Authorial Voice in John Dowland's *First Booke of Songes or Ayres*." *Renaissance Studies* 26, no. 1 (2012): 13–33. ISSN 0269–1213. CB361 .R474.

A wonderfully detailed examination of Dowland's *First Booke* as a singular entity, from prefatory material to conscious ordering of songs, that "creates an alternative kind of (material) performance space in which meaning might be reciprocally informed by the relationship between sounding performances of the songs, or indeed memories of particular performance, and their 'silent,' visual representation and positioning within the book." Demonstrates various levels of meaning for different readers/singers within Dowland's collection. Contends the courtly elite, from whom most of the original poetry likely originated, knew of direct associations hidden within the lyrics. For a wider audience, Dowland's volume created a semblance of authorship and respectability for its composer, while allowing a glimpse of courtly activity.

395   Goodwin, Chris. " 'Will You Go Walk the Woods So Wild?' and the Question of 'Popular' Music." *Lute News: The Lute Society Magazine* 64 (December 2002): 10–18. ML5 .L885.

Considers the history, context, and many variants of the popular tune "Will you go walk the woods so wild," which is used as a countermelody in Dowland's *Earl of Essex Galliard*/"Can she excuse" (D42). Uses the Dowland composition as a starting point from which to examine other popular songs that may have survived from the Henrician period.

396   Greer, David. "A Dowland Curiosity." *The Lute: The Journal of the Lute Society* 27 (1987): 42–4. ISSN 0952–0759. ML5 .L89.

Reviews an arrangement by twentieth-century Irish composer Hamilton Harty of a song ascribed to John Dowland, but not found elsewhere in Dowland manuscripts or prints. The piece is titled "Adieu, sweet Amaryllis." The author considers issues of attribution, but no definitive identification is made.

397   Greer, David. "The Lute Songs of Thomas Morley." *Lute Society Journal* 8 (1966): 25–37. ISSN 0460–007X. ML5 .L89.

Considers Morley's only published lute song-air book, with inevitable comparisons to Dowland's compositions. Gives focused consideration to the composers' respective settings of "I saw my lady weep" (D141).

398   Greer, David. "The Part-Songs of the English Lutenists." *Proceedings of the Royal Musical Association* 94 (1967–1968): 97–110. ISSN 0080–4452. ML5 .R888.

A lecture transcript that examines songs printed with the choice of performance either as part song or lute song. The author comments on multiple composers, but firmly believes that Dowland's works, even those printed in his later volumes, were written first as lute songs and that words were added to additional voice parts to widen the audience for commercial sales.

399   Gross, Harvey. "Technique and *Epistémè*: John Dowland's 'Can She Excuse My Wrongs.'" *Bulletin of Research in the Humanities* 86, no. 3 (1983–1985): 318–34. ISSN 0160–0168. Z881 .N6B.

A reading of "Can she excuse my wrongs" (D42) that considers structure, rhythm, melody, poetics, and rhetorical devices, while maintaining that the piece stands on its own as a single musico-poetic text. The musical harmonic analysis may seem anachronistic, but the author states he places this piece within the early Baroque period, and therefore subjects it to major-minor rather than modal analysis, a choice that is at times successful and at other times puzzling. Addresses the B-flat question raised in **416**.

400   Harper, John. "A New Way of Making Ayres? Thomas Campion: Towards a Revaluation." *The Musical Times* 110, no. 1513 (March 1969): 262–3. ISSN 0027–4666. ML5 .M85.

Though this article focuses on Dowland's contemporary Thomas Campion, the author's argument is couched in the idea that it is unfair to judge Campion's music in comparison with Dowland's.

401   Henning, Rudolf. "A Possible Source of *Lachrymae*?" Translated by Uta Henning and John E. Hancock. *Lute Society Journal* 16 (1974): 65–7. ISSN 0460–007X. ML5 .L89.

Suggests Cipriano de Rore's "Quando lieta speri," with its lyric "Lagrime," is a source from which Dowland's *lachrimae* theme was inspired, though there is no concrete evidence that Dowland knew this madrigal.

402   Hill, Cecil. "Dowland." *The Musical Times* 105, no. 1453 (March 1964): 199. ISSN 0027–4666. ML5 .M85.

Argues for the earlier Fellowes theory that Dowland's lute song-airs were originally written for four voice parts and later rearranged for solo voice and lute. Functions as a response to Poulton's criticism of this statement in an earlier article by the author (**292**).

403 Kerman, Joseph. *The Elizabethan Madrigal: A Comparative Study*. New York: American Musicological Society, 1962. xii, 318 p. ML2631 .K47.

In spite of its title, this book encompasses all Elizabethan secular song types, including not only madrigals, but also consort songs and lute songs. Comments on Dowland and his music are scattered throughout, though little is presented that is not found in subsequent studies of more depth. That said, this book is a standard in the literature of Elizabethan music, and should be valued for its historical significance. The reader, however, should engage in further research to confirm that information offered reflects the latest scholarly stance.

404 Knispel, Claudia. "Die Intavolierungen der Dowlandschen Ayre 'Come Again' im Lautenbuch der Elisabeth von Hessen." *Concerto: das Magazin für alte Musik* 6 (1989): 9–13. ISSN 0177-5944. ML169.8 .C66. In German.

Examines multiple versions of Dowland's "Come again" (D60) found in Kassel, Landesbibliothek, 4° Mus. 108.1 (**164**). Comments on Dowland's time in the Landgrave of Hesse's court and defends the versions against previous accusations of being "inaccurate."

405 Kozel, David. "Melancholy in the Music of John Dowland and Benjamin Britten." *Hudba-Integrácie-Interpretácie* 19 (2016): 59–80.

A three-part article, in which the author: attempts to define the nature of melancholy; presents a surface-level exposition on John Dowland's melancholic works (ending with a short analysis of "Come heavy sleep," D138); and examines Britten's *Nocturnal*, op. 70, which is based on "Come heavy sleep." Each section reads like an introduction, providing little elaborative detail. As such, the article might serve as fodder for those looking to continue the work started here. The journal is Slovakian, but the article is in English.

406 Leech-Wilkinson, Daniel. "My Lady's Tears: A Pair of Songs by John Dowland." *Early Music* 19, no. 2 (May 1991): 227–33. ISSN 0306-1078. ML5 .E18.

Posits "I saw my lady weep" (D141), the opening song in Dowland's *Second Booke*, as an introduction to the second song, "Flow my tears" (D15). The author then examines possible connections of the piece to Morley's setting in his own *First Booke of Ayres*, published the same year. Evidence presented is highly conjectural, but the author argues his case logically and confidently. David Pinto responds to the article in "Dowland's Lachrymal Airs," *Early Music* 20, no. 3 (August 1992): 525, questioning assumptions and drawing attention to Joan Wess's work on the same pieces in **434**.

407 Malhomme, Florence. "Le Madrigal Anglais: Influences et Age d'Or (1593–1622): Problématique générale et approche analytique." ["The Madrigal English:

Influences and Golden Age (1593–1622): General Problem and Analytical Approach."] *Musurgia* 4, no. 4 (1997): 7–28. ISSN 1257-7537. ML5 .M9845. In French.

Compares musical styles of the madrigal, the lute song-air, and other early modern English secular works. Includes descriptive examples of selected songs borrowed from Thurston Dart's *Invitation to Madrigals*, Vol. 2 (London: Stainer and Bell, 1962) at the end. Provides a basic description of "Wilt thou unkind" (D135), the example chosen to represent Dowland.

408   McGrady, Richard. "Coperario's *Funeral Teares.*" *Music Review* 38 (1977): 163–76.

The final portion of this article compares Dowland's setting of "In darkness let me dwell" (D201) with John Coprario's earlier lute song setting that commemorated the death of Charles Blount, first Earl of Devonshire.

409   Mellers, Wilfrid. "The Double Man: John Dowland, Hamlet, and Seventeenth Century Melancholy." *Margin* 7 (1988): 53–64. ISSN 0950-5091. NX456 .M357.

Opening with a parallel to Shakespeare's *Hamlet*, this article examines Dowland and his music as two-edged: joyful, religious, and love-filled on one side, and melancholic and death-infused on the other. The article focuses on four of Dowland's most well-known songs: "Flow my tears" (D15), "I saw my lady weep" (D141), "Weep you no more sad fountains" (D174), and "In darkness let me dwell" (D201).

410   Mellers, Wilfrid. "Words and Music in Elizabethan England." In *The New Pelican Guide to English Literature. Volume 2: The Age of Shakespeare*. Revised and Expanded. Edited by Boris Ford, 165–94. Harmondsworth, UK: Penguin Books, 1982. ISBN 0140222650. PR83 .N49.

Briefly analyzes "Shall I sue" (D156), proclaiming the song an exemplary setting that considers both textual and musical affect. First printed in 1955.

411   Meyer, Jeffrey Thore. "The Tonal Language of John Dowland's Lutesongs: Character of the Airs and Constructive Use of Gestures." PhD Diss., University of Minnesota, 1999. UMI 9929512.

Describes Dowland's "compositional choices through the use of gestures" specific to the composer's lute songs, as a means to "clarify and deepen poetic meaning." In doing so, Dowland's lute songs are situated against English theoretical treatises printed in the late sixteenth and early seventeenth centuries (Bathe, *A Brief Introduction to the Skill of Song*, 1584; Morley, *A Plaine and Easie Introduction to Practicall Musicke*, 1597; Campion, *A New Way of Making Fowre Parts in Counter-point*, 1613–1614; Butler, *The Principles of Musik in Singing and Setting*, 1636). Compositions are contextualized by their "air," determined by the number of flats in the key signature and by tonal center, the author assiduously avoiding anachronistic common-practice vocabulary in an effort to view the music as the composer did, suggesting an alternate way to analyze these songs.

412   Newcomb, Wilburn W. *Lute Music of Shakespeare's Time; William Barley: A New Booke of Tabliture, 1596*. University Park: Pennsylvania State University Press, 1966. xxxviii, 115 pp. MT640 .B17.

A basic edition of Barley's 1596 lute anthology, which contains three Dowland pieces for lute (*Lachrimae* D15, *Piper's Pavan* D8, and *Fortune* D62), and four for orpharion (*Solus cum Sola* D10, *Galliard* D42, *Go from my Window* D64, and *Mistress Winter's Jump* D55). Barley is likely the volume to which Dowland referred when he complained in his *First Booke* preface that his works were being circulated with errors. The editor often refers to the Dowland songs in his opening section defining "The Musical Forms."

413   Nitz, Martin. "John Dowland, Jacob van Eyck und die künstlerische Freiheit." *Tibia* 40, no. 3 (2015): 517–19. ISSN 0176–6511. ML929 .T5. In German.

A comparison, highlighting variants of the melody line of Dowland's "Flow my tears" (D15) found in Jacob van Eyck's 1644/1655 *Der Fluyten Lust-Hof*.

414   Nuzzo, Claudio. "John Dowland e l'Ayre: Origini e Sviluppo di una Forma Poetico-Musicale." *Hortus Musicus: Trimestrale di Musica Antica* 2, no. 6 (April–June 2001): 14–19. ISSN 1129–4965. In Italian.

An overview article that fashions the ayre as the perfect synthesis of music and poetry, positioning Dowland as a leader in the English lute song school who combined English, French, and Italian musical traits. Continues on to discuss for whom lute song-airs were composed, metric rhyme schemes and forms, and the development of monody.

415   Poulton, Diana. "Dowland's Songs and their Instrumental Forms." *Monthly Musical Record* 81 (1951): 175–80. ML5 .M6.

One of Poulton's earliest articles. Describes the forms in which Dowland's music appeared and discusses seven lute song-airs that also appear as consort music or as lute solos.

416   Poulton, Diana. "John Dowland's 'Can She Excuse My Wrongs'—B Flat or Natural?" *The Lute: Journal of the Lute Society* 9 (1967): 41–4. ISSN 0952–0759. ML5 .L89.

Considers whether a flat, added to the first "B" in the voice part of "Can she excuse" (D42) in the first modern critical edition of Dowland's *First Booke of Songes*, was the composer's original or revised intention, or simply a mistake in the lute tablature of Dowland's print. Includes a list of concordances with their markings, and arrives at the conclusion that the "B" in the voice part was never intended to be flatted.

417   Rooley, Anthony. " 'I must complain': A Comparative Study in Variant Settings." In *Essays on Renaissance Music in Honour of David Fallows*. Edited by Fabrice Fitch and Jacobijn Kiel, 233–48. Woodbridge, UK: Boydell, 2011. ISBN 9781843836193. ML172 .E877.

Compares musical settings of a Thomas Campion poem—one by Dowland (D176) and one by Campion. (Two other anonymous settings survive.) Analyzes musical rhetoric, as well as textual context, and attempts a chronological dating of all the settings. Declares Dowland's setting superior, although the author stresses that is not the point of the article.

418   Rooley, Anthony. "Time Stands Still: Devices and Designs, Allegory and Alliteration, Poetry and Music and a New Identification in an Old Portrait." *Early Music* 34, no. 3 (August 2006): 443–60. ISSN 0306–1078. ML5 .E18.

Revisits the circumstances of the first performance of "His golden locks" (D137), the retirement observance of Sir Henry Lee, who for many years was the queen's champion at the tilts. The author not only places Dowland's song from the *First Booke* as the version used for Lee's celebration, but also suggests Dowland was a participant in the performance, though there is no concrete evidence of either. (Many scholars think the version was likely that of Dowland's, but there is no way to know for sure.) Rooley then explores "Time's eldest son" (D145), a song included in Dowland's *Second Booke*, presenting the work as part of "a through-composed trilogy," portraying an aged Lee in agreement with a third song, "Far from triumphing court" (D199) from *A Musicall Banquet*. Two other pieces from the *Third and Last Booke* are also suggested as having possible Lee associations. The larger article focuses on Lee portraiture and an illustration printed on the title page of Dowland's *First Booke*.

419   Ruff, Lillian M., and D. Arnold Wilson. "Allusion to the Essex Downfall in Lute Song Lyrics." *The Lute: Journal of the Lute* 12 (1970): 31–6. ISSN 0460–007X. ML5 .L89.

A continuation of the pair's earlier, often-cited *Past & Present* article (420), providing further evidence for their thesis, that many vernacular songs of the late sixteenth and early seventeenth centuries were commentaries on the Earl of Essex and his downfall. Among the most important discoveries is that of a commonplace book containing lyrics of six Dowland songs, copied from the first and second songbooks, including "Come again, sweet love" (D60), "Can she excuse my wrongs" (D42), "Sleep wayward thoughts" (D133), "Sorrow stay" (D142), "O sweet woods" (D147), and "A shepherd in a shade" (D154). The article then links the listed songs to individuals who knew Dowland's compositions, rather than to Dowland himself.

420   Ruff, Lillian M., and D. Arnold Wilson. "The Madrigal, the Lute Song and Elizabethan Politics." *Past & Present* 44 (August 1969): 3–51. ISSN 0031–2746. D1 .P37.

This article, cited in many subsequent pieces of scholarship, examines Elizabethan secular song as an extension of political associations of the time, specifically those related to the pro-Essex faction in the Elizabethan court. While the first half of the article focuses on madrigals, the second section considers the lute song, beginning with the role William Barley's *New Booke of Tabliture* had in motivating Dowland's *First Booke*. Then works from all of Dowland's lute song-air volumes are prominently featured as the authors attempt to tie lyrics to pro-Essexian sentiment. The argument is continued in **419**. Includes a useful table and graph indicating when lute songs were published from 1596 through 1632, and by whom.

421 Rupp, Suzanne. "'Sinner's Sighs'—The Devotional Lute Songs of John Dowland and Thomas Campion." In *Gesang zur Laute*. Edited by Nicole Schwindt, 191–206. Kassel: Bärenreiter, 2002. (Trossinger Jahrbuch für Renaissancemusik 2.) ISBN 376181612X, 9783761816127. ML1013 .G47.

Posits six devotional lute songs of *Pilgrimes Solace* as both a marketing ploy to seize on heightened interest in Protestant public-private devotional music and a representation of Dowland's own personal devotional journey.

422 Smith, James Gordon. "John Dowland: A Reappraisal of His Ayres." DMA Diss., Indiana University, 1973.

An in-depth study of the lute song-airs included in Dowland's four printed volumes, with poetic, metrical, and musical analysis, transcriptions of and commentary on selected pieces, and many charts comparing the songs of each collection. Argues that these songs should only be considered in their original printed versions, which provide options for various combinations of performers (or in the words of the author, "publications which are deliberately ambiguous in performance specifications"), rather than the either-or approach (i.e. lute song or multi-voice air) reflected in critical editions of Dowland's music published to the time the dissertation was written.

423 Sommerrock, Ulrich. *Das Englische Lautenlied (1597–1622) Eine Literaturwissenschaftlich-Musikologische Untersuchung*. Regensburg: S. Roderer, 1990. ISBN 3890734715. vii, 264 p. ML2831 .S6 1990. In German.

A rhetorical-musical study of English lute songs, in which Dowland's airs are analyzed both for language used and in the context of topics such as the pastoral, death, melancholy, spirituality, and gender. Consideration is given to both primary and secondary source literature on these subjects. Includes a comparison of Dowland's and Coprario's versions of "In darkness let me dwell" (D201). This edition is a print of the author's dissertation of the same year.

424 "The Songs of Dowland." *The Musical Times* 71, no. 1044 (February 1, 1930): 174–5. ML5 .M85.

Report of a paper introducing Dowland and his music, given by Edmund Fellowes at the 56th Musical Association meeting. Presents some concepts that have been superseded by more recent scholarship. Though the content is at times questionable, the article serves as a starting point from which to view the immense strides made in Dowland scholarship over the last eighty-five plus years.

425 Spencer, Robert. "Dowland's Can She Excuse?: The Case for Reinstalling the B Flat." In *La Musique, de tous les Passetemps le plus Beau: Hommage à Jean-Michel Vaccaro*. Edited by François Lesure, Henri Vanhulst, and Victor Coelho, 333–41. Paris: Klincksieck, 1998. ISBN 2252032049. ML172 .M92.

Reconsiders the B-flat versus B-natural issue in the opening melody line of "Can she excuse my wrongs" (D42), discussed previously by Poulton in 1967 (**416**) and re-visited by Gross in 1983 (**399**). Outlines the history of the note as presented in primary and secondary source editions of Dowland's music. The author disagrees with Poulton and recommends that B-flat be utilized, based on his assertion that the piece was first composed for lute solo, thereby suggesting it should conform to the original lute tablature.

426 Spencer, Robert. "Singing Lute Songs: A Final Word." *The Lute: The Journal of the Lute Society* 25 (1985): 81. ISSN 0952–0759. ML5 .L89.

Argues that the second voice/bass parts of the first eight lute song-airs of Dowland's *Second Booke* were never truly intended for singing.

427 Spink, Ian. *English Song: Dowland to Purcell*. London: B. T. Batsford, 1974. Reprinted with corrections New York: Taplinger, 1986. 310 p. ISBN 0800823966. ML2831 .S68.

Dowland and his music serve as the starting point for this stylistic survey of seventeenth-century English monodic tradition. The first chapter (pp. 15–37) is primarily devoted to Dowland's lute songs, as the author states the composer "achieve[d] an intensity of expression unequalled in England until Purcell." Many Dowland musical examples, from all four of his songbooks, are excerpted for use as examples of the composer's compositional technique.

428 Taylor, Andrew. "The Sounds of Chivalry: Lute Song and Harp Song for Sir Henry Lee." *Journal of the Lute Society of America* 25 (1992): 1–23. ISSN 0076–1524. ML1 .L75.

Within this well-written article, the author details and contextualizes the song, "His golden locks Time hath to silver turned" (D137), sung at the retirement tilt of Queen Elizabeth's champion Sir Henry Lee. Dowland later included a musical setting of this text in his *First Booke*, and many believe that this was the setting sung seven years earlier at the tilt.

429 Teo, Kenneth S. "Chromaticism in Thomas Weelkes's 1600 Collection: Possible Models." *Musicology Australia* 13, no. 1 (1990): 2–14. ISSN 0814–5857. ML5 .M897.

Makes a case that Weelkes borrowed musical ideas from songs in Dowland's first songbook, as well as from works by Morley and Italian composers represented in manuscripts circulating throughout England.

430 Teo, Kenneth K. S. "Dowland and 'Cease Sorrows Now.'" *Studia Musicologica Academiae Scientiarum Hungaricae* 36, no. 1/2 (1995): 5–10. ISSN 0039–3266. ML5 .S8.

More deeply explores an idea introduced in the author's 1990 article (**429**), that Dowland's songs, such as "All ye whom love" (D134), served as inspiration for the chromaticism demonstrated in Weelkes's early works.

431 Traficante, Frank. "Music for the Lyra Viol: The Printed Sources." *The Lute Society Journal* 8 (1966): 7–24. ISSN 0460–007X. ML5 .L89.

Within this article, the author briefly considers Dowland's prefatory statement in the songbook *A Pilgrimes Solace*, which rebukes Tobias Hume's earlier assertion that the viol could produce music of the same quality as the lute. Also provides possible reasons for a seven-year delay in response by Dowland (see especially pp. 11–14).

432 Walls, Peter. *Music in the English Courtly Masque 1604–1640*. Oxford: Clarendon, 1996. xix, 372 p. ISBN 0198161417. ML1731.7 .E5 W35.

Though not Dowland-centric, this book positions a few pieces from *A Pilgrimes Solace* as masque songs. Includes a very brief analysis (pp. 67–8) of "Up merry mates" (D196). Otherwise, Dowland is treated mostly in passing.

433 Warner, Sylvia Townsend. "Madrigalists and Lutenists (Continued)." *The Musical Times and Singing Class Circular* 63, no. 950 (April 1, 1922): 234–7. ML5 .M85.

This early twentieth-century article comments on airs and their place in early modern English music, briefly using Dowland's first songbook as an example. Supports Fellowes's assertion that Dowland can be considered "the greatest song-writer that this country has yet produced" (**390**).

434 Wess, Joan. "Musica Transalpina, Parody, and the Emerging Jacobean Viol Fantasia." *Chelys: The Journal of the Viola da Gamba Society* 15 (1986): 3–25. ISSN 0952–8407. ML749.5 .C5.

Asserts that Dowland and other English composers used a parody technique, borrowing musical material from *Musica Transalpina* (1588) and other Italian madrigal collections. "I saw my lady weep" (D141) is compared with Ferrabosco's "Vidi pianger" as one example.

Lyrics

see also **269, 350, 393, 394, 473**

435 Clayton, Thomas. " 'Sir Henry Lee's Farewell to the Court': The Texts and Authorship of 'His Golden Locks Time Hath to Silver Turned.'" *English Literary Renaissance* 4, no. 2 (March 1974): 268–75. ISSN 0013–8312. PR1 .E43.

Considers the authorship of the text of "His golden locks" (D137), which received its second public printing in Dowland's *First Booke*. The author concludes that the lyrics were written by Sir Henry Lee to commemorate his own retirement.

436 Doughtie, Edward. *Lyrics from English Airs 1596–1622*. Cambridge, MA: Harvard University Press, 1970. xvii, 657 p. ISBN 0674539761. PR1181 .D6.

Anthologizes the texts of Elizabethan-Jacobean English lute song-air collections (with the exception of those by Campion), including lyrics from Dowland's four songbooks, *A Musicall Banquet*, and Barley's *New Booke of Tabliture*. This volume has reached the level of canon, serving as the impetus for many studies of the lyrics of Dowland and others. Texts include both song lyrics and prefatory material of collections. The author's critical commentary provides information on printers, dedicatees, and others associated with each volume, musical borrowings, extant copies (known to the time of publication), variants, and a host of other helpful information. The book's introduction includes a valuable primer on the history of the lute song-air, providing important social and cultural contextualization while also considering the texts' placement within England's literary tradition. This work is an extension of the author's 1963 dissertation (**438**).

437   Doughtie, Edward. "Nicholas Breton and Two Songs by Dowland." *Renaissance News* 17, no. 1 (Spring 1964): 1–3. ISSN 0277–903X. CB361 .R45.

Attributes one, and possibly two, lyrical texts, set by Dowland in *A Pilgrim's Solace*, to poet Nicholas Breton: "From silent night" (D189) and "Thou mighty God" (D193).

438   Doughtie, Edward Orth. "Poems from the Songbooks of John Dowland." PhD Diss., Harvard University, 1963. UMI 0257319.

On the poetry set by Dowland, see **436**, which supersedes information presented here. This dissertation, however, also contains a substantial Dowland biography, contextualizes Dowland's music in relation to humanism and the Reformation, and provides contemporaneous mentions of Dowland not included in the later published anthology, but then superseded by **264**.

439   Fellowes, Edmund, ed. *English Madrigal Verse 1588–1632*. 3rd ed. Revised and enlarged by Frederick W. Sternfeld and David Greer. Oxford: Clarendon, 1967. xxx, 798 p. PR1195 .M2 F4.

An anthology of Elizabethan-Jacobean madrigal and lute song lyrics. Includes the texts of all four Dowland songbooks and *Musicall Banquet* in modernized English (pp. 454–511). Commentary on editions, poetry, sources, and other relevant information is provided in the back of the volume. The first edition appeared in 1920, and has been updated and expanded since.

440   Fischlin, Daniel T. " 'The Consent of Speaking Harmony': The Literary Aesthetics of the English Air." *Journal of the Lute Society of America* 19 (1986): 29–57. ISSN 0076–1524. ML1 .L75.

In this study of late sixteenth- and early seventeenth-century printed lute song-air lyrics, the author attempts to identify reasons composers selected texts for their compositions, and explores an effort to represent the "divine" through words that speak to an inexpressibility to do so. Dowland and his works are referenced repeatedly. Readers with little musical background are cautioned, as the article is written in the context of literary studies, and references to musical elements and genres are at times tenuous. Like Fischlin's other articles, this item became a chapter in his later book (**442**), which presents a more complete place to start.

441 Fischlin, Daniel T. "'The Highest Key of Passion': Inexpressibility and Metaphors of Self in John Dowland's *The First Booke of Songes or Ayres*." *Journal of the Lute Society of America 20–21* (1987–1988): 46–86. ISSN 0076-1524. ML1 .L75.

This article uses Dowland's *First Booke* to comment upon late sixteenth-century use of "metaphors of self in the lyrics of the English air." The focus is solely on poetic texts, rather than music, and assumes a foundational understanding of theories of literary analysis. Interested researchers might rather consult Fischlin's later monograph (**442**).

442 Fischlin, Daniel T. *In Small Proportions: A Poetics of the English Ayre 1596–1622*. Detroit: Wayne State University Press, 1998. 404 p. ISBN 0814326935. ML2531.2 .F57.

Dowland figures prominently in this monograph that attempts to place lute song-air lyrics as a category of overlooked literary verse, serving as a bridge between Elizabethan poetry and metaphysical poetry. The author asserts that texts can be viewed as a source of social and cultural commentary on the era. Emphasis is placed primarily on lyrics, without as much consideration of the music. As such, the author's expertise in literary rhetoric is apparent, but musicological considerations are sometimes misguided. Dowland is mentioned throughout and is the main focus of chapter 2, "'The Highest Key of Passion': Self, Metaphor, and Inexpressibility in John Dowland's *The First Booke of Songes or Ayres*," which is essentially a revision of the author's 1987 *JLSA* article (**441**), presenting lute song lyrics as a self-fashioning metaphor. Likewise, other chapters are largely reprints of the author's earlier articles: chapter 1 (**440**), chapter 3 (**465**), and chapter 4 (**444**).

443 Fischlin, Daniel T. "Music and Metrics: Idiom and English Air." *Mosaic: An Interdisciplinary Critical Journal 24*, no. 2 (Spring 1991): 19–42. ISSN 0027-1276. PN2 .M68.

An analysis of English airs based solely on metrical stress, without consideration of any additional musical elements. Uses several Dowland lyrics as examples, including "Weep you no more sad fountains" (D174), "Think'st thou then by thy feigning" (D130), and "Come heavy sleep" (D138).

444 Fischlin, Daniel. "'Sighes and Teares Make Life to Last': The Purgation of Grief and Death through Trope in the English Ayre." *Criticism 38*, no. 1 (Winter 1996): 1–25. ISSN 0011-1589. PN2 .F592.

Places the lute song-air as an appropriate medium for mourning in early modern England, especially songs that replicate the sounds of weeping and other standard presentations of expressions of grief. Appears in the author's later book (**442**) as chapter 2.

445 Gibson, Kirsten. "John Dowland and the Elizabethan Courtier Poets." In **270**: 239–53.

Notes that only fourteen of eighty-eight printed Dowland songs have lyrics securely attributed to courtiers of Elizabeth's reign, including those by Edward Dyer, Henry Lee, and Fulke Greville. The author contextualizes the texts' purposes and presentation within circles surrounding Robert Devereux, second Earl of Essex, and Robert Sidney.

446 Gibson, Kirsten. " 'So to the wood went I': Politicizing the Greenwood in Two Songs by John Dowland." *Journal of the Royal Musical Association* 132, no. 2 (2007): 221–51. ISSN 0269-0403. ML28 .L8 M8.

An important study that uses principles of intertextuality to contextualize Dowland's compositions "Can she excuse my wrongs" (D42) and "O sweet woods" (D147) as reflections of courtly desire for solitude and privacy, as well as feelings related to exile. Connects the songs to the figures of Philip Sidney and Robert Devereux, second Earl of Essex, through their own poetic texts, specific biographical aspects of their lives, and titles of solo lute versions of Dowland songs. The author argues that associated texts were understood by readers of the time in a way that is difficult for listeners today to discern.

447 Hurst-Wajszczuk, Kristine. "Dowland Lute Songs and the Cult of Elizabeth." *Journal of Singing* 63, no. 5 (May-June 2007): 523–30. ISSN 1086-7732. ML27 .U5 N2652.

Presents the case that many of Dowland's lyrics allude to Robert Devereux, Earl of Essex. This article, aimed at singers interested in contextualizing Dowland's songs, relies heavily on the scholarship of Ruff and Wilson (**419, 420**) and Christopher Haigh (*The Reign of Elizabeth I*, Athens: University of Georgia Press, 1985), which readers might rather consult from the start.

448 Klotz, Sebastian. " 'Were euery thought an eye'—Musical *Actio* and the Crisis of Visionary Language in Dowland's Lute Songs." In *Gesang zur Laute.* Edited by Nicole Schwindt, 179–89. Kassel: Bärenreiter, 2002. (Trossinger Jahrbuch für Renaissancemusik 2.) ISBN 376181612X, 9783761816127. ML1013 .G47.

Claims that Dowland's lyrics represent a new-to-the-time English philosophy, in which descriptions of bodily reception via eye and ear imply an intimate sensuality closely tied to melancholy. Does not consider the musical aspects of Dowland's songs.

449 Leach, Elizabeth Eva. "The Unquiet Thoughts of Edmund Spenser's Scudamour and John Dowland's *First Booke of Songes.*" In *Uno Gentile et Subtile Ingenio: Studies in Renaissance Music in Honour of Bonnie J. Blackburn.* Edited by M. Jennifer Bloxam, Gioia Filocamo, and Leofranc Holford-Strevens, 513–20. Turnhout: Brepols, 2009. ISBN 9782503531632. ML172 .G32.

Attempts to connect the opening song of Dowland's *First Booke* (D125) to Canto V of Spenser's fourth *Fairie Queene* book through textual comparison and other points of reference in the two artists' lives.

450 Lindley, David. "A Dowland Allusion in Herbert's 'Grief.'" *Notes and Queries* 31 (June 1984): 238–9. ISSN 0029–3970. AG305 .M7.

A short letter proposing that lyrics to "Come heavy sleep" (D138) were the inspiration for George Herbert's poem, "Grief."

451 Main, C. F. "New Texts of John Donne." *Studies in Bibliography* 9 (1957): 225–33.

Mentions verse found within an early seventeenth-century commonplace book (Harvard MS Eng 686) that conflates lyrics of Dowland's "Sweet stay awhile" (D182) and a fragmentary paraphrase of John Donne's "Break of day." Elaborates on other instances in which the two pieces of poetry are placed together.

452 Manning, Rosemary. "Lachrimae: A Study of John Dowland." *Music & Letters* 25, no. 1 (January 1944): 45–53. ISSN 0027–4224. ML5 .M64.

Muses upon Dowland's lyrics as representative of the composer's personal melancholy, leading the author to believe that Dowland may have served as his own lyricist. The age of this article and its lack of citation should give researchers pause, though the ideas contained within may encourage further exploration.

453 May, Stephen W. "The Poems of Edward DeVere, Seventeenth Earl of Oxford and of Robert Devereux, Second Earl of Essex." *Studies in Philology* 77, no. 5 (1980): 1–132. ISSN 0039–3738. P25 .S8.

This journal issue is in fact an edition of Oxford's and Essex's poems. Though only a small part of the article, an important note of commentary disputes Poulton's and others' attribution of "Can she excuse" (D42) lyrics to the Earl of Essex, based on the author's evaluation of poetic style (see pp. 114–15 in the section "Poems Wrongly Attributed to Essex"). Dowland's name is mentioned several other times within the issue, but with little substantial information attached.

454 Schleiner, Louise. *Cultural Semiotics, Spenser, and the Captive Woman.* Bethlehem, PA: Lehigh University Press, 1995. 278 p. ISBN 093422336X. PR2367 .W6 S35.

Briefly presents the text of Dowland's "Say Love, if ever thou didst find" (D166) as an example of a "courtly moon" trope, with a protagonist that fulfills the same role as the Cynthia character poet John Lyly used to symbolize Queen Elizabeth (pp. 150–1).

455 Schleiner, Louise. "Jacobean Song and Herbert's Metrics." *SEL Studies in English Literature, 1500–1900* 19, no. 1 (Winter 1979): 109–26. ISSN 0039–3657. PR1 .S82.

Uses the text of Dowland's "To ask for all thy love" (D183) to demonstrate a distinct Herbert poetic meter. The article, however, does not focus on Dowland.

456 Schleiner, Louise. *The Living Lyre in English Verse from Elizabeth through the Restoration.* Columbia: University of Missouri Press, 1984. 218 p. ISBN 0826204414. ML2831 .S3.

Classifies early modern English verse into three categories: song-influenced, speech-shaped, and declamatory or oratorical. Dowland is referenced infrequently, though some of his song lyrics are used as examples, including "Come away, come sweet love" (D131), "O sweet woods" (D147), "Say Love, if ever thou didst find" (D166), and "To ask for all thy love" (D183).

457   Scholl, Evelyn H. "English Metre Once More." *Publications of the Modern Language Association of America* 63, no. 1 (March 1948): 293–326. ISSN 0030–8129. PB6 .M6.

Examines metrical accents within the English language through lute song lyrics. Selected Dowland works serve as examples. There is some repetition from the author's previous article (**458**), and it is unclear whether the author relies solely on transcriptions from Fellowes's editions (which do not always align with spellings of the originals), or if original prints were consulted.

458   Scholl, Evelyn H. "New Light on Seventeenth Century Pronunciation from the English School of Lutenist Song Writers." *Publications of the Modern Language Association* 59, no. 2 (June 1944): 398–445. PB6 .M6.

Many Dowland lyric examples are used within this study that attempts to determine pronunciation standards, especially stress and abbreviation, through an examination of how English lyrics are set rhythmically in lute songs.

459   Smith, Bruce R. "Landscape with Figures: The Three Realms of Queen Elizabeth's Country-House Revels." *Renaissance Drama* n.s. 8 (1977): 57–115. ISSN 0486–3739. PN1785 .R4.

Within a larger topic, elaborates on events surrounding texts Dowland set (perhaps for the occasions mentioned, perhaps later) that are recorded as being used in Elizabethan theatrical entertainments. Considers "Far from triumphing court" (D199), "His golden locks" (D137), "My heart and tongue were twins" (D195), and "O sweet woods" (D147).

460   Troost, Linda V. "The Dowland Reference in Chapman's *The Widow's Tears*." *American Notes & Queries* 22, no. 3–4 (November–December 1983): 36–7. ISSN 0003–0171. AG305 .A42.

Expands on a footnote found in George Chapman, *The Widow's Tears*, ed. Akihiro Yamada (London: Methuen, 1975), xxxii, which states that several lines from the last act of the early seventeenth-century play are borrowed from Dowland's song "Say Love, if ever thou didst find" (D166), equating a character in the play with a virtuous Elizabeth I.

461   Walls, Peter. "'Music and Sweet Poetry'? Verse for English Lute Song and Continuo Song." *Music & Letters* 65, no. 3 (July 1984): 237–54. ISSN 0027–4224. ML5 .M64.

Places selected Dowland lyrics alongside verse of recognized Elizabethan-Jacobean poets, most especially John Donne, contextualizing Dowland's air texts within the literary culture of the time.

Music and Text

see also entries in **Lute Song-Airs,** *and* **554, 564**

462 Bronson, Bertrand Harris. *The Ballad as Song.* Berkeley and Los Angeles: University of California Press, 1969. xii, 324 p. ISBN 0520013999. ML3553 .B76.

A short section of this volume considers the textual-musical relationship of stressed syllables in selected Dowland songs, including "Can she excuse my wrongs" (D42), "Come away, come sweet love" (D131), "Come again, sweet love doth now invite" (D60), "Now cease my wand'ring eyes" (D150), "Flow my tears" (D15), "Wilt thou unkind" (D135), and "Now O now I needs must part" (D23). The author suggests that the importance of musical stress over textual stress implies the poetry may have been written by Dowland himself. He goes on to compare Dowland's settings with those of his contemporary Thomas Campion, noting the higher literary quality of Campion's creations (see especially pp. 297–303), a subjective response with which some Dowland scholars may disagree.

463 Davis, Walter R. "Melodic and Poetic Structure: The Examples of Campion and Dowland." *Criticism* 4, no. 2 (Spring 1962): 89–107. ISSN 0011–1589. PN2 .F592.

Analyzes musical and textual connections in lute song-airs by Dowland and Campion. The author states his aim is to move beyond simple analysis of word painting, but the musical analysis remains quite basic, considering the text only in combination with melodic lines. He lands upon the idea that Campion uses contrast to structure his musical choices, while Dowland depends more upon what he terms "continuous development" based on repetition. The main issue with the author's argument is his assumption that Dowland's music was written simultaneously with the text, when several of his examples may first have been conceived as lute solos and later adapted as lute song-airs.

464 Doughtie, Edward. "Sibling Rivalry: Music vs. Poetry in Campion and Others." *Criticism* 20, no. 1 (Winter 1978): 1–16. ISSN 0011–1589. PN2 .F592.

Compares Thomas Campion's settings of his personally penned verse to that of other composers who set the same lyrics. In Dowland's case, this results in an evaluation of the two composers' versions of "I must complain" (D176), Dowland's found in his *Third Booke.*

465 Fischlin, Daniel. "'Tis Like I Cannot Tell What': Desire, Indeterminacy, and Erotic Performance in the English Ayre." *Modern Language Quarterly* 56, no. 4 (1995): 395–491. ISSN 0026–7929. PB1 .M642.

Argues that lute song-airs exemplify a rhetorical gesture in early poetry that creates a paradoxical sense of self and other. The author further believes that the aspect of performance adds an inherent extra-erotic element to verse. Several of Dowland's song texts are used as examples. Adapted to become chapter 3 of the author's later book (**442**), which is recommended as a better alternative, as some information is updated and corrected.

466 Horner, Bruce. "Negotiating Traditions of English Song: Performance, Text, History." *Mosaic: An Interdisciplinary Critical Journal* 27, no. 3 (September 1994): 19–44. ISSN 0027-1276. PN2 .M68.

In this article that evaluates songs as texts (that is, as a single unit of combined music and lyrics), the author argues that songs allowed composers to establish an artistic self. Further, Dowland's lute song-airs are placed within a courtly domain, in which each performance could be evaluated in its social context. The author reinterprets Dowland's lute songs not so much as inherently melancholic, but as a means for members of court to express discontent or other feelings to royals and fellow court members.

467 Horner, Bruce Merle. "The Rhetorics of Seventeenth-Century English Songs." PhD Diss., University of Pittsburgh, 1988.

Attempts to define early English songs as "rhetorical acts," differentiated by associations with the places in which they were presented. Traditional genres are studied to determine how they were perceived differently by various socio-cultural groups. Chapter 5 focuses on Dowland, as well as Thomas Campion and Henry Lawes, as a composer of songs intended for court performance, with courtly themes and concerns. The author characterizes these pieces as isolation-ist, assuming that lutenist and singer were intended to be one and the same, which may or may not be the case. These concepts are distilled in **466**.

468 Ing, Catherine. *Elizabethan Lyrics: A Study of the Development of English Metres and their Relation to Poetic Effect.* London: Chatto and Windus, 1951. 252 p. Reprinted New York: Barnes and Noble, 1969. PR525 .V4.

Traces various poetic meters employed by early modern English authors, as well as poetic relationships to musical setting. Several Dowland songs, such as "Weep you no more sad fountains" (D174), are cited as examples.

469 Iovan, Sarah. "Music and Performative Poetics in Early Modern English Lyrics." PhD Diss., University of Wisconsin-Madison, 2013. UMI 3588727.

This dissertation, written as a requirement for an English doctoral degree, moves beyond examining the textual-musical relationship found within songs to con-sider the individual voices of the singer and the lute itself, the ways each com-plicates understanding of a composition, and their dependence upon each other. The author allocates a full chapter to Dowland's lute songs, with special emphasis on "In darkness let me dwell" (D201) and "Weep you no more sad fountains" (D174). Iovan also devotes quite a bit of space to Ornithoparcus's and Dowland's "understanding of musical voices" to foreground this discussion.

470 Iovan, Sarah. "Performing Voices in the English Lute Song." *SEL Studies in English Literature 1500-1900* 50, no. 1 (Winter 2010): 63–81. ISSN 0039-3657. PR1 .S82.

An excellent primary source based commentary on early artistic product and its enhancement within a performative sphere. Defines song as, "the site of the intersection between words and music." Continues on to position performance as a third entity that must be considered when contextualizing lute song. Uses Dowland's translation of *Micrologus* to illuminate sixteenth-century thought on music alone, singular poetry, and combined presentation. "Weep you no more sad fountains" (D174) is offered as an example through which the author presents her theory.

471　Jorgens, Elise Bickford. " 'Let Well-Tun'd Words Amaze': Attitudes Toward Poetry in English Solo Song from John Dowland to Henry Lawes." PhD Diss., City University of New York, 1975.

A close study of early seventeenth-century accompanied song with an emphasis on musical-textual setting. Comments both on common conventions and individual composers' styles. Dowland figures prominently and his songs are used continuously as examples, especially within chapter 3, which examines compositions inspired by dance forms, and chapter 5, which creates a new categorization of songs called "Pathetic Airs," encompassing works that are especially affective and do not necessarily follow more conventional structures of other songs of the era. Superseded by the author's monograph (**474**).

472　Jorgens, Elise Bickford. "On Matters of Manner and Music in Jacobean and Caroline Song," *English Literary Renaissance* 10, no. 2 (Spring 1980): 239–64. ISSN 0013–8312. PR1 .E43.

Describes Dowland's text setting as semantic rather than poetic, that is, rhythmically situated with careful thought as to how the text will be perceived upon listening. Contends this practice sometimes lessens the effectiveness of later strophic verses. Portions of this article are reprinted in the author's 1982 monograph (**474**).

473　Jorgens, Elise Bickford. " 'Sweet Stay Awhile': Six Musical Interpretations." *Centerpoint* 2, no. 2 (Spring 1977): 1–10. ISSN 0098–924X. AP2 .C373.

After arguing that the text for "Sweet stay awhile" (D182) was likely *not* written by John Donne, as it is attributed in many early musical and literary editions, the author describes six musical settings of the poem from the first half of the seventeenth century. Proclaims Dowland's "best of the six." The other five, including one by Orlando Gibbons, draw comparisons to Dowland's version.

474　Jorgens, Elise Bickford. *The Well-Tun'd Word: Musical Interpretations of English Poetry 1597–1651.* Minneapolis: University of Minnesota Press, 1982. xx, 298 p. ISBN 0816610290. ML3849 .J67.

The author views Dowland as the foremost composer of lute songs, and hence, his compositions play a large part in this full-length monograph that examines the relationship between musical settings and the verses they set. Considers meter, textual stress, syntax, and form. Dowland's music and lyrics are used as examples throughout and featured especially within chapters on "Meter and Rhythm," "Lines and Stanzas," "Measured Music," "Dance Songs," and "Pathetic Airs." This volume is one of the first to present an in-depth study of the relationship between Dowland's texts and his music.

475   Klotz, Sebastian. "Gestures of Commitment and Gestures of Detachment: Reconsidering Music and Rhetoric in the Elizabethan Madrigal and Ayre." *Dutch Journal for Musicology/Muziek & Wetenschap* 4, no. 1-2 (1994): 3-31. ISSN 0925-725X. ML5 .M9963.

Attempts to situate a rhetorical analysis of music outside traditional examinations of musical gestures, and with consideration of renaissance primary source treatise content. Dowland's "In darkness let me dwell" (D201) is briefly mentioned as an example of rhetorical declamation resulting from performance, not from individual words.

476   Maynard, Winifred. "Dowland, Ferrabosco, and Jonson: Ayres and Masque Songs." Chapter 4 in *Elizabethan Lyric Poetry and its Music*. Edited by Winifred Maynard, 113-49. Oxford: Clarendon, 1986. ISBN 0198128444. ML79 .M4 1986.

The first fifteen pages of this chapter put forth a general reflection on Dowland's lute song-air lyrics, with special consideration of their associations with dance forms and Elizabethan celebrations, including the retirement of Sir Henry Lee.

477   Mellers, Wilfrid. *Harmonious Meeting: A Study of the Relationship between English Music, Poetry, and Theatre, c. 1600-1900*. London: Dobson, 1965. 317 p. ML3849 .M5.

A preface describes this book as "an exploration of the relationship between English music, poetry, and theatre by way of a detailed commentary on specific pieces." Chapter 8 (pp. 81-94) explores "Four Ayres of John Dowland," discussing "Shall I sue" (D156), "Flow my tears" (D15), "I saw my lady weep" (D141), and "In darkness let me dwell" (D201). The author does, indeed, produce analyses that demonstrate musico-texual synthesis. Chapter 9 (pp. 95-103) examines "Me, me, and none but me" (D164), "Come heavy sleep" (D138), and "Thou mighty God" (D193), as examples of the "Choral Ayre," which is described as "lute ayres that Dowland arranged as part-songs." Readers should note that descriptive harmonic analysis is anachronistic and that these pieces were never "choral," in the sense that they were not envisioned by the composer for a choir with multiple singers on each part. Still, there is value in the analyses presented. In chapters 10 and 12, Dowland—though not the main focus—is repeatedly evoked in comparison to Henry Lawes and Henry Purcell.

478   Pattison, Bruce. "Literature and Music in the Age of Shakespeare." *Proceedings of the Musical Association* 60 (1933-1934): 67-86. ISSN 0958-8442. ML5 .R888.

This lecture transcript is one of the first pieces of scholarship to address the importance of considering lyrics and music jointly in Elizabethan song.

479   Pattison, Bruce. *Music and Poetry of the English Renaissance*. London: Methuen, 1948. ix, 220 p. Reprinted Folcroft, PA: Folcroft, 1971. ML286.2 .P3.

While most of the information on Dowland and his works found within this volume is covered in more detail in other sources, the author successfully contextualizes Dowland's music and lyrics and that of his contemporaries within social, cultural, and literary circles of the time.

480 Pinnock, Andrew, and Bruce Wood. "A Mangled Chime: The Accidental Death of the Opera Libretto in Civil War England." *Early Music* 36, no. 2 (May 2008): 265–84. ISSN 0306–1078. ML5 .E18.

Though not the main point of this article, the authors contend that John Dowland and his contemporaries often overlooked natural spoken metrical accents to accommodate musical lines, using "If floods of tears" (D148) from the *Second Booke* as an example.

481 Ratcliffe, Stephen. "Echoes." *Conjunctions* 16 (1991): 280–95. ISSN 0278–2324. PN6010.5 .C66.

This disjointed, poetic article, found in a creative writing journal, explores musical affect through gestural melodic and intervallic tropes that enhance the meaning of verse. No particular song receives any sort of in-depth treatment, but at least four of Dowland's songs are referenced. Includes no historical or analytical analysis, but may provide colorful references.

482 Toft, Robert. "Musicke a Sister to Poetrie: Rhetorical Artifice in the Passionate Airs of John Dowland." *Early Music* 12, no. 2 (May 1984): 191–9. ISSN 0306–1078. ML5 .E18.

Explains musico-textual rhetoric in late renaissance English music as portrayed in Henry Peacham's *The Compleat Gentleman* (1622). Then details how Dowland used specific rhetorical gestures, especially ones that employ repetition or restatement, to heighten listeners' emotional responses to his songs "Sorrow stay" (D142) and "In darkness let me dwell" (D201).

483 Wells, Robin Headlam. "The Art of Persuasion." *The Lute: Journal of the Lute Society* 16 (1974): 67–9. ISSN 0952–0759. ML5 .L89.

A short article that defines Dowland's "Come again, sweet love" (D60) as a seduction song. The author contends the meaning of the air's penultimate textual line is accentuated through the composer's choice of sequential, ascending musical melodic movement.

484 Wells, Robin Headlam. *Elizabethan Mythologies: Studies in Poetry, Drama, and Music.* Cambridge: Cambridge University Press, 1994. xviii, 287 p. ISBN 0521433851. PR428 .M8 W45.

Synthesizes and elaborates on many ideas presented in the author's earlier articles. Chapter 8, "Dowland, Ficino, and Elizabethan Melancholy," expands upon theories offered in **485**, reflecting on Anthony Rooley's writings (**314**) to consider if Dowland's melancholic work was steeped in Hermetic neoplatonism, and weighing such considerations against typical conventions of the time. Chapter 4 echoes **486**.

485   Wells, Robin Headlam. "John Dowland and Elizabethan Melancholy." *Early Music* 13, no. 4 (November 1985): 514–28. ISSN 0306–1078. ML5 .E18.

A reaction to Anthony Rooley's **314**, in which author Wells suggests that Dowland's use of rhetorical devices was not an outgrowth of Hermetic neoplatonism, but simply a reflection of musico-rhetorical conventions of the time, taken to new heights by an especially gifted composer.

486   Wells, Robin Headlam. "The Ladder of Love: Verbal and Musical Rhetoric in the Elizabethan Lute-Song." *Early Music* 12, no. 2 (May 1984): 173–89. ISSN 0306–1078. ML5 .E18.

Using textual examples, the author provides a solid overview of rhetorical devices found in Elizabethan texts that were commonly acknowledged in educated, humanist circles. Wells then applies the same principles to Dowland's airs, while maintaining that words were all-important—music serving to enhance textual meaning, not through word painting, but through gestural amplification. Some information in this article is expanded upon in **484**.

CONSORT MUSIC

see also **289, 301, 303, 349, 352, 365, 510, 572, 573**. *For Dowland's* Lachrimae *(1604) volume, see also* **4** *and* **230**.

487   Bianco, Aurelio. *"Nach englischer und frantzösischer Art": vie et oeuvre de Carlo Farina: avec l'édition des cinq recueils de Dresde.* Turnhout: Brepols, 2010. 299 p. ISBN 9782503533650. ML410 .F221 B53. In French.

This monograph on seventeenth-century Italian composer and violinist Carlo Farina positions Dowland's 1604 *Lachrimae* in its proper place as the inspiration for many continental compositions utilizing a melancholic view within the pavane form. More specifically, the author directly credits the four-note descending tear motive so closely associated with Dowland. The book goes on to demonstrate Farina's use of the theme in his pavanes, though there is some question as to if he was inspired by Dowland's original music, or simply by the trend that developed in the music of others of the time (see pp. 92–9).

488   Bryan, John. "'Their Last Foile and Polishment': Aspects of Compositional Refinement in the Consort Dances of Dowland and Holborne." In **270**: 219–37.

A contrapuntal, structural, and textural analysis of the dances of Dowland's *Lachrimae* (1604) volume, with some comparison to Anthony Holborne's 1599 collection of consort pieces.

489   Fleming, Michael, and John Bryan. *Early English Viols: Instruments Makers and Music.* New York: Routledge, 2016. xxi, 373 p. ISBN 9781472468543. ML927 .V5 B79.

Though Dowland is associated more with the lute than viols, the *Lachrimae* collection ensured his inclusion in any conversation related to standard viol repertoire. Dowland's compositions are briefly discussed throughout this work, and special attention is given to advice mined from the "Necessary Observations" sub-section titled "Of setting the right sizes of Strings upon the Lute" from Robert Dowland's 1610 *Varietie of Lute Lessons*, indicating the information is valuable for viol and other strings as well (see pp. 289–92).

490　Goodwin, Christopher. "Some Recent Dowland Discoveries." *Lute News: The Lute Society Magazine* 68 (December 2003): 12–20. ML5 .L885.

A bit of a miscellany of information, including consideration of possible lute parts for songs in Morley's *Consort Lessons* (no copies of the lute partbook have survived); an Ian Payne observation of a probable musical pun related to *Solus cum sola* (D10) and *Solus sine sola*; and the proportionally large number of Dowland works (compared to other composers) dedicated to or that reference women, with contextual musings on each.

491　Hauge, Peter. "Dowland's Seven Tears, or the Art of Concealing the Art." *Dansk Årbog for Musikforskning* 29 (2001): 9–36. ISSN 0416–6884. ML5 .D109.

Closely analyzes the seven pavans of *Lachrimae* (1604) structurally, musically, and with reference to the "Flow my tears" (D15) text. In a reading unlike Holman (**493**) or Pinto (**498**), the author presents the collection as a reflection of contemporaneous universal-spiritual vs. earthly-human dichotomies, with levels of influence and importance represented by the compositions included.

492　Holman, Peter. "The Crying Game." *BBC Music Magazine* 7, no. 1 (1998): 27–8. ISSN 0966–7180. ML5 .B349.

An understandable, abbreviated overview of the early modern concept of melancholy as related to Dowland's seven *Lachrimae* pavans. Written for a general audience.

493　Holman, Peter. *Dowland: Lachrimae (1604)*. Cambridge: Cambridge University Press, 1999. xvi, 100 p. (Cambridge Music Handbooks). ISBN 0521581966. ML410 .D808 H65.

This concise volume is part of the Cambridge Music Handbooks series, which features analysis and contextualization of important Western art music compositions. In this case, the showcased work is Dowland's only volume of consort music, *Lachrimae*. Holman's book—the first and only monograph to highlight the 1604 *Lachrimae* collection—provides a concentrated overview of the musical work, as well as analyses of its individual components. The author examines *Lachrimae's* background, its importance within the context of early English printing, its format, organization, and place in consort repertoire, and provides an exploration of Dowland's favored dance types. Each of Dowland's seven pavans is closely analyzed. In doing so, the author theorizes that these pieces function as individual, recognizable parts of a spiritual cycle related to the melancholy for which Dowland is so well known. The book is geared toward a general musical readership, although it would be especially useful for performers who are preparing works from *Lachrimae*.

494   Holman, Peter. *Four and Twenty Fiddlers: The Violin at the English Court, 1540–1690*. Oxford: Clarendon, 1993. xxvii, 491 p. ISBN 019816145X. ML756 .H64.

Includes a brief section (pp. 160–70) that focuses primarily on individual pieces of the 1604 *Lachrimae* volume appearing in various consort versions in German manuscripts and prints of the 1590s through 1620s.

495   Holman, Peter. "Reflections on John Dowland." *Early Music Review* 55 (November 1999): 9–11. ISSN 1355-3437. ML5 .E195.

This sort of stream-of-consciousness article presents the musings of one expert on the state of Dowland studies. Focuses include the composer's religion, discoveries of new Dowland primary sources (since the publication of Poulton's monograph, **264**, until this article was written), updates needed for full representation of Dowland's music in modern editions (specifically Poulton and Lam, **221**, and Edgar Hunt's *Complete Consort Music*, **222**), and an interpretation of *Lachrimae* (1604). This last topic was included in anticipation of the publication of the author's *Lachrimae* monograph (**493**).

496   Jones, Allan Clive. "Warlock, Dowland, and Segovia." *Classical Guitar Magazine* 29, no. 9 (May 2011): 24–9; 29, no. 10 (June 2011): 16–19; 29, no. 11 (July 2011): 16–20. ISSN 0950-429X.

A three-part article tracing internationally renowned guitarist Andrés Segovia's access to the music of John Dowland, of which he recorded three pieces. Though this number is quite limited, the author contends that it is important to understand how Segovia knew of the music. "Part 1: Dowland Restored" introduces Philip Heseltine (1894–1930), who produced both Dowland literature and musical editions under the name Peter Warlock, and his relationship to Andrés Segovia (1893–1987). "Part 2: Warlock the Editor" discusses Heseltine's methodology when transcribing and editing Dowland's music from the original tablature. "Part 3: Dowland's Mysterious 'Galliard'" explores how Andre Segovia might have accessed Dowland music that he recorded, finding a connection to early twentieth-century guitar-music editor Hans Dagobert Brüger, who transcribed several pieces from van Hove's 1612 printed anthology (**27**). The author also considers early twentieth-century editions of Dowland's music, including those by Heseltine, whose work is often overshadowed by early music giant Edmund Fellowes. Written for a general audience who may be unfamiliar with Dowland's work, the final part also provides a clear overview of *Lachrimae* (1604), its contents, how they appeared visually, and how this format affected later transcription.

497   Ludwig, Loren Monte. "'Equal to All Alike': A Cultural History of the Viol Consort in England, c. 1550–1675." PhD Diss., University of Virginia, 2011. UMI 3467465.

Chapter 2, "Melancholy, Mourning, and Mimesis: The Viol Consort and English Sadness," examines Dowland's 1604 *Lachrimae* as an example of how consort playing functioned as an outlet for a sort of communal melancholy. The larger thesis considers the ways viol consorts served social and cultural needs of the era.

498   Pinto, David. "Dowland's Tears: Aspects of 'Lachrimae.'" *The Lute: Journal of the Lute Society* 37 (1997): 44–75. ISSN 0952-0759. ML5 .L89.

Argues that Dowland's *Lachrimae* (1604) was not delineative of melancholic states, but a Catholic-hued reflection of the seven penitential psalms. Suggests that Dowland was inspired by a Lassus psalm cycle featuring a theme identical to the *lachrimae* motive. The author also contends Dowland's pavan series served as a coded appeal to Queen Anne's Roman Catholic sensibilities. An appendix includes a detailed exploration of the pieces' ties to the original dance form utilized for their structures.

499   Rooley, Anthony. "A Portrait of Sir Henry Umpton." In *Companion to Medieval and Renaissance Music*. Edited by Tess Knighton and David Fallows, 85–92. Berkeley: University of California Press, 1992. ISBN 0520210816. ML172 .C65.

Examines *Sir Henry Umpton's Funerall* (D120), discusses the composition's potential origins and uses, and compares the consort setting to Anthony Holborne's *The Countess of Pembroke's Funerall*.

500   Schab, Alon. "Dowland's *Lachrimae*: A Passionate Interpretation." *The Musical Times* 157, no. 1935 (Summer 2016): 17–35. ISSN 0027-4666. ML5 .M85.

Refashions the seven pavans of *Lachrimae* (1604) and *Semper Dowland, semper dolens* (D9) alongside Croce's seven penitential psalms, as music used within an imagined Catholic Maundy Thursday service for Queen Anne. While the author is thorough in his argument, all evidence presented is purely conjectural, making for a thought-provoking, but not completely established scenario.

PSALMS

501   Hamlin, Hannibal. "Psalm Culture in Early Modern England." PhD Diss., Yale University, 2000. UMI 9973692.

The seven funeral psalms composed upon the death of Henry Noel are analyzed within this wide-ranging thesis (pp. 176–97). The author depicts the set as a "bridge" between secular and sacred music and between Protestant and Catholic practices.

502   McCoy, Stewart. "New Ballad, Dance and Masque Tunes, and a Dowland Intabulation, in a Recently Discovered Lute Book." *Lute News: The Lute Society Magazine* 74 (July 2005): 8–13. ML5 .L885.

Overview of a (then) newly discovered seventeenth-century lute manuscript, Yale University Osborn fb7 (**206**), which contains an intabulation of one of Dowland's Psalm 100 harmonizations (D206), the first-known instance of an extant primary source lute version of the psalm setting. A transcription is included.

KEYBOARD ARRANGEMENTS

503   Hogwood, Christopher. "John Dowland on the Keyboard." In **270**: 255–72.

Author Hogwood, an especially respected modern interpreter of early music, provides an overview of keyboard pieces arranged by other composers that were based upon Dowland's lute music. Especially valuable is an appendix of contemporaneous keyboard arrangements of Dowland's music with concordances to the original lute versions.

504   Hogwood, Christopher. "The Keyboard Music of John Dowland." In *De Clavicordio VII: The Clavichord and the Lute: Proceedings of the VII International Clavichord Symposium, Magano, 7–10 September 2005.* Edited by Bernard Brauchli, Alberto Galazzo, and Judith Wardman, 195–211. Magano: Musica Antiqua a Magnano, 2006. ISBN 9788890026942. ML651 .I57 C42.

Comments on contemporaneous keyboard arrangements made of Dowland's lute solos and airs. Includes an appendix listing primary sources, both print and manuscript, in which such arrangements are found.

505   Mangsen, Sandra. *Song Without Words: Keyboard Arrangements of Vocal Music in England, 1560–1760.* Rochester, NY: University of Rochester Press, 2016. xvii, 263 p. ISBN 9781580465496. ML728 .M36.

One section of this monograph provides a general overview of seventeenth-century keyboard arrangements of *Lachrimae Pavan* (D15), by composers such as Byrd, Farnaby, Morley, and Sweelinck. Includes musical examples for comparison and a table of selected versions and their sources (pp. 36–55).

ORNITHOPARCUS, HIS MICROLOGUS

see also **315, 469, 470, 563, 576.** *For Dowland's original volume, see* **228.**

506   Cockman, Irwen. "Robert Peilin (c. 1575–c. 1638) a Josseffüs, ei Draethawd ar Gerddoriaeth." ["Robert Peilin (c. 1575–c. 1638) and his essay on music, Josseffüs."] *Hanes cerddoriaeth cymru/Welsh Music History* 4 (2000): 39–87. ISSN 1362-0681. ML289 .W454. In Welsh.

This essay presents information on Welsh harpist Robert Peilin, who translated Dowland's version of *Andreas Ornithoparcus, His Micrologus* into his native tongue. Though most of the article is not related to Dowland, the author does examine which parts of Dowland's translation Peilin included, as well as additions and changes he made.

507   DeFord, Ruth I. "Tempo Relationships between Duple and Triple Time in the Sixteenth Century." *Early Music History* 14 (1995): 1–51. ISSN 0261-1279. ML169.8 .E15.

Not Dowland-centric, but utilizes several quotes from Dowland's translation of Ornithoparcus's *Micrologus*.

508   Godt, Irving. "New Voices and Old Theory." *The Journal of Musicology* 3, no. 3 (1984): 312–9. ISSN 0277–9269. ML1 .J693.

Though not focused on Dowland, this article highlights that the composer-writer, in his translation of Ornithoparcus, advocated for use of the monochord to teach basic theoretical concepts.

509   Smith, James G. "Da Capo." *The Choral Journal* 15, no. 2 (October 1974): 17. ISSN 0009–5028. ML1 .C656.

An editorial column drawing attention to Dowland's translation of *Andreas Ornithoparcus, His Micrologus* as a reference for performance practice in renaissance singing.

510   Wilson, Christopher R. "Shakespeare and Early Modern Music." In *The Edinburgh Companion to Shakespeare and the Arts*. Edited by Mark Thornton Burnett, Adrian Streete, and Ramona Wray, 119–41. Edinburgh: Edinburgh University Press, 2011. ISBN 9780748635238. PR3091 .E35.

Briefly quotes parts of Dowland's translation of Ornithoparcus's *Micrologus*, as explanation of Elizabethan concepts of the forces that shaped music. Also mentions use of the *lachrimae* theme within a 2002 Globe Theatre production of *Twelfth Night*.

8

Secondary Source Bibliography
Source Studies, Print and Manuscript Culture, Performance Practice, Influence, and Legacy

SOURCE STUDIES

General

see also **264, 345, 354, 368, 493, 494, 502**

511 Hulse, Lynn. "Hardwick MS 29: A New Source for Jacobean Lutenists." *The Lute: Journal of the Lute Society* 26, no. 2 (1986): 62–72. ISSN 0952–0759. ML5 .L89.

Details the contents of the title manuscript, which belonged to William Cavendish, first Earl of Devonshire, and was later housed at Chatsworth House in Derbyshire. Briefly provides information on John and Robert Dowland's individual positions in the Cavendish household, including payments received between 1612 and 1616, and an inventory of the contents of Cavendish's library, which included several Dowland prints.

512 Lumsden, David. "The Sources of English Lute Music (1540–1620)." PhD Diss., University of Cambridge, 1955.

In a massive two-volume dissertation, the author attempts to create the first comprehensive thematic catalogue of extant English lute music (known to that date), including music not only by Dowland, but all composers of the time. The document's importance was long lasting, and until **221**, Dowland's lute solos were often referred to by their "Lumsden" number. Though more recent research has revealed additional sources, as well as new information related to the ones listed, this work still impresses as a means of comparing Dowland's prolific output to others of his era. Researchers seeking details are advised to consult later options, but Lumsden's contribution to Dowland scholarship should not be overlooked, as it served as a launching point for more complete studies undertaken later in the century.

513 Newton, Richard. "English Lute Music of the Golden Age." *Proceedings of the Musical Association* 65 (1938–1939): 63–90. ISSN 0958-8442. ML5 .R888.

This early twentieth-century article serves as one of the first well-rounded introductions to print and manuscript volumes of Elizabethan-Jacobean lute music, including those featuring Dowland's works. Though subsequent articles provide more detailed cataloguing of individual anthologies, this essay, which was originally presented aurally with accompaniment by a young Diana Poulton, is a good general overview of some important primary sources.

514 Spring, Matthew. *The Lute in Britain: A History of the Instrument and its Music.* Oxford: Oxford University Press, 2001. xxxii, 536 p. ISBN 0198166206. ML1010 .S77.

Although this volume spans lute history from before 1500 through the seventeenth century, Dowland and his works are proportionally afforded quite a bit of attention. Much information is provided on Elizabethan and Jacobean manuscript and print sources in which Dowland's music appears, with descriptions and both textual and notated comparisons of selected source variants. Dowland's print anthologies are described on pp. 264–73. The non-Dowland portions of this book should also prove valuable to those interested in historical lute culture, as they provide a solid grounding in English lute conventions, traditions, composers, and iconic works.

515 Steur, Peter, and Markus Lutz. *Musik für Lauteninstrumente: Eine Datenbank der Manuskripte und Drucke für Lauteninstrumente.* http://mss.slweiss.de.

A database of over 35,000 lute compositions found in more than 450 manuscript and print sources, including over 360 individual entries for Dowland. Offers incipits of lute tablature for each work. Most useful is a concordance feature that provides links to equivalent pieces in other collections. There is a search/limit function, but it is not especially intuitive and can be a bit difficult to use. Offers choice of German or English text.

516 Ward, John M. "The British Broadside Ballad and Its Music." *Journal of the American Musicological Society* 20, no. 1 (Spring 1967): 28–86. ISSN 0003-0139. ML27 .U5 A83363.

Offers additional concordances of ballad tunes catalogued in Claude Simpson's broadside ballad volume, including Dowland's *Frog Galliard* (D23) and *Lord Willoughby* (D66), as well as the composer's setting of *Walsingham* (D67).

Print Sources

517 Coelho, Victor, and Keith Polk. *Instrumentalists and Renaissance Culture, 1420–1600: Players of Function and Fantasy.* Cambridge: Cambridge University Press, 2016. 331 pp. ISBN 9781107145801. ML3795 .C635 2016.

One very small section, or "case study" as it is titled, of this full-length book on renaissance instrumental music is devoted to Robert Dowland's *Varietie of Lute Lessons*, with mention of the decided proportion of space given in the 1610 volume to father John's solo lute works, as opposed to other composers (pp. 126–30). Useful for contextualization of this important anthology and John Dowland's contributions to lute repertoire of the era.

518   Greer, David. *Manuscript Inscriptions in Early English Printed Music.* Burlington, VT: Ashgate, 2015. xx, 206 p. (Music and Material Culture Series.) ISBN 9781472445872. ML93 .G74.

This volume catalogues marginalia and other additions written in early volumes of music. Though not about Dowland specifically, Dowland print volumes are included among sources found in libraries throughout the world, with indications of names, musical incipits, and poetry added.

519   Groot, Simon. "De Liederen in de 'Nederlantsche Gedenck-clank' van Adriaen Valerius." *Tijdschrift van de Koninklijke Vereniging voor Nederlandse Muziekgeschiedenis* 51, no. 2 (2001): 131–48. ISSN 1383–7079. ML27 .N4 V44.

An overview of the history of Valerius's anthology (**47**), which includes over seventy-five musical pieces—some by Dowland, apparently copied from Dowland's printed songbooks. The author identifies only three Dowland songs, "Now O now I needs must part" (D23), "Come again" (D60), and "Flow my tears" (D15) (all with Dutch words in this volume), though others have been cited by various scholars.

520   Robison, John O. "Elias Mertel's *Hortus Musicalis Novus* and Progressive Tendencies in the Late Renaissance Lute Fantasia." *Journal of the Lute Society of America* 17–18 (1984–1985): 26–41. ISSN 0076–1524. ML1 .L75.

Study of a 1615 publication (**29**) of over three hundred lute preludes and fantasias that includes versions of two unattributed Dowland works. Dowland's pieces are not considered within the article, but listed in the concordance table following.

521   Russell, John F. "John Dowland's 'Lachrimae,' Etc." *The Musical Times and Singing Class Circular* 67, no. 998 (April 1, 1926): 353. ML5 .M85.

A letter from a librarian at the Henry Watson Music Library, Manchester, informing the readership of surviving copies of Dowland publications housed at the library.

522   "Studies in the Lute and its Music: Prospects for the Future." *Journal of the Lute Society of America* 17–18 (1984–5): 118–32. ISSN 0076–1524. ML1 .L75.

This report details a forum held at the 1986 annual meeting of the American Musicological Society and sponsored by the Lute Society of America, providing a list of hundreds of suggested topics related to the lute that deserve further scholarly consideration. Unfortunately, the person tasked with compiling a list related to English Renaissance topics was not available to complete the project and subjects involving Dowland are scare. One exception is the suggestion of further exploration of Johann Daniel Mylius's 1622 print *Thesaurus gratiarum* (**31**, reprinted 1644), which contains at least five pieces by Dowland (p. 123).

Manuscripts

see also **285, 299, 345, 354**

523 Chan, Mary. "*Cynthia's Revels* and Music for a Choir School: Christ Church Manuscript Mus 439." *Studies in the Renaissance* 18 (1971): 134–72. ISSN 0081–8658. D223 .S8.

This article argues the titled manuscript represents music sung by one particular choir school. Includes a source study and catalogue of the manuscript (**131**), which contains six pieces by Dowland, including "Now O now I needs must part" (D23), "Flow my tears" (D15), "Come ye heavy stars of night" (D151), "Sorrow stay" (D142), "If my complaints" (D19), and "Can she excuse" (D42), each of which the author categorizes as a political song based on secondary source writings, especially those of Ruff and Wilson (see **419, 420**).

524 Charteris, Richard. "Manuscript Additions of Music by John Dowland and his Contemporaries in Two Sixteenth-Century Prints." *Consort* 37 (1981): 399–401. ISSN 0268-9111. ML5 .C664.

Inventories manuscript additions in two Dublin library sources, Marsh Library Z4.3.1–5 and Trinity College Library B.1.32 (now OLS 192.n.40, no. 1) (**73, 77**), both of which contain one or more copied parts from Dowland airs.

525 Charteris, Richard. "New Connections between Eastern Europe and Works by Philips, Dowland, Marais and Others." *Chelys* 29 (2001): 3–27. ISSN 0952-8407. ML749.5 .C5.

Surveys printed collections found in a Kraków library that contain manuscript additions, including one, Biblioteka Jagiellońska, Mus. ant. pract. H 540 (**187**), that contains copied consort parts for a *Lachrimae pavan*, similar to the one found in Dowland's 1604 edition. Reprinted in Richard Charteris, *Giovanni Gabrieli and His Contemporaries: Music, Sources, and Collections* (Farnham: Ashgate, 2011). ISBN 9781409403692. ML410 .G118 C486.

526 Craig-McFeely, Julia. *English Lute Manuscripts and Scribes 1530–1630: An Examination of the Place of the Lute in 16th- and 17th-Century English Society through a Study of the English Lute Manuscripts of the So-Called "Golden Age," including a Comprehensive Catalog of Sources*. Oxford: Self-Published, 2000. www.ramesescats.co.uk/thesis/.

An extensive study of early lute manuscripts in which, though not Dowland-centered, the composer's music figures prominently. The author addresses dating, scribal practices, manuscript development and use, ownership, and dissemination. Important manuscripts are closely examined and many tables detail their contents. The appendices, which attempt comprehensive cataloguing of all English lute manuscripts of the time, are invaluable, updating and clarifying work begun by Lumsden in **512**. This website is an expansion of the author's 1993 University of Oxford PhD dissertation, available at www.cs.dartmouth.edu/~wbc/julia/.

527   Goodwin, Christopher. "Who Owned the Folger Dowland Lute Book? A Solve-It-Yourself Historical Puzzle." *Lute News: The Lute Society Magazine* 65 (April 2003): 15–20. ML5 .L885.

A call for genealogical reader assistance in deducing whose names or initials are inscribed on flyleaves of the Folger-Dowland Lute Book (**212**) and the Margaret Board Lute Book (**120**). Offers up some initial suggestions, but arrives at no conclusions.

528   Harwood, Ian. "The Origins of the Cambridge Lute Manuscripts." *The Lute Society Journal* 5 (1963): 32–48. ISSN 0460–007X. ML5 .L89.

Details the provenance of the largest English collection of early seventeenth-century lute music, a set of four manuscript books known as the "Matthew Holmes Lute Books," as well as a set of four partbooks for broken consort (lute, bass viol, recorder, and cittern), and a solo cittern volume, all housed at Cambridge University Library and all containing Dowland works. Also authenticates the scribal hand of collector Holmes.

529   Kenny, Elizabeth. "Revealing Their Hand: Lute Tablatures in Early Seventeenth-Century England." *Renaissance Studies* 26, no. 1 (February 2012): 112–37. ISSN 0269–1213. CB361 .R474.

An original and informative explanation of primary source information that can be gleaned from pedagogical lute tablature manuscripts. Selected works in the Mynshall Lute Book (**118**), which contains many Dowland compositions, as well as the M. L. Lute Book (**107**), the Folger-Dowland Lute Book (**212**), and the Marsh Lute Book (**72**) serve as examples to elucidate the author's ideas on manuscripts as musico-archaeological objects.

530   Nordstrom, Lyle. *The Bandora: Its Music and Sources.* Warren, MI: Harmonie Park, 1992. xiv, 147 p. (Detroit Studies in Music Bibliography 66.) ISBN 0899900607. ML128 .B235 N67.

Five Dowland works for bandora solo are included in a thematic index found within this book. None are likely original to Dowland, but are arrangements of his works. Also included are consort versions of Dowland-inspired pieces that call for bandora. Concordances are provided.

531   Nordstrom, Lyle. "The Cambridge Consort Books." *Journal of the Lute Society of America* 5 (1972): 70–103. ISSN 0076–1524. ML1 .L75.

A description and index of Cambridge University Library manuscripts Dd.3.18 (lute), Dd.5.20 (bass viol), Dd.5.21 (recorder), and Dd.14.24 (cittern), a set of consort partbooks containing multiple Dowland works (**58**, **61**, **62**, **65**, respectively).

532 Oboussier, Philippe. "Turpyn's Book of Lute-Songs." *Music & Letters* 34, no. 2 (April 1953): 145–9. ISSN 0027–4224. ML5 .M64.

An overview of a manuscript lute book (**70**) held in the library of King's College, Cambridge, of which three of twelve musical works are Dowland compositions.

533 Poulton, Diana. "Checklist of Some Recently Discovered English Lute Manuscripts." *Early Music* 3, no. 2 (April 1975): 124–5. ISSN 0306–1078. ML5 .E18.

This article provides annotations describing six lute manuscripts "discovered" in the 1970s, four of which contain pieces by Dowland: the Mynshall Lute Book (c. 1597–1599); the Sampson Lute Book (c. 1609); the Margaret Board Lute Book (c. 1620–1630); and the Trumbull Lute Book (c. 1610). The first three were once part of the private collection of Robert Spencer, and are now held in London's Royal Academy of Music Library (**118**, **119**, **120**). The last is housed at Cambridge University Library, Add. 8844 (**56**).

534 Robinson, John H., and Richard Charteris. "A Selection of Lute Solos from the Lute Book of Wolfgang Hoffmann von Grünbühel." *Lute News: The Lute Society Magazine* 84 (December 2007): suppl. 1–20. ML5 .L885.

Overview, basic inventory, and transcription of the title manuscript (**158**, Berlin Preussischer Kulturbesitz, N. Mus. ms. 479). Footnotes to the introduction include a concordance list for the *Frog Galliard* (D23) and *Lachrimae Pavan* (D15), the two Dowland pieces contained within the described manuscript.

535 Rudén, Jan Olof. "Per Brahe's Lute Book." *Svensk Tidskrift för Musikforskning* (1977): 47–62. ISSN 0081–9816. ML5 .S968.

A descriptive source study of a manuscript housed in a Swedish archive (**194**) that includes a number of Dowland lute solos, though Dowland is only briefly mentioned. Provides musical incipits.

536 Sheptovitsky, Levi. "The Cracow Lute Tablature (Second Half of the 16th Century): Discussion and Catalogue: Lvov State Ivan Franco University, Ms 1400/1." *Musica Disciplina* 48 (1994): 69–97. ISSN 0077–2461. ML5 .M722.

Identifies three Dowland fantasias, not previously noticed, in a large volume of lute tablature with international representation (**199**).

537 Spencer, Robert. "Three English Lute Manuscripts." *Early Music* 3, no. 2 (April 1975): 119–24. ISSN 0306–1078. ML5 .E18.

Describes three manuscript lute books, then in the possession of the author, all of which contain lute works attributed to Dowland: The Mynshall Lute Book (c. 1597–1599), the Sampson Lute Book (c. 1609), and the Margaret Board Lute Book (c. 1620–1630). This last source includes diagrams and lesson notes, perhaps in the hand of Dowland. All three books are now housed in London's Royal Academy of Music Library (**118**, **119**, **120**).

538 Spencer, Robert. "The Tollemache Lute Manuscript." *The Lute Society Journal* 7 (1965): 38–9. ISSN 0460–007X. ML5 .L89.

Catalogues the contents of a manuscript, also known as the Sampson Lute Book (**119**), purchased by the author and previously owned by Lord Tollemache of Helmington Hall, Suffolk. Includes at least five Dowland works. Now part of the collection of the Royal Academy of Music Library, London.

539 Ward, John M. "The Fourth Dublin Lute Book." *The Lute Society Journal* 11 (1969): 28–46. ISSN 0460–007X. ML5 .L89.

Inventories the contents of the Marsh Lute Book (**72**), a manuscript that includes several Dowland pieces.

540 Ward, John M. "The Lute Books of Trinity College, Dublin. II: Ms. D.1.21 (The So-Called Ballet Lute Book)." *The Lute Society Journal* 10 (1968): 15–32. ISSN 0460–007X. ML5 .L89.

A detailed description and catalogue of a late sixteenth-/early seventeenth-century manuscript lute anthology (**74**) that includes copies or arrangements of at least four different Dowland works. Now shelved as MS 408.

541 Ward, John M. "The So-Called 'Dowland Lute Book' in the Folger Shakespeare Library." *Journal of the Lute Society of America* 9 (1976): 4–29. ISSN 0076–1524. ML1 .L75.

An analysis and inventory of a lute manuscript (**212**) that includes multiple pieces written in Dowland's hand or signed by the composer. Ward believes that the book was originally owned by a student of Dowland's and later found its way into possession of the Dowland family before being auctioned by Sotheby in the 1920s. Provides analysis of the many scribal hands that contributed to the manuscript and suggests one belongs to John Dowland and another possibly to son Robert.

PRINT AND MANUSCRIPT CULTURE

see also **315, 316, 421**

542 Coral, Lenore. "A John Playford Advertisement." *Royal Musical Association Research Chronicle* 5 (1965): 1–12. ISSN 1472–3808. ML5 .R14.

Discusses a bibliographical list of English books printed between 1571 and 1638 (including all four of Dowland's songbooks, *Lachrimae*, *Micrologus*, and Robert Dowland's books) that was included as part of an advertisement by John Playford, c. 1650.

543 Dowling, Margaret. "The Printing of John Dowland's *Second Booke of Songs or Ayres*." *The Library* 4s. 12, no. 4 (March 1932): 365–80.

A compelling rendering of the events surrounding printing and publication of Dowland's second songbook volume, pieced together through surviving court documents. Illuminates the different roles of composer, publisher, patent holder, printer, and workers; typical amounts that each might receive; and expectations of each in terms of responsibilities and reward. Offers helpful insights into the conventions of early English printing. The incident is explored further in **551** and **552**.

544   Freeman, Graham. "The Transmission of Lute Music and the Culture of Aurality in Early Modern England." In *Beyond Boundaries: Rethinking Music Circulation in Early Modern England*. Edited by Linda Phyllis Austern, Candace Bailey, and Amanda Eubanks Winkler, 42–53. Bloomington: Indiana University Press, 2017. ISBN 9780253024794. ML286.2 .B49.

Presents the pedagogical methods and conventions attached to surviving lute tablature manuscripts to explain why so few volumes of lute solos were printed during the "Golden Age." Dowland's *Lachrimae Pavan* (D15) is featured as an example of how individuals adapted pieces of music to fit their skill level or personal interests.

545   Gibson, Kirsten. "'How Hard an Enterprise It Is': Authorial Self-Fashioning in John Dowland's Printed Books." *Early Music History* 26, no. 1 (2007): 43–89. ISSN 0261–1279. ML169.8 .E15.

This important article uses Dowland and his printed songbooks to comment upon self-promotion by late sixteenth- and early seventeenth-century composers through the press. Explores how Dowland utilized works disseminated in print to control public perception and reputation, maintain artistic autonomy and authorship recognition, and create a personal material legacy, while still adhering to traditional expectations of patron flattery and servant loyalty. The author is especially adept at reviewing different outcomes and philosophies of print and manuscript dissemination in a manner accessible to those unfamiliar with conventions of the time.

546   Hill, Cecil. "William Stansby and Music-Printing." *Fontes Artis Musicae* 19, no. 1–2 (1972): 7–13. ISSN 0015–6191. ML5 .F66.

An overview of the career of an early modern English printer who received transfer of ownership of several of Dowland's musical volumes after the deaths of printers who first issued them.

547   Mann, Joseph Arthur. "'Both Schollers and Practicioners': The Pedagogy of Ethical Scholarship and Music in Thomas Morley's 'Plaine and Easie Introduction to Practicall Musicke." *Musica Disciplina* 59 (2014): 53–92. ISSN 0077–2461. ML5 .M722.

Quotes several passages excerpted from Dowland song collections' prefatory material to align Dowland's consternation over other musicians' actions with accusations Morley makes of "unethical scholarship" in the latter's famous theoretical treatise.

548 Murray, Tessa. "Peter Short and the Printing of Dowland's *First Booke of Songs*." *The Lute: The Journal of the Lute Society* 53 (2013): 1–17. ISSN 0952–0759. ML5 .L89.

Examines dedicatory epistle texts, as well as physical attributes such as paper type, to attempt a chronological ordering of music volumes printed by Peter Short in 1597. Suggests Dowland's volume was printed last that year. The author contends that the printer improved his processes through his earlier volumes, to the benefit of Dowland. Further, she explores reasons that Dowland may have chosen Short as printer for his project, rather than Thomas East or William Barley, and considers how Short may have contributed to Dowland's choice to use tablebook format.

549 Murray, Tessa. *Thomas Morley: Elizabethan Music Publisher*. Woodbridge, UK: Boydell, 2014. xviii, 265 p. ISBN 9781843839606. ML427 .M67 M87.

Devotes several pages to consideration of mutual influences on, similarities to, and differences between Morley's *Canzonets or Litle Short Aers to Five and Sixe Voices* and Dowland's *First Booke*, which were both issued in 1597 and both dedicated to Sir George Carey, Baron Hunsdon (pp. 80–3). Also examines the ways in which Dowland's *First* and *Second Booke*s may have influenced Morley's *First Booke of Ayres* (pp. 146–9).

550 Oswell, Michelle Lynn. "The Printed Lute Song: A Textual and Paratextual Study of Early Modern English Song Books." PhD Diss., University of North Carolina at Chapel Hill, 2009. UMI 3366401.

Focuses on the non-musical aspects of early modern English music anthologies, including lute books such as those by Dowland. The author interprets the title page border of Dowland's *First Booke*, which is not original to printer Peter Short, and the volume's dedicatory epistle, note to the reader, rhetoric, and other extratextual components, comparing and contrasting them with other musical anthologies of the era, most especially those of Robert Jones.

551 Smith, Jeremy L. "The Hidden Editions of Thomas East." *Notes* 2s. 53, no. 4 (June 1997): 1059–1091. ISSN 0027–4380. ML27 .U5 M695.

Briefly recounts events described in Dowling's 1932 article (**543**), adding contextualization of East's printing practices.

552 Smith, Jeremy L. *Thomas East and Music Publishing in Renaissance England*. Oxford: Oxford University Press, 2003. 233 p. ISBN 0195139054. ML427 .E27 S65.

Within this volume, the author elaborates on information provided in **551**, reviewing the Eastland-East litigious suit first discussed in **543**. Utilizes physical evidence from Dowland's 1600 song collection, such as type decay and paper identification, to help date other works printed by Thomas East. Also considers possible connections of the 1600 anthology to political events surrounding the alleged uprising of the Earl of Essex, building on **420** to explore the role established print culture played in the matter (pp. 107–11).

553   Wilson, Christopher R. "Thomas Campion's 'Superfluous Blossomes of His Deeper Studies': The Public Realm of His English Ayres." In *Beyond Boundaries: Rethinking Music Circulation in Early Modern England.* Edited by Linda Phyllis Austern, Candace Bailey, and Amanda Eubanks Winkler, 54–66. Bloomington: Indiana University Press, 2017. ISBN 9780253024794. ML286.2 .B49.

Explores Campion's self-proclaimed reluctance to publish his lute song-airs, briefly comparing the composer's self-representation and motives with those of Dowland and Robert Jones.

PERFORMANCE PRACTICE AND PERFORMANCE GUIDES

General

see also **373, 374, 489**

554   Bose, Mishtooni. "Humanism, English Music, and the Rhetoric of Criticism." *Music & Letters* 77, no. 1 (February 1996): 1–21. ISSN 0027-4224. ML5 .M64.

Points out flaws in lute song-air analyses that insist upon applying conventional rhetorical gestures, identified both in traditional literary and musicological studies, as directives for performance. The author's reasoning is that such practice implies that renaissance musicians understood and analyzed pieces in such a manner prior to performance, a view that cannot be verified.

555   Conlon, Joan Cantoni. "Early Instruments and Choral Music." *Choral Journal* 20, no. 1 (September 1979): 5–11. ISSN 0009-5028. ML1 .C656.

Briefly and simply suggests how to perform "Come again sweet love" with period instruments.

556   Kenny, Elizabeth. "The Uses of Lute Song: Texts, Contexts and Pretexts for 'Historically Informed' Performance." *Early Music* 36, no. 2 (May 2008): 285–99. ISSN 0306-1078. ML5 .E18.

Reminds modern performers that, in spite of many publications suggesting domestic performance was the main intention of composers, manuscripts show that some compositions were performed with much more complexity, indicative of professional performance within theatrical and other settings. This view is intended to encourage thoughtful consideration of ornamentation and other performer-determined musical choices when learning and performing pieces by Dowland and his contemporaries.

557   Rooley, Anthony. *Performance: Revealing the Orpheus Within.* Longmead, UK: Element Books, 1990. x, 142 p. ISBN 1852301600. ML3830 .R73.

This performance practice guide helps situate early modern English music within popular philosophy of the time, especially that espoused by followers of Ficino. Dowland, his writings, and his music are referenced repeatedly throughout, perhaps not surprisingly in a book written by a recognized professional lutenist who references Orpheus in the title. Dowland, however, is not specifically a main focus of this book. An appendix provides lyrics to songs included in a program titled, "Lute-Songs on the Theme of Mutability and Metamorphosis by John Dowland and his Contemporaries," which features three Dowland songs.

558 Tomlinson, Gary. "The Historian, the Performer, and Authentic Meaning in Music." In *Authenticity and Early Music: A Symposium*. Edited by Nicholas Kenyon, 115–36. Oxford: Oxford University Press, 1988. Reprinted 2002. ISBN 0198161522. ML457 .A98.

Advocates a method of contextualization, using contemporaneous meaning beyond the music itself, to enhance historically informed performance. Within the larger non-Dowland-centric article, the author uses a brief example of Dowland scholarship, highlighting publications of the 1980s by Robin Headlam Wells (**486**), Anthony Rooley (**314**), and Robert Toft (**482**) for their consideration of extra-musical aspects of Dowland's songs.

Singing

see also **425, 447, 457, 470, 509**

559 Gillespie, Gail. "Let the Singer Beware: Linguistic Pitfalls in Facsimile Lute Songs." *Lute Society of America Quarterly* 38 (May–August 2003): 6–7. ISSN 1547–982X. ML1 .L88.

A very basic introduction to early English typography for vocalists, addressing spelling variants, abbreviations, and grammatical conventions. While any composer of the era's songs might have been used, the author chooses to cite lyric examples from Dowland's first songbook.

560 Hawn, C. Michael. "Baroque Corner: The Lute Songs of John Dowland." *The NATS Journal* 43, no. 3 (January–February 1987): 24–5. ISSN 0884–8106. ML27 .U5 N2652.

A brief introduction to Dowland's lute songs for vocalists, advocating study of these compositions as means to enhance expressive singing. Includes a list of several recommended performance editions of Dowland's music.

561 Pilkington, Michael. *Campion, Dowland, and the Lutenist Songwriters*. Bloomington: Indiana University Press, 1989. x, 179 p. (English Solo Song: Guides to the Repertoire). ISBN 0253346959. ML128 .S3 P54.

A repertoire guide intended for singers. Lists Dowland lute songs from the composer's four printed songbooks, as well as *Musicall Banquet* (see pp. 74–108). Entries include title, suggested voice type, difficulty rating, duration, musical considerations such as range, key, and meter, and other pertinent information, enhanced by editorial commentary.

562   Rooley, Anthony. "Practical Matters of Vocal Performance." Chapter 4 in *A Performer's Guide to Renaissance Music*. 2nd ed. Edited by Jeffrey Kite-Powell, 42–51. Bloomington: Indiana University Press, 2007. ISBN 9780253348661. ML457 .P48.

Emphasizes the importance of rehearsal in crafting historically informed performances. Dowland's "Go crystal tears" (D129) is used as an example for one process of preparing an SATB version of the song. Considers lyrical syntax, textual and musical meaning, diction and stress, dynamics, vibrato, and ensemble.

563   Spencer, Robert. "Performance Style of the English Lute Ayre c. 1600." *The Lute: The Journal of the Lute Society* 24, no. 2 (1984): 55–68. ISSN 0952-0759. ML5 .L89.

A guide for singers of lute song-airs that considers performance choices, supported by primary source writings of the era including Dowland's *Andreas Ornithoparcus, His Micrologus*. The author uses several Dowland songs as examples. Anthony Rooley responds in "The Art of Singing," *The Lute: The Journal of the Lute Society* 25 (1985): 31–9, commending Spencer's gathering of material, adding information he feels is pertinent, and condemning Spencer's first interpretation as being biased due to individual preference. Together, these articles bring up difficult issues surrounding historically informed performance practice in the modern age.

564   Toft, Robert. *Tune Thy Musicke to Thy Hart: The Art of Eloquent Singing in England 1597–1622*. Toronto: University of Toronto Press, 1993. viii, 104 p. ISBN 0802028489. ML457 .T6.

An Elizabethan-Jacobean performance practice guide that relies heavily on primary sources to suggest a method of song preparation based on the early rhetorical practices of *elocutio* and *pronunciatio*. Dowland songs receive special treatment, as the author states: "nowhere is the connection between rhetorical delivery and compositional procedure more apparent than in his solo songs." The composer's works are featured as examples throughout, and the final portion of this book uses "Sorrow stay" (D142) and "In darkness let me dwell" (D201) to illustrate and apply concepts previously introduced in the book.

565   Toft, Robert. *With Passionate Voice: Re-Creative Singing in 16th-Century England and Italy*. New York: Oxford University Press, 2014. ix, 329 p. ISBN 9780199382026. ML1620.2 .T64.

This book is essentially a performance practice manual devoted to pronunciation, embellishment, and elocution of sixteenth-century music. Dowland's songs are heavily featured, and references to Dowland and his music are found throughout. The volume should be highly valued by singers who want to perform Dowland works with a view towards replicating singing philosophies of the time. For technical aspects such as tone and vibrato production, however, performers will need to look elsewhere. The publisher offers a companion website with musical examples at http://global.oup.com/us/companion.websites/9780199382033/.

Instruments

see also **489**, **493** *and* **Temperament and Tuning**

566 Abbott, Djilda, and Ephraim Segerman. "Gut Strings." *Early Music* 4, no. 4 (1976): 430–7. ISSN 0306–1078. ML5 .E18.

Prepares performers to use gut strings on early instruments. Includes several Dowland primary source quotes.

567 Acker-Johnson, Jesse. "A Guide to the Interpretation of John Dowland's 'Queen Elizabeth's Galliard p. 41,' 'Lachrimae Pavan p. 15,' 'Farewell Fantasy p. 3,' and 'Forlorn Hope Fancy p. 2' Transcribed for Guitar." DM Diss., Florida State University, 2015. UMI 3705765.

An aid for guitarists who wish to perform Dowland works. Provides adaptation recommendations to play more "lute-like," instructions for ornamentation, and transcriptions of selected solos, arranged in treble clef for guitarists' convenience.

568 Gill, Donald. "The Elizabethan Lute." *The Galpin Society Journal* 12 (May 1959): 60–2. ISSN 0072–0127. ML5 .G26.

This very brief article asserts that the seven-course lute was the standard instrument used in Elizabethan England, and is therefore best suited for most of Dowland's works, with exceptions noted.

569 Irvine, Robin. "The Lute's Lower Courses." *Early Music* 8, no. 3 (July 1980): 428–9. ISSN 0306–1078. ML5 .E18.

A letter referencing Dowland's words from *Varietie of Lute Lessons* (1610), asserting that the musician advocated for the use of octave, rather than unison, tuning in the lower lute strings.

570 North, Nigel. "Searching for Dowland." In **270**: 301–5.

Considers fingering technique, tempo, and style in Dowland lute solos. Written by a respected modern performing lutenist.

571 Poulton, Diana. "Graces of Play in Renaissance Lute Music." *Early Music* 3, no. 2 (April 1975): 107–14. ISSN 0306–1078. ML5 .E18.

Explores the use of ornaments in Italian, French, and English sixteenth- and seventeenth-century lute music. Evidence is provided through primary source music and treatises of the time, including those by Robert and John Dowland.

572 Rastall, Richard. "Spatial Effects in English Instrumental Consort Music, c. 1560–1605." *Early Music* 25, no. 2 (1997): 268–88. ISSN 0306–1078. ML5 .E18.

One section of this article considers the physical arrangement of players necessitated by the tablebook format of Dowland's *Lachrimae* volume, and how such ordering affects imitative aspects of the music. Later in the essay, the author suggests configurations for modern consort performance.

573   Schoedel, William R. "A Walk Through John Dowland's *Lachrimae*." *VdGSA News* 53, no. 4 (Winter 2016): 13–14.

A very brief article that translates the titles of Dowland's seven *Lachrimae* (1604) pavans, associating each with the lyrics of one of Dowland's lute song-airs to suggest an affective mood for chamber players to simulate when playing individual movements.

574   Shepherd, Martin. "Dowland's Lutes." 2008. www.luteshop.co.uk/dowland/dlutes.html.

The "Articles" section of this website, maintained by a modern lutenist and luthier, includes several essays related to Dowland, including a brief commentary on the kinds of lutes Dowland would have played, with sections on number of courses, stringing and tension, fretting, and pitch, and a brief guide to embellishing Dowland's music. Links to sound clips are provided.

575   Spencer, Robert, Anthony Rooley, and Peter Phillips. "Approaches to Performance: The Lutenists' View." *Early Music* 7, no. 2 (April 1979): 225–35. ISSN 0306–1078. ML5 .E18.

Phillips interviews Spencer and Rooley on recommendations for modern programming and performance on the lute. Though not Dowland-centered, the renaissance lute master often frames the discussion and non-Dowland-specific content is still relevant and applicable to performance of Dowland works.

Temperament and Tuning

see also **568, 569, 574**

576   Barbour, J. Murray. *Tuning and Temperament: A Historical Survey*. East Lansing: Michigan State College Press, 1953. xii, 228 p. Reprinted Mineola, NY: Dover, 2004. ISBN 0486434060. ML3809 .B234.

Though Dowland is addressed only sporadically in this volume (see especially pp. 153–5), the information is valuable, providing an interpretation of the lutenist-composer's tuning method by converting interval ratios into cents, and revealing a closeness (though modified) to Pythagorean tuning, as filtered through Ornithoparcus.

577   Coakley, Chris J. "Dowland's Lute Tuning and Other Ancient Methods, including Gerle's." *Fellowship of Makers and Researchers of Historical Instruments Quarterly* 123 (February 2013): 16–43. ML26 .F4863.

Provides a detailed mathematical analysis of Dowland's system for lute tuning and fret positioning, as presented in Robert Dowland's *Varietie of Lute Lessons* (1610). Consideration is given to the influence that Hans Gerle may have had on Dowland's method. This very technical article also includes suggestions for how a simplified and improved version of Dowland's system can be used by modern performers.

578   Dolata, David. *Meantone Temperaments on Lutes and Viols*. Bloomington: Indiana University Press, 2016. xx, 280 p. ISBN 9780253021236. MT165 .D65.

Dowland's system of fretting, as explained in son Robert's *Varietie of Lute Lessons*, is referenced multiple times in this monograph on early temperament. One especially useful tool is the book's accompanying webpage, which includes streaming audio examples. Performance clips of "Tarleton's Riserrectione" (D59), demonstrating aural differences between 1/4-comma, 1/6-comma, and 1/8-comma meantone and equal temperaments, are of special notice. A score within the text guides listener-readers to chords deserving close listening attention (pp. 152–4).

579   Lindley, Mark. *Lutes, Viols, and Temperaments*. Cambridge: Cambridge University Press, 1984. 134 p. ISBN 0521246709. ML3809 .L42.

Devotes several pages in chapter 6 to clarification of Dowland's *Varietie of Lute Lessons* fretting instructions, identifying confusing statements and explaining why they do not work.

580   Mitchell, David. "Fretting and Tuning the Lute." Appendix 2 in **264**, 456–65.

Labeled "A discussion, with special reference to John Dowland's instructions in *Varietie of Lute-Lessons*," this essay attempts to aid modern lutenists in deciphering the questions related to fretting and temperament, first addressed by Dowland in print in 1610, through illustrations depicting physical positioning of frets and mathematical tables related to tuning.

581   Richman, James. "Temperament: Not Just a Numbers Game." *Early Music America* 12, no. 3 (Fall 2006): 25–7, 46–9, 51. ISSN 1083–3633. ML1 .E15.

Attempts to elucidate meantone temperament for performers of early music. The final paragraph paraphrases Barbour's explanation of Dowland's tuning (see **576**) as described in *Varietie of Lute Lessons*.

INFLUENCE, LEGACY, AND SCHOLARSHIP

see also **276, 305, 391, 396, 405, 424, 450, 478, 487, 495, 496, 506, 556**

582   Brown, Richard. "Joyce's Englishman: 'That Het'rogeneous Thing' from Blake and Dowland to Defoe's 'True-Borne Englishman.'" Chapter 1 in *Joyce, Ireland, Britain*. Edited by Andrew Gibson and Len Platt, 33–49. Gainesville: University Press of Florida, 2006. ISBN 0813030153. PR6019 .O9 Z666.

Cites Joyce's appreciation for Dowland and other Elizabethan music, and provides examples from Joyce's writings to assert the author used Dowland and his songs to reference "Englishness," in what might be perceived as a non-Irish nationalist stance.

583   Burke, Karen M. "The Cadenza for Oboe in Beethoven's Fifth Symphony." *The Beethoven Journal* 15, no. 2 (Winter 2000): 64–5. ISSN 1087–8262.

This extremely circumstantial essay attempts to link the downward descending passage found in Beethoven's Fifth Symphony oboe cadenza to the *lachrimae* motive, claiming that Dowland's music would have been known in Vienna in the early nineteenth century. Evidence of Beethoven's knowledge of the piece or composer, however, is lacking in any of the composer's sketches or correspondence.

584   Dwyer, Benjamin. " 'Within it lie ancient melodies': Dowland's Musical Rhetoric and Britten's *Songs from the Chinese*." *The Musical Times* 153, no. 1919 (Summer 2012): 87–102. ISSN 0027-4666. ML5 .M85.

This article explores Dowland's possible uses of musical rhetoric. These principles are then overlaid onto a Britten song cycle in an effort to portray the influence the renaissance composer had on his twentieth-century countryman. The author's main point: "Britten assimilated Dowland's virtuosity in musical rhetoric so acutely and instinctively that it became an inherent aspect of his own compositional technique." Much of the author's theory related to rhetorical gestures seems to be based on Robert Toft's writings (**482** and **564**), and some assertions need further support. Readers are advised to consult **554** for alternate considerations.

585   Goodwin, Christopher. "Lanier's 1613 Portrait: A Suggested Reading." *Lute News: The Lute Society Magazine* 93 (2010): 6–8. ML5 .L885.

Offers a thoughtful interpretation of a seventeenth-century portrait of musician Nicholas Lanier. Suggests that clues within the painting indicate Lanier may have been trying to portray himself as "a new John Dowland."

586   Goss, Stephen. "Come, Heavy Sleep: Motive and Metaphor in Britten's *Nocturnal*, opus 70." *Guitar Forum* 1 (September 2001): 53–75.

Examines the ways in which Dowland's song "Come heavy sleep" (D138) influenced Benjamin Britten's guitar composition *Nocturnal after John Dowland*, op. 70, specifically the first movement entitled "Musingly." A close, interconnecting reading of the two pieces would have been quite beneficial, but this article's section on Dowland's song gets mired down in identification of melancholic musical tropes, many of which are not directly linked to either piece. The author, however, is quite correct in his assertion that this composition, connecting two great English composers, deserves more critical attention.

587   Hooper, Emma. "Somewhere a Place for Us: How Intratextual Music-Association Conveys Characteral Identity in *The Time of Singing* by Powers." *JMM: The Journal of Music and Meaning* 11 (2012–2013): 1–21. ISSN 1603-7170. ML3800.

Considers the ways in which Dowland's "Time stands still" (D161) represents a 2003 fictional character who adopts the work as his signature song.

588   Mason, Dorothy E. *Music in Elizabethan England*. Washington: Folger Shakespeare Library, 1958. 36 p. (Folger Booklets on Tudor and Stuart Civilization.) ML286.2 .M35.

A short but charming overview of Elizabethan music, with a few mentions of Dowland's importance. The mini-"exhibit" after the introduction includes a facsimile page from the *First Booke of Songes or Ayres* (1600) and a facsimile page from "A manuscript commonplace book, partly in the hand of John Dowland," both housed at the Folger Shakespeare Library.

589 Paterson, Adrian. "'After Music': *Chamber Music*, Song, and the Blank Page." In *The Poetry of James Joyce Reconsidered*. Edited by Marc C. Conner, 117–43. Gainesville: University Press of Florida, 2012. ISBN 9780813039763. PR6019 .O9 Z78226.

After acknowledging Joyce's fascination with Elizabethan music, especially works by John Dowland, the author explores how the famous writer likely accessed Dowland's lyrics and music. Elaborates on ways in which Dowland's influence manifested itself in Joyce's own poetry, especially that found in his *Chamber Music* anthology.

590 Pears, Peter. "John Dowland." In *New Aldeburgh Anthology*. Edited by Ariane Bankes and Jonathan Reekie, 199–200. Woodbridge, UK, and Rochester, NY: Aldeburgh Music/Boydell, 2009. ISBN 9781843834397. ML38 .A66 N49.

An endearing essay reprinted from the *Aldeburgh Anthology* (1972). Describes Dowland's works as "the first great art songs of modern times," going on to state none so great appeared again until Schubert. Written in the style of a program note or performance introduction.

591 Rupprecht, Philip. *Britten's Musical Language*. Cambridge: Cambridge University Press, 2001. x, 358. (Music in the Twentieth Century.) ISBN 0521631548. ML410 .B853 R8.

Includes an analysis of twentieth-century British composer Benjamin Britten's *Lachrymae: Reflections on a Song of Dowland* for viola and piano. Attempts to isolate Dowland's voice and direct quotations (of both the *lachrimae* theme and "If my complaints") from Britten's personal compositional language, describing a sort of discourse between the two (pp. 14–21). Features musical examples.

592 Savage, Roger. "This is the Record of John: Eight Decades of Dowland on Disc." In **270**: 281–94.

A history of Dowland recordings, from 1925 through 2010, including 78, LP, and CD formats.

593 Valk, Reinier de. "Celebrating Dowland's 450th." *Early Music* 41, no. 3 (August 2013): 538–40. ISSN 0306–1078. ML5 .E18.

Reports on activities of a Cambridge, UK two-day conference featuring Dowland scholarship, performance, and discussion. Valuable as a record of contemporary interest within Dowland studies.

594 Wiebe, Heather. "'Now and England': Britten's *Gloriana* and the 'New Elizabethans.'" *Cambridge Opera Journal* 17, no. 2 (July 2005): 141–72. ISSN 0954–5867. ML1699 .C36.

Briefly comments upon the second lute song of Britten's *Gloriana* as a reflection of his relationship with the Fitzwilliam *Lachrymae*, drawing upon Philip Rupprecht's analysis in **591**.

DOWLAND-INSPIRED POETRY

595 Greening, John. *Accompanied Voices: Poets on Composers from Thomas Tallis to Arvo Pärt*. Woodbridge, UK: Boydell, 2015. xx, 214 p. ISBN 9781783270156. PR1195 .M7 A34.

This poetry anthology consists of verses inspired by composers of the last five hundred years. Includes three poems, "O Dowland, Old John Dowland," "Mrs John Dowland," and "John Dowland on the Lute: A Round of Variations," by modern poets Hal Summers, Pauline Stainer, and N. S. Thompson, respectively (pp. 5–7).

596 Hill, Geoffrey. "Lachrimae or Seven tears figured in seven passionate Psalms." In *Tenebrae*, 15–21. Boston, MA: Houghton Mifflin, 1979. 48 p. ISBN 0395276101. PR6015 .I4735 T4.

A contemporary suite of seven poems, four of which adopt titles from Dowland's *Lachrimae* pavans. All consist of spiritual or somber subject matter. The four with Dowland titles are reprinted in *Before the Door of God: An Anthology of Devotional Poetry*, eds. Jay Hopler and Kimberly Johnson, 333–5 (New Haven, CT: Yale University Press, 2013).

597 Mathews, Harry. *Trial Impressions*. Providence: Burning Deck, 1977. PS3563 .A8359 T7.

A suite of twenty-nine contemporary poems, plus one of Dowland's lyrics, fashioned as a theme and diverse set of variations on Dowland's "Dear if you change" (pp. 241–55). The complete set is analyzed for macro- and microstructures in Joseph M. Conte, *Unending Design: The Forms of Postmodern Poetry* (Ithaca, NY: Cornell University Press, 1991), xii, 314 p. ISBN 0801424690. PS325 .C65.

598 Smith, Jordan. "A Song of Dowland's on the Stereo." *The Kenyon Review* ns. 11, no. 1 (Winter 1989): 33. ISSN 0163-075X. AP2 .K426.

An original poem that opens with the first three lines of text of "I saw my lady weep," before taking a fully contemporary turn.

599 Stainer, Pauline. "Mrs John Dowland." In *Sighting the Slave Ship*. Newcastle upon Tyne: Bloodaxe Books, 1992. 80 p. ISBN 1852241764. PR6069 .T1848.

A contemporary, original poem presenting the perspective of Mrs. Dowland, about whom no primary source evidence exists, except as related to her role in selling the rights to her husband's second songbook. Reprinted in a collected anthology of the same author, *The Lady and the Hare: New and Selected Poems* (Northumberland, UK: Bloodaxe Books, 2003) and **595**.

9

Recordings

Dowland's compositions are found in thousands of recorded collections. This selective discography features recordings that are primarily or wholly devoted to Dowland's music, using instrumental and vocal combinations common to early modern England. For individual songs or performers, see **Composition/Collection** and **Performer Indexes**.

COMPREHENSIVE COLLECTIONS

600 *John Dowland: The Collected Works.* 12 CDs. Éditions de l'Oiseau-Lyre, 1997, 2007.

The only collection attempting comprehensive coverage of all Dowland works. Includes lute solos and duos, lute song-airs, consort music, sacred music, and keyboard music. Individual volumes were previously released as analog and compact discs, 1967–1980. Performers: The Consort of Musicke [Anthony Rooley (director), Emma Kirkby, Glenda Simpson (sopranos), John York Skinner (countertenor), Martyn Hill (tenor), David Thomas (bass), Catherine Mackintosh, Polly Waterfield, Roderick Skeaping, Ian Gammie, Trevor Jones, and Jane Ryan (viols, violins), Bernard Thomas, Baldrick Deerenberg (flutes, recorders), Jakob Lindberg, Anthony Rooley, Christopher Wilson, and Julian Creme (lutes, other plucked strings), Alan Wilson (organ, virginal)], Colin Tilney (harpsichord), Anthony Bailes, Jakob Lindberg, Nigel North, Anthony Rooley, Christopher Wilson (solo lutes). Recorded at Decca Studios, West Hampstead, London. Notes by Peter Holman and Anthony Rooley in English, French, German, and Italian.

Includes: (CD 1 *Dowland: First Booke of Songes* **659**): D19, D23, D24, D26, D42, D60, D125, D126, D127, D128, D129, D130, D131, D132, D133, D134, D135, D136, D137, D138, D139; (CD2 *Dowland: Second Booke of Songes* **662**): D15, D141, D142, D143, D144, D145, D146, D147, D148, D149, D150, D151, D152, D153, D154, D155, D156, D157, D158, D159; (CD 3 *The Third Booke of Songs* **680**): D160, D161, D162, D163, D164, D165, D166, D167, D168, D169, D170, D171, D172, D173, D174, D175, D176, D177, D178, D179, D180; (CD 4 *A Pilgrimes Solace* I–XVI **661**): D34, D181, D182, D183, D184, D185, D186, D187, D188, D189, D190, D191, D192, D193; (CD 5 *A Pilgrimes Solace* XVII–XXI **661** / *Dowland: Keyboard Transcriptions* **694**): D194, D195, D196, D197, D198 / D8, D10, D15, D19, D23, D42, D48, D95; (CD 6 *Dowland: Mr. Henry Noell Lamentations 1597* **693** / *Dowland: Lachrimae 1604* **684**): D212, D213, D214, D215, D216, D217, D218 / D9, D14, D15, D19, D26, D29, D34, D38, D40, D42, D52, D114, D115, D116, D117, D118, D119, D120, D121, D122, D123; (CD 7 *Psalms and Sacred Songs* **693** / *Dowland: A Miscellany* **604**): D142, D203, D204, D205, D206, D207, D208, D209, D210, D211 / D8, D10, D15, D19, D20, D37, D42, D43, D60, D66, D142; [CDs 8–11: Originally released as a 5-LP set, *Dowland: Complete Lute Music* **620**] (CD 8): D1, D6, D12, D13, D15, D18, D21, D25, D27, D29, D32, D41, D42, D45, D47, D49, D60, D68, D69, D71, D75, D79, D96, D97, D98, D99, D100; (CD 9): D5, D8, D9, D15, D16, D19, D20, D22, D23, D24, D31, D33, D34, D46, D48, D53, D54, D63, D64, D66, D67, D72, D73, D76, D78, D81, D111; (CD 10): D2, D3, D4, D10, D11, D15, D23, D28, D30, D35, D38, D40, D42, D50, D52, D55, D56, D57, D58, D65, D77, D61, D70, D94, D95, D120; (CD 11 *Dowland: Complete Lute Music* **620** / *Dowland: Consort Musicke* **682**): D7, D14, D17, D26, D36, D43, D44, D51, D59, D62, D80 / D8, D14, D15, D19, D22, D23, D38, D39, D41, D42, D52, D62, D81, D95, D109, D114; (CD 12 *Dowland: Consort Musicke* **682** / *Dowland: A Musicall Banquet 1610*): D52, D94, D185, D200 / D199, D200, D201.

MIXED GENRES

601 *Best of Dowland*. CD. Naxos, 2009.

Lute solos, lute songs, consort music. Compiled from previous Naxos recordings. Performers: Catherine King (mezzo-soprano), Steven Rickards (countertenor), Jacob Heringman, Dorothy Linell, Nigel North (lutes), Rose Consort of Viols (viols). Notes by Keith Anderson. Includes D3, D7, D9, D10, D14, D15, D38, D39, D40, D41, D48, D60, D128, D134, D141, D166, D201.

602 *Burst Forth My Tears: The Music of John Dowland*. 2 CDs. Naxos, 2010.

Lute solos, lute song-airs, consort music. Compilation from previous recordings. Performers: Catherine King (mezzo-soprano), Nigel North, Jacob Heringman (lutes), Rose Consort of Viols (viols). Includes D1, D14, D15, D17, D33, D75, D128, D154, D190.

603 *Come Away, Come Sweet Love.* CD. Stradivarius series. Milano Dischi, 2002.

Lute solos, lute song-airs, consort music. Performers: Roberta Invernizzi (soprano), Accademia Strumentale Italiana (Alberto Rasi, director). Notes by Hugh Ward-Perkins in Italian, English, and French. Includes D9, D15, D19, D26, D38, D42, D47, D115, D123, D131, D134, D136, D138, D142, D166, D173.

604 *Dowland: A Miscellany.* LP. Éditions de l'Oiseau-Lyre, 1979.

Lute and bandora solos, lyra viol solos, recorder solos, consort songs, consort music. Performers: Consort of Musicke [John York Skinner (countertenor), Polly Waterfield (treble viol), Roderick Skeaping (alto viol), Ian Gammie (treble viol, lyra viol), Trevor Jones, Jane Ryan (bass viol), Baldrick Deerenberg (tenor recorder), Jakob Lindberg (lute, bandora), Christopher Wilson (lute), Anthony Rooley (lute, director)]. Notes by Anthony Rooley in English, French, and German. Includes D8, D10, D15, D19, D20, D37, D42, D43, D60, D66, D142.

605 *Dowland: Ayres.* CD. Voix Baroque series 18. Naïve, 2004, 2008.

Lute solos, lute song-airs, consort music. Performers: Gérard Lesne (alto), Jacob Heringman (lute), Ensemble Orlando Gibbons (instruments). Recorded October 2002 at the Priory of Froville, France. Includes D15, D19, D23, D24, D34, D42, D60, D98, D129, D131, D138, D149, D158, D187, D189, D190, D191, D192, D193.

606 *Dowland: Consort Music and Songs.* CD. Early Music series. Naxos, 1997.

Lute solos, lute songs, and consort music. Performers: Catherine King (mezzo-soprano), Jacob Heringman (lute), Rose Consort of Viols (viols). Recorded March 12–14, 1995 at St. Andrew's Church, Toddington, Gloucestershire, England. Notes by John Bryan. Includes D4, D9, D13, D14, D19, D26, D29, D34, D38, D40, D42, D52, D73, D120, D121, D122, D123, D128, D134, D154, D182, D190.

607 *Dowland: In Darkness Let Me Dwell.* CD. Harmonia mundi, BMG, 2008, 2013.

Lute solos, lute songs, consort songs, consort music. Performers: Dorothee Mields (soprano), Hille Perl (viol), Lee Santana (lute), Sirius Viols (viol consort). Recorded 2007 in Sengwarden, Germany. Notes by Hille Perl in German, English, and French. Includes D2, D3, D9, D15, D19, D42, D114, D118, D119, D138, D142, D158, D161, D189, D201.

608 *Dowland: Lute Songs, Lute Solos.* 2 LPs, CDs. Harmonia mundi, 1978, 1989, 1996, 2003.

Lute solos, lute song-airs, consort music. Also issued as individual albums. Performers: Alfred Deller (countertenor), Robert Spencer (lute), Consort of Six [Trevor Jones, Jane Ryan (viols), Peter Davies (flutes), Nigel North (lute), Ian Harwood (cittern), Robert Spencer (lute, bandora)]. Recorded September 1977. Notes by Robert Spencer in English, French, and German. Includes (Disc 1): D15, D19, D20, D23, D39, D41, D42, D48, D50, D58, D62, D99, D131, D135, D142, D164, D166, D168, D174, D190, D192; (Disc 2): D8, D19, D25, D37, D42, D47, D54, D55, D56, D59, D60, D61, D66, D138, D141, D156, D167, D188, D189, D201.

609   *Dowland: Passionate Pavans and Galliards.* CD. Naxos, 2000.

Lute solos, lute song-airs, keyboard. Performers: Queen's Chamber Band [Julianne Baird (soprano), Marshall Coid (countertenor), Jerry Willard (lute), Elaine Comparone (virginal, director)]. Notes by Elaine Comparone. Recorded May 2000 at Town Hall, New York City. Includes D1, D5, D15, D15 (arr. Byrd), D19, D23, D26, D42, D60, D66, D142, D158, D161, D178, D187, D201.

610   *Dowland: Tears of the Muse.* CD. Atma, 1998.

Lute solos, lute songs, consort songs, consort music. Performers: Daniel Taylor (countertenor), Andreas Martin (lute), Les Voix Humaines [Margaret Little, Susie Napper (viols)]. Recorded October 1997 at Église Saint-Augustin, Mirabel, Québec, Canada. Notes by Daniel Taylor in English and French. Includes D15, D42, D60, D64, D118, D141, D142, D161.

611   *Farewell, Unkind: Songs and Dances of John Dowland.* CD. Erato, 1996.

Lute song-airs, lute solos, consort music, and psalms. Performers: Anne Azéma (soprano), Karen Clark (mezzo-soprano), William Hite (tenor), Joel Frederiksen (bass, lute), Boston Camerata (Joel Cohen, director). Recorded May 23–26, 1995 at Campion Center, Weston, MA. Notes by Jan Nuchelmans. Includes D19, D23, D24, D41, D42, D48, D59, D60, D123, D129, D131, D133, D135, D138, D159, D166, D173, D174, D186, D190, D192, D199, D200, D206.

612   *Flow My Teares: Songs by John Dowland.* CD. Atrium, 1998; Warner Classics, 2005.

Airs, consort songs, solo lute, consort music. Performers: Mikael Samuelson, Freddie Wadling (voice), Forge Players. Recorded at Studioatrium, Kista, Stockholm, Sweden. Includes D9, D15, D19, D40, D52, D60, D120, D122, D125, D134, D138, D168, D169.

613   *John Dowland (1563–1626).* LP. Alpha Brussels, 1976.

Lute solos, lute song-airs, consort music. Performers: Ensemble Musica Aurea [Anne Verkinderen (soprano), Anne-Marie Sonneveld, Jérôme Lejeune, Shige Sennari (viols), Janine Rubinlicht, Martin Sonneveld (violins), Philippe Lemaigre (lute), Huguette Lallemend (keyboard)]. Recorded 1976 in Ghent. Notes by Jérôme Lejeune in Dutch, English, French, and German. Includes D9, D13, D15, D19, D23, D25, D29, D41, D42, D44, D59, D121, D122, D123, D142, D151, D156, D192.

614   *John Dowland's Lachrimae or Seaven Teares.* CD. Amon Ra, 1992.

Lute song-airs, consort music. Performers: Caroline Trevor (alto), Jacob Heringman (lutes), Rose Consort of Viols [Alison Crum (treble and alto viols), John Bryan (tenor viol), Susanna Pell, Elizabeth Liddle, Sarah Groser (bass viols)]. Recorded October 1991 at Forde Abbey, Chard, Dorset, England. Notes by Elizabeth Liddle. Released as streaming audio by Naxos as *Dowland, J.: Chamber and Vocal Music,* Naxos, 2009. Includes D15, D114, D115, D116, D117, D118, D119, D129, D138, D141, D142, D189.

615 *Lachrimæ: John Dowland.* CD. Atma classique, 2018.

Lute solos, consort music. Performers: Nigel North (lute), Les Voix Humaines [Mélisande Corriveau, Felix Deak, Margaret Little, Rafael Sanchez-Guevara, Susie Napper (viols)]. Recorded July 2017 at Église Saint-Augustin, Mirabel, Quèbec, Canada. Notes by François Filiatrault in French and English. Includes D13, D14, D15, D19, D26, D34, D42, D46, D114, D115, D116, D117, D118, D119, D123, D185.

616 *Seaven Teares: Music of John Dowland.* CD. Harmonia mundi, 2002.

Lute songs, consort songs, consort music. Performers: Ellen Hargis (soprano), The King's Noyse [David Douglass (violin and director), Robert Mealy, Margriet Tindemans, Scott Metcalfe (violas), Emily Walhout (bass violin), Paul O'Dette (lute)]. Recorded June 12–14, 2000 at Seiji Ozawa Hall, Tanglewood, Lenox, MA. Notes by Scott Metcalfe in English, French, and German. Includes D9, D14, D15, D19, D26, D29, D34, D38, D40, D42, D52, D114, D115, D116, D117, D118, D119, D121, D123, D129, D138, D141, D142.

617 *Treasures from My Minde: Songs and Instrumental Pieces by John Dowland.* CD. Virgin Classics, 1999.

Lute solos, lute songs, consort music. Performers: Virelai [Catherine King (mezzo-soprano), William Lyons (flutes, recorders), Jacob Heringman (lutes), Susanna Pell (viols, lute, recorder), Sarah Cunningham (viols/harp)]. Recorded June 1996 and January–February 1997 at St. Andrew's Church, Toddington, Gloucestershire, England. Notes by Tim Crawford. Includes D1, D15, D19, D23, D24, D38, D42, D52, D60, D65, D95, D122, D131, D142, D149, D161, D188, D189, D190, D201.

618 *Tunes of Sad Despaire.* CD. Satirino, 2012.

Lute solos, lute song-airs, consort music. Performers: Dominique Visse (counter-tenor), Renaud Delaigue (bass), Éric Bellocq (lute, orpharion), Fretwork [Asako Morikawa, Reiko Ichise, Richard Tunnicliffe, Richard Boothby (viols)]. Recorded September 18–20, 2011 at Église de Marols, Loire, France. Notes by Richard Langham Smith. Includes D12, D15, D19, D23, D79, D94, D129, D134, D138, D139, D142, D149, D188, D189, D191, D201.

LUTE SOLOS

see also **Combined Lute Solos and Lute Song-Airs**

619 *Dances of Dowland.* LP, CD. RCA Red Seal, 1968, 1993, 2013.

Performer: Julian Bream (lute). Recorded in 1967 at Wardour Chapel (Chapel of All Saints), Wardour Castle, Wiltshire, Dorset, England. Notes by Shirley Fleming. Includes D9, D15, D22, D23, D25, D38, D42, D43, D44, D47, D51, D54, D57, D58, D111, D119.

620   *Dowland: Complete Lute Music.* 5 LPs, CDs. Florilegium series. Éditions de l'
Oiseau-Lyre, 1980, 1990.

Reissued as CDs 8–11 in **600**. Performers: Anthony Bailes, Jakob Lindberg,
Nigel North, Anthony Rooley, Christopher Wilson (lutes). Notes by Anthony
Rooley in English, French, and German. (Disc 1, Anthony Bailes): D1, D12,
D13, D15 (arr. Sturt), D25, D32, D42, D47, D49, D69, D71, D75, D96, D97,
D98, D99, D100; (Disc 2, Nigel North): D6, D9, D15, D18, D21, D23, D27, D29,
D31, D34, D41, D42, D45, D46, D60, D63, D68, D72, D78, D79; (Disc 3, Jakob
Lindberg): D5, D8, D16, D19, D20, D22, D24, D33, D48, D53, D54, D64, D66,
D67, D73, D76, D81, D94, D111; (Disc 4, Anthony Rooley): D3, D4, D11, D15 (arr.
Cozens), D23, D30, D35, D40, D42, D50, D52, D55, D56, D57, D58, D65, D77,
D95, D120; (Disc 5, Christopher Wilson): D2, D7, D10, D14, D17, D26, D28,
D36, D38, D43, D44, D51, D59, D61, D62, D70, D80.

621   *Dowland: The Complete Solo Lute Music.* 4 CDs. BIS, 1995, 2008.

Performers: Jakob Lindberg (lutes, orpharion). Recorded October 4–7, November
1–4, November 28–30, and December 8–10, 1994 at Djursholms Kapell, Sweden.
Notes by Jakob Lindberg in English, German, and French. (Disc 1): D1, D3, D14,
D15, D16, D17, D26, D27, D28, D29, D36, D38, D40, D41, D42, D43, D44, D45,
D46, D47, D51, D54, D111. (Disc 2): D2, D4, D6, D7, D11, D18, D32, D33, D34,
D35, D57, D58, D59, D62, D67, D69, D70, D73, D76, D77, D80. (Disc 3): D8,
D9, D10, D12, D19, D20, D21, D22, D24, D25, D30, D31, D49, D50, D52, D56,
D61, D63, D64, D65, D72, D75, D78, D81, D113. (Disc 4): D5, D9, D10, D13,
D23, D39, D42, D48, D53, D55, D60, D64, D66, D68, D71, D79, D94, D95, D96,
D97, D98, D99, D100, D103, D106, D107.

622   *Dowland: A Dream.* CD. Paris: Näive Astrée, 2005.

Performer: Hopkinson Smith (lute). Recorded in July 2004 in Beinwil,
Switzerland. Notes by Hopkinson Smith. Includes D1, D3, D6, D9, D15, D23,
D25, D28, D40, D42, D43, D45, D47, D54, D56, D62, D75, D95, D97.

623   *Dowland: Fantasies and Dances for the Lute.* LP. Arch, 1977; Musical Heritage
Society, 1981.

Performer: Joseph Bacon (lute). Recorded November–December 1976 at
Montgomery Chapel, San Francisco Theological Seminary, San Anselmo, CA.
Includes D1, D4, D6, D7, D18, D19, D28, D34, D40, D45, D57, D71, D96.

624   *John Dowland: Complete Lute Music.* 4 CDs. Early Music series. Naxos, 2009.

Each CD originally released individually in volumes 1–4, 2006–2007. Performer:
Nigel North, lute. Recorded July 23–26, 2004, June 16–19, 2005, June 29–July 1,
2006, and June 28–July 1, 2007 at St. John Chrysostom Church, Newmarket,
Ontario, Canada. Notes by Nigel North. (Disc 1, *Dowland: Fancyes, Dreams
and Spirits (Lute Music 1)*): D1, D2, D3, D4, D5, D6, D32, D45, D50, D52,

D54, D55, D56, D57, D58, D59, D61, D65, D73, D75, D98, D99; (Disc 2, *John Dowland: Dowland's Tears (Lute Music 2)*): D8, D9, D13, D14, D15, D16, D18, D19, D29, D30, D33, D34, D42, D46, D120, D141; (Disc 3, *Dowland: Pavans, Galliards and Almains (Lute Music 3)*): D10, D11, D12, D17, D25, D28, D36, D38, D39, D43, D44, D47, D48, D49, D51, D53, D94, D95, D96, D111; (Disc 4, *Dowland: The Queen's Galliard (Lute Music 4)*): D20, D21, D22, D23, D24, D26, D27, D31, D35, D40, D41, D42, D60, D62, D63, D64, D66, D67, D68, D69, D70, D79, D97, D100.

625 *John Dowland: Complete Lute Works.* 5 CDs. Harmonia mundi, 1997.

Each CD originally released individually, 1995–1997. Performer: Paul O'Dette (lute, orpharion). Recorded June 30–July 2, June 22–24, July 3, and October 20–21, 1994 and September 23–25, 1995 at Campion Center, Boston, MA, and September 12–15, 1996 at Seiji Ozawa Hall, Tanglewood, Lenox, MA. Notes by Robert Spencer and Paul O'Dette in English, French, and German. (Disc 1): D3, D5, D12, D18, D23, D25, D27, D29, D30, D35, D36, D43, D48, D49, D50, D51, D55, D56, D61, D64, D66, D75, D79, D104, D106; (Disc 2): D1, D4, D8, D10, D11, D15, D19, D20, D21, D22, D26, D31, D32, D34, D42, D47, D54, D57, D68, D70, D80, D109, D111, D113; (Disc 3): D2, D7, D9, D13, D14, D16, D31, D33, D40, D41, D44, D45, D52, D53, D59, D62, D65, D67, D81, D97, D99; (Disc 4): D6, D15, D17, D23, D24, D28, D38, D42, D46, D58, D60, D66, D69, D71, D82, D94, D95, D96, D98, D100; (Disc 5): D1, D15, D19, D39, D42, D44, D72, D73, D76, D77, D78, D84, D93, D103, D107, D120.

626 *Julian Bream Plays Dowland.* LP. Westminster, 1965.

Performer: Julian Bream (lute). Notes by J. Robison. Includes D1, D2, D3, D9, D15, D25, D40, D41, D49, D54, D56, D57, D61, D120.

627 *Lute Music of John Dowland.* CD. Dorian Sono Luminus, 1991.

Performer: Ronn McFarlane (lute). Notes by Ronn McFarlane. Includes D1, D5, D8, D9, D12, D15, D19, D20, D23, D25, D39, D41, D42, D45, D47, D48, D54, D55, D56, D58, D59, D61, D62, D64, D66, D79, D98, D99.

628 *Lute Music of John Dowland.* LP, CD. RCA Red Seal, 1976, 2013.

Performer: Julian Bream (lute). Recorded April 1976 at Wardour Chapel, Dorset, England. Notes by Basil Lam. Includes D2, D3, D5, D8, D13, D19, D26, D33, D37, D46, D66, D73.

629 *My Favorite Dowland.* CD. Harmonia mundi, 2014.

Performer: Paul O'Dette (lute). Recorded January 2012 at Sauder Hall, Goshen College, IN. Notes by Paul O'Dette in English, French, and German. Includes D1, D2, D3, D5, D6, D9, D14, D15, D18, D23, D40, D41, D42, D45, D46, D47, D54, D55, D57, D58, D67, D80, D95.

630 *Semper Dowland Semper Dolens.* 2 CDs. San Lorenzo de El Escorial: Glossa, 2003, 2013.

Performers: José Miguel Moreno (lute), Eligio Quinteiro (theorbo and gittern). Recorded September 2002 at Iglesia de San Miguel, Cuenca, Spain. Notes by Reduán Ortega. Includes D1, D5, D6, D9, D10, D12, D14, D15, D23, D33, D39, D40, D41, D42, D47, D48, D51, D52, D54, D55, D58, D59, D62, D64, D65, D66, D77, D79, D93, D95, D98, D103.

631 *Such Sweet Sorrow: Lute Pieces by John Dowland.* CD. Centaur, 1999.

Performer: John Paul (lute). Notes by Anden Houben. Includes D4, D8, D9, D13, D14, D15, D19, D20, D23, D29, D31, D32, D33, D37, D38, D40, D42, D45, D46, D53, D57, D61, D62, D64, D66, D67, D69, D79, D80, D81, D97, D99.

632 *Two Loves: A Sequence of Poetry and Music by William Shakespeare and John Dowland.* CD. RCA Red Seal, 1989, 2013.

Performers: Peggy Ashcroft (poetic recitation), Julian Bream (lute). Recorded April 22, September 20–22, 1988 at Wardour Chapel (Chapel of All Saints), Wardour Castle, Wiltshire, Dorset, England. Notes by Julian Bream. Includes D7, D9, D15, D25, D34, D40, D44, D54, D59, D61, D69, D97.

COMBINED LUTE SOLOS AND LUTE SONG-AIRS

see also separate **Lute Solos** *and* **Lute Song-Airs** *sections*

633 *The Art of Melancholy.* CD. Hyperion, 2014.

Lute solos, lute songs. Performers: Iestyn Davies (countertenor), Thomas Dunford (lute). Recorded April 6–8, 2013 at Potton Hall, Dunwich, Suffolk, England. Notes by Robert Savage. Includes D9, D15, D23, D42, D55, D60, D62, D128, D129, D131, D134, D138, D141, D142, D153, D161, D162, D166, D201.

634 *Awake, Sweet Love: The Music of John Dowland.* CD. Arabesque Recordings, 1991.

Lute solos, lute song-airs. Performers: Julianne Baird (soprano), David Tayler (lute and orpharion), Robert DeCormier Singers (Robert DeCormier, director). Recorded January 8–10, 1991 at Concordia College, Bronxville, NY. Notes by Edward Taylor. Includes D15, D19, D23, D24, D59, D60, D130, D134, D137, D139, D141, D144, D147, D149, D157, D161, D168, D174, D178, D187, D201.

635 *Blissful Kisses: Music by John Dowland.* CD. Musicaphon, 2011.

Lute solos, lute songs. Performers: Fortune's Musicke [Hanna Thyssen (soprano), Susanne Peuker (lute)]. Recorded August 17–18, 2011 at Kirche St. Nikolai, Mahndorf, Bremen, Germany. Notes by Marcus Stäbler in German and English. Includes D6, D9, D15, D19, D23, D24, D39, D42, D60, D64, D98, D131, D137, D142, D149, D161, D177, D182, D187.

636   *Dowland: Ayres and Lute Lessons.* LP, CD. Harmonia mundi, 1982, 1989.

Lute solos, lute song-airs. Performers: Deller Consort [Rosemary Hardy (soprano), Mark Deller (countertenor, director), Paul Elliott (tenor), Michael George (bass), Robert Spencer (lute)]. Recorded July 1981. Notes by Robert Spencer in French, English, and German. Includes D9, D19, D26, D60, D129, D132, D134, D135, D138, D139, D154, D165, D168, D182, D187.

637   *Dowland: Flow My Tears and Other Lute Songs.* CD. Naxos, 1997.

Lute solos, lute songs. Performers: Steven Rickards (countertenor), Dorothy Linell (lute). Recorded March 1 and October 26–30, 1995 at Fordham Town Hall, New York City. Notes by Dorothy Linell and Keith Anderson. Reissued as CD 1 in the set *Songs of Tears, Dreams, and Spirits: The Lute Music and Songs of John Dowland*, Naxos, 2007. Includes D15, D19, D23, D25, D42, D60, D62, D70, D130, D135, D137, D138, D141, D142, D149, D161, D164, D165, D166, D186, D200, D201.

638   *Dowland: Lachrimæ.* CD. Alpha, 2013, 2016.

Lute solos, lute song-airs. Performers: Thomas Dunford (lute), Ruby Hughes (soprano), Reinoud van Mechelen, Paul Agnew (tenors), Alain Buet (bass). Recorded July 11–12, 2012 at L'église Évangelique Luthèrienne de l'Ascension, Paris, and August 21–22, 2012 at Studio 4, Flagey, Belgium. Notes by Gabrielle Oliveira Guyon in French, English, and German. Includes D9, D15, D23, D25, D40, D42, D60, D62, D75, D98, D129, D141, D142.

639   *Dowland: Tell Me True Love.* CD. Harmonia Mundi, 2016.

Lute solos, lute song-airs. Performers: Ensemble Phoenix Munich [Joel Frederiksen (bass, lute, director), Ziv Brah (lute), Ryosuke Sakamoto (lute, viol), Alexandra Polin, Elizabeth Rumsey, Domen Marinčič (viols)]. Recorded November 15–17, 2015 at Kapelle des Malteserstifts St. Josef, Starnberg-Percha, Germany. Includes D6, D15, D23, D34, D37, D42, D59, D98, D127, D133, D134, D139, D149, D165, D166, D178, D187, D189, D192, D200, D201.

640   *English Orpheus: Songs for Voice and Lute.* LP, Cassette, CD. Virgin Classics, 1989, 1993, 2000.

Lute solos, lute song-airs. Performers: Emma Kirkby (soprano), Anthony Rooley (lute, orpharion). Recorded September 1988 at Forde Abbey, Chard, Somerset. Notes by Anthony Rooley in English, French, and German. Includes D9, D24, D34, D42, D44, D55, D99, D127, D134, D142, D143, D144, D150, D153, D160, D162, D164, D178, D186, D193.

641   *Fine Knacks for Ladies.* CD. Collegium Vocale Bydgoszcz, 2012.

Lute solos, lute song-airs. Performers: Patrycja Cywińska-Gacka (soprano), Janusz Cabała (countertenor), Michał Zieliński (tenor, director), Łukasz Hermanowicz (bass), Magdalena Tomsińska (lute), Marcin Zalewski (viol). Recorded Summer 2012 at St. Kazimierz Królewicz Church, Kruszyn, Poland.

Notes by Michał Zieliński in Polish. Includes D19, D23, D48, D54, D60, D81, D98, D99, D126, D127, D131, D137, D149.

642   *First Booke of Songs: John Dowland.* CD. My Lord Chamberlain's Consort, 2003.

Lute solos, lute song-airs. Performers: My Lord Chamberlain's Consort [Marcia Young (soprano, early harp), Drew Minter (countertenor, early harp), Philip Anderson (tenor), Grant Herreid (tenor, lute), Pat O'Brien (lute, cittern), Andy Rutherford (lute), Rosamund Morley (viol), Kurt-Owen Richards (bass)]. Recorded January 13–16, 2003 in New York. Includes D19, D23, D24, D26, D37, D42, D60, D125, D126, D127, D128, D129, D130, D131, D132, D133, D134, D135, D136, D137, D138, D139.

643   *Fortune My Foe: Songs of John Dowland.* CD. Koch International, 1992.

Lute solos, lute song-airs. Performers: Echos Muse [Janet Humberger (soprano), Paul Elliot (tenor), Wendy Gillespie (viol), Margriet Tindemans (viol), David Tayler (lute)]. Recorded January 13–15, 1992 at St. Steven's Episcopal Church, Belvedere, CA. Includes D15, D23, D62, D130, D131, D138, D139, D141, D142, D150, D154, D166, D167, D174, D178, D182, D189, D200, D201.

644   *John Dowland: A Pilgrimes Solace.* CD. Mignarda, 2013.

Lute solos, lute song-airs. Performers: Mignarda [Donna Stewart (voice), Ron Andrico (lute), Alex Korolov, Alexander Rakov (viols)]. Notes by Ron Andrico and Edward Doughtie. Includes D34, D98, D100, D182, D181, D183, D186, D187, D188, D189, D190, D193.

645   *John Dowland: Awake, Sweet Love.* CD. Schumacher, 2014.

Lute solos, lute songs. Performers: David Munderloh (tenor), Julian Behr (lute). Recorded February 4–6, 2014 at Kirche St. Pantaleon, Solothurn, Switzerland. Notes by Christian Kelnberger and Anthony Rooley in German and English. Includes D10, D15, D24, D26, D34, D42, D47, D78, D130, D131, D134, D138, D139, D141, D142, D144, D150, D154, D161, D201.

646   *John Dowland: In Darkness.* CD. Stradivarius, 2015.

Lute solos, lute songs. Performers: Michael Chance (countertenor), Paul Beier (lute). Includes D5, D6, D34, D38, D46, D94, D96, D98, D100, D111, D182, D186, D187, D191, D193, D199, D200, D201.

647   *John Dowland: Lute Songs and Dances.* LP. Orion, 1972.

Lute solos, lute songs. Performers: Hayden Blanchard (tenor), Frederick Noad (lute), Ruth Adams (viol). Includes D24, D39, D42, D48, D49, D58, D59, D60, D64, D129, D130, D131, D132, D135, D138.

648   *John Dowland: Lute Songs and Lute Solos.* LP. Musical Heritage Society, 1973.

Lute solos, lute songs. Performers: Willard Cobb (tenor), Deborah Minkin (lute). Notes by Jürgen Thym. Includes D15, D46, D52, D59, D66, D115, D131, D134, D138, D194, D201.

649 *Julian Bream in Concert: Lute Music by Dowland and Byrd; Six Lute Songs by Dowland.* LP, CD. RCA Victor, 1965; Sony, 2013.

Lute solos, lute songs. Performers: Peter Pears (tenor), Julian Bream (lute). Recorded April 4–6, 1963 at Wellesley College, MA, and October 10, 1963 at Wigmore Hall, London. Notes by John Gruen. Includes D14, D19, D41, D45, D59, D66, D135, D142, D145, D166, D178, D201.

650 *Songs and Dances of John Dowland.* LP. Turnabout, 1973.

Lute solos, lute songs. Performers: Hugues Cuénod (tenor), Joel Cohen (lute), Christiane Jaccottet (virginal). Recorded 1971 in Rivaz, Switzerland. Notes by Joel Israel Cohen. Includes D23, D24, D34, D42, D50, D55, D60, D61, D62, D70, D130, D131, D142, D149, D152, D165, D166, D168, D173, D174, D186.

651 *Songs from the Labyrinth.* CD. Deutsche Grammophon, 2007.

Lute solos, lute song-airs. CD accompanying DVD documentary (**695**). Performers: Sting (voice, lute), Edin Karamazov (lute). Recorded at St. Luke's Church, Old Street, London. Notes by Sting. Includes D2, D6, D15, D40, D42, D60, D66, D67, D135, D138, D149, D158, D174, D178, D201.

652 *Sorrow Stay: John Dowland.* CD. ABC Classics series. Australian Broadcasting Corporation, 2012.

Lute solos, lute songs. Performers: Justin Burwood (tenor), Rosemary Hodgson (lute). Recorded at St. Fidelis' Catholic Church, Coburg, Melbourne, Australia. Notes by Rosemary Hodgson and Grantley McDonald. D9, D15, D23, D34, D127, D129, D134, D141, D142, D151, D161, D167, D174, D182, D200, D201.

653 *Sweet Stay Awhile: Songs and Lute Pieces by John Dowland.* CD. EMI Classics, 1998.

Lute solos, lute songs. Performers: Charles Daniels (tenor), David Miller (lute). Includes D9, D15, D42, D71, D131, D134, D138, D141, D150, D156, D158, D164, D167, D176, D179, D182, D193.

LUTE SONG-AIRS

see also **Combined Lute Solos and Lute Song-Airs**

654 *Ayres and Lute-Lessons.* LP, CD. Saga, 1977, 1994. Reissued with added material as *John Dowland: Lute Songs*, Alto, 2009.

Performers: James Bowman (countertenor), Robert Spencer (lute). Recorded at Eltham College, London. Notes by Robert Spencer. Includes D9, D15, D21, D24, D34, D42, D48, D60, D129, D142, D149, D156, D164, D165, D167, D168, D187, D200.

655 *Ayres for Four Voices, Vol. I.* LP. Collectors series. Westminster, 1958, 1970.

Performers: Golden Age Singers [Margaret Field-Hyde (soprano, director), John Whitworth (countertenor), René Soames (tenor), Gordon Clinton (baritone)],

Julian Bream (lute), Edith Steinhauser (treble viol), Beatrice Reichert (alto viol), Rieda Litschauer (tenor viol), Ernst Knava (bass viol). Notes by Ed Cray. Includes D24, D60, D127, D131, D133, D138, D147, D148, D149, D152, D153, D156, D165, D168, D172, D181, D183, D184.

656   *Ayres for Four Voices, Vol. II.* LP. Collectors series. Westminster, 1958, 1974.

Performers: Golden Age Singers [Margaret Field-Hyde (soprano, director), John Whitworth (countertenor), René Soames (tenor), Gordon Clinton (baritone)], Julian Bream (lute), Edith Steinhauser (treble viol), Beatrice Reichert (alto viol), Rieda Litschauer (tenor viol), Ernst Knava (bass viol). Notes by Nigel Fortune. Includes D19, D34, D128, D130, D132, D134, D139, D151, D154, D157, D166, D167, D170, D171, D173, D180, D185.

657   *Ayres for Four Voices, Volume 3.* LP. Collectors series. Westminster, 1958.

Performers: Golden Age Singers [Margaret Field-Hyde (soprano, director), John Whitworth (countertenor), René Soames (tenor), Gordon Clinton (baritone)], Julian Bream (lute), Edith Steinhauser (treble viol), Beatrice Reichert (alto viol), Rieda Litschauer (tenor viol), Ernst Knava (bass viol). Includes D23, D26, D129, D155, D158, D169, D174, D176, D179, D182, D187, D192, D193, D194.

658   *Ayres for Four Voices, Volume 4.* LP. Westminster, 1958.

Performers: Golden Age Singers [Margaret Field-Hyde (soprano, director), John Whitworth (countertenor), René Soames (tenor), Gordon Clinton (baritone)], Julian Bream (lute), Edith Steinhauser (treble viol), Beatrice Reichert (alto viol), Rieda Litschauer (tenor viol), Ernst Knava (bass viol). Notes by Nigel Fortune. Includes D42, D125, D126, D135, D136, D137, D146, D150, D159, D164, D175, D177, D178, D186, D191, D195.

659   *Dowland: First Booke of Songes.* LP, CD. Florilegium series. 1976, 1989, 2003, 2007, 2016.

Reissued as CD 1 in **600**. Performers: Consort of Musicke [Emma Kirby (soprano), John York Skinner (countertenor), Martyn Hill (tenor), David Thomas (bass), Catherine Mackintosh, Polly Waterfield, and Ian Gammie (tenor viols), Trevor Jones (bass viol), Anthony Rooley (lute, director)]. Recorded in 1976 at Decca Studio no. 3, West Hampstead, London. Notes by Anthony Rooley in English, French, and German. Includes D19, D23, D24, D26, D42, D60, D125, D126, D127, D128, D129, D130, D131, D132, D133, D134, D135, D136, D137, D138, D139.

660   *Dowland: First Booke of Songes.* CD. ASV, 1993.

Performers: Rufus Müller (tenor), Christopher Wilson (lute). Recorded in Toddington Church, Gloucestershire, England. Includes D19, D23, D24, D26, D42, D60, D125, D126, D127, D128, D129, D130, D131, D132, D133, D134, D135, D136, D137, D138, D139.

661 *Dowland: A Pilgrimes Solace 1612.* 2 LPs. Florilegium series. Éditions de l'Oiseau-Lyre, 1981.

Reissued on CDs 4 and 5 in **600**. Performers: Consort of Musicke [Emma Kirby (soprano), John York Skinner (countertenor), Martyn Hill (tenor), David Thomas (bass), Catherine Mackintosh, Polly Waterfield, and Ian Gammie (tenor viols), Trevor Jones (bass viol), Anthony Rooley (lute, director)]. Notes by Anthony Rooley in English, French, and German. Includes D34, D181, D182, D183, D184, D185, D186, D187, D188, D189, D190, D191, D192, D193, D194, D195, D196, D197, D198.

662 *Dowland: Second Booke of Songes.* 2 LPs, CD. Florilegium series. Éditions de l'Oiseau-Lyre, 1977, 1991.

Reissued as CD 2 in **600**. Performers: Consort of Musicke [Emma Kirby (soprano), John York Skinner (countertenor), Martyn Hill (tenor), David Thomas (bass), Catherine Mackintosh, Polly Waterfield, and Ian Gammie (tenor viols), Trevor Jones (bass viol), Anthony Rooley (lute, director)]. Notes by Anthony Rooley in English, French, and German. Includes D15, D141, D142, D143, D144, D145, D146, D147, D148, D149, D150, D151, D152, D153, D154, D155, D156, D157, D158, D159.

663 *Dowland Ayres: 1er Livre/1st Book.* CD. Pierre Verany, 1994, 2013.

Performers: John Elwes (tenor), Matthias Spaeter (lute). Includes D19, D23, D24, D26, D42, D60, D125, D126, D127, D128, D129, D130, D131, D132, D133, D134, D135, D136, D137, D138, D139.

664 *Dowland's Vocal Music.* LP. EMI Odeon Records, 1965.

Performers: Janet Baker, Wilfred Brown, Grayston Burgess, April Cantelo, Gerald English, Christopher Keyte, Jantina Noorman (voice), Raymond Leppard (director). Notes by Diana Poulton. Includes D129, D142, D149, D156, D166, D173, D174, D184, D185, D187, D192, D194, D196, D197, D200, D203, D206.

665 *First Booke of Songs or Ayres.* CD. BIS, 1988, 1990.

Performers: Roger Covey-Crump (tenor), Jakob Lindberg (lute). Recorded November 27–29, 1988 at the Petrus Church (Petruskyrkan), Stocksund, Sweden. Notes in English, French, and German by Diana Poulton. Includes D19, D23, D24, D26, D42, D60, D125, D126, D127, D128, D129, D130, D131, D132, D133, D134, D135, D136, D137, D138, D139.

666 *Flow My Teares: John Dowland: Songs from the First Booke of Songs 1597 and the Second Booke of Songs 1600.* CD. Metronome, 1995.

Performers: Paul Agnew (tenor), Christopher Wilson (lute). Recorded March 1995 at St Andrew's Church, Toddington, Gloucestershire, England. Includes D15, D19, D24, D42, D60, D127, D129, D133, D134, D141, D142, D145, D148, D149, D151, D156.

667   *Honey from the Hive: Songs by John Dowland.* CD. BIS, 2005.

Performers: Emma Kirkby (soprano), Anthony Rooley (lute). Recorded April 2004, Länna Church, Sweden. Notes by Anthony Rooley. Includes D15, D42, D137, D141, D142, D143, D144, D145, D147, D149, D160, D161, D162, D163, D164, D165, D166, D177, D199.

668   *In Darknesse Let Me Dwell: John Dowland: Songs from a Musicall Banquet 1610, The Third and Last Booke of Songs 1605, A Pilgrimes Solace.* CD. Metronome Recordings, 1996.

Performers: Paul Agnew (tenor), Christopher Wilson (lute). Notes by Robert Spencer. Includes D34, D161, D162, D165, D166, D167, D168, D170, D174, D176, D184, D186, D192, D193, D200, D201.

669   *J. Dowland: Airs et Madrigaux.* LP. Amadeo, 1966. Reissued as *Awake Sweet Love: Airs & Partsongs.* LP, CD. Vanguard Classics, 1966, 1999.

Performers: Deller Consort [Honor Sheppard (soprano), Alfred Deller (counter-tenor), Desmond Dupré (lute), Beatrice Reichert (viol), Viktor Redtenbacher (violin)]. Notes by Theodor Guschlbauer in French. Recorded in Vienna. Includes D15, D19, D24, D41, D42, D60, D133, D135, D142, D149, D164, D167, D188, D192, D201.

670   *John Dowland: Ayres.* CD. Reflexe series. EMI, 1989, 2016.

Performers: Hilliard-Ensemble (Paul Hillier, director). Recorded March 1986 at Abbey Road Studio No. 1, London. Notes by Simon Heighes. Includes D23, D24, D129, D137, D154, D168, D181, D187, D193, D197, D198, D212, D213, D214, D215, D216, D217, D218.

671   *John Dowland: First Booke of Ayres.* LP. Dover, 1958, 1966.

Performers: Pro Musica Antiqua of Brussels [Elisabeth Verlooy (soprano), Jeanne Deroubaix (contralto), René Letroye, Franz Mertens (tenors), Willy Pourtois (bass), Michel Podolski (lute), Silva Devos (recorder), Janine Tryssesoone, Gaston Dome, André Douvère (viols), Safford Cape (director)]. Includes D19, D23, D24, D26, D37, D42, D60, D125, D126, D127, D128, D129, D130, D131, D132, D133, D134, D135, D136, D137, D138, D139.

672   *John Dowland: First Booke of Songes or Ayres.* CD. Signum Classics, 2018.

Performers: Grace Davidson (soprano), David Miller (lute). Recorded April 26–28, 2016 at Ascot Priory, Berkshire, England. Notes by Christopher Goodwin. Includes D19, D23, D24, D26, D42, D60, D125, D126, D127, D128, D129, D130, D131, D132, D133, D134, D135, D136, D137, D138, D139.

673   *John Dowland: Lute Songs.* LP, CD. Lyrichord, 1958, 1994.

Performers: Russell Oberlin (countertenor), Joseph Iadone (lute). Includes D9, D15, D42, D60, D141, D156, D167, D174, D193, D199, D200, D201.

674 *John Dowland: Music of Love and Friendship.* LP. Lyrichord, 1963. Reissued as *Dowland: Vocal Music.* CD. Naxos, 2008.

Performers: Saltire Singers, Desmond Dupré (lute). Includes D19, D23, D130, D139, D149, D164, D165, D166, D168, D182, D187, D191, D194.

675 *John Dowland: Second Booke of Songs or Ayres (1600).* CD. Dux Recording Producers, 2015.

Performers: Schoole of Night [Maria Skiba (soprano), Frank Pschichholz (lute, director)]. Recorded August 1–5, 2013 at Studio Polskiego, Warsaw. Notes by Rebekah Ahrendt. Includes D13, D15, D141, D142, D143, D144, D145, D146, D147, D148, D149, D150, D151, D152, D153, D154, D155, D156, D157, D158, D159.

676 *John Dowland: Songs for Tenor and Lute.* CD. Virgin Classics, 1988.

Performers: Nigel Rogers (tenor), Paul O'Dette (lute). Recorded November 1987 at St. Barnabas Church, London. D15, D19, D24, D26, D34, D131, D135, D138, D141, D142, D149, D156, D165, D166, D174, D175, D182, D183, D184, D185.

677 *John Dowland Lute Songs and Ayres: Elizabeth and Essex Songs.* CD. Centaur, 2007.

Performers: Kristine Hurst (soprano), Ben Cohen (lute). Notes by Kristine Hurst. Includes D15, D19, D23, D26, D42, D60, D137, D142, D147, D161, D162, D163, D166, D170, D174, D177.

678 *Music of Love and Friendship.* LP, CD. Lyrichord, 1963, 1998.

Performers: Saltire Singers [Patricia Clark (soprano), Jean Allister (contralto), Edgar Fleet (tenor), Frederick Westcott (bass)], Desmond Dupré (lute). Notes by David Josephson. Includes D19, D23, D130, D139, D149, D164, D165, D166, D168, D182, D187, D191, D194.

679 *Selected Works by John Dowland.* LP. Archive Production, 1966. Reissued as *I Saw My Lady Weep: Dowland Songs and Lachrimae.* CD. ArkivMusic, Deutsche Grammophon, 2002.

Performers: Studio der Frühen Musik [Andrea von Ramm (mezzo-soprano), Grayston Burgett (countertenor), Nigel Rogers (tenor), Karl-Heinz Klein (bass), Sterling Scott Jones, Laurentius Strehl, Kurt Haselhort, Hans-Peter Winkel, Johannes Finck (viols), Thomas E. Binkley (director)]. Recorded August 31–September 3, 1964 at Musikhochschule, Grosser Saal, Munich. Notes by Larry Palmer in English, French, and German. Includes D42, D114, D119, D141, D142, D151, D156, D164, D187, D188, D193, D201.

680 *Third Booke of Songs.* LP, CD. Florilegium series. Éditions de l'Oiseau-Lyre, 1977, 1991.

Reissued as CD 3 in **600**. Performers: Consort of Musicke [Emma Kirby (soprano), John York Skinner (countertenor), Martyn Hill (tenor), David Thomas (bass), Catherine Mackintosh, Polly Waterfield, and Ian Gammie (tenor viols), Trevor Jones (bass viol), Anthony Rooley (lute, director)]. Notes by Anthony Rooley in English, French, and German. Includes D160, D161, D162, D163, D164, D165, D166, D167, D168, D169, D170, D171, D172, D173, D174, D175, D176, D177, D178, D179, D180.

681 *Time Stands Still: Songs by John Dowland.* CD. Euterpe musica, 2002.

Performers: Johan Linderoth (tenor), Inger Alebo (lute). Includes D19, D24, D26, D127, D129, D131, D137, D141, D142, D161, D184.

CONSORT MUSIC

682 *Dowland: Consort Musicke.* LP. Florilegium series. Éditions de l'Oiseau-Lyre, 1977.

Reissued on CDs 11 and 12 of **600**. Notes by Anthony Rooley in English, French, and German. Performers: Consort of Musicke [Catherine Mackintosh, Polly Waterfield (treble viols, violins), Ian Gammie (tenor viol), Trevor Jones (tenor, bass viols, viola), Jane Ryan (bass viol), Bernard Thomas (flute), Jakob Lindberg (bandora), Julian Creme (cittern), Alan Wilson (virginal, organ), Anthony Rooley (lute, director)]. Notes by Anthony Rooley in English, French, and German. Includes D8, D14, D15, D19, D22, D23, D38, D39, D41, D42, D52, D62, D81, D94, D95, D109, D114, D185, D200.

683 *Dowland: Lachrimae (1604).* CD. Virgin Classics, 1993.

Performers: Fretwork [Richard Boothby, Richard Campbell, Wendy Gillespie, Julia Hodgson, William Hunt (viols)], Christopher Wilson (lute). Notes by Peter Holman. Includes D9, D14, D15, D19, D26, D29, D34, D38, D40, D42, D52, D114, D115, D116, D117, D118, D119, D120, D121, D122, D123.

684 *Dowland: Lachrimae 1604.* LP, CD. Florilegium series. Éditions de l'Oiseau-Lyre, 1976, 1989. 2016.

Reissued on CD 6 of **600**. Notes by Anthony Rooley in English, French, and German. Performers: Consort of Musicke [Catherine Mackintosh, Polly Waterfield (treble viols, violins), Ian Gammie, Trevor Jones (tenor viols), Jane Ryan (bass viol), Julian Creme (lute), Anthony Rooley (lute, director)]. Recorded February 26–28, 1976 at Decca Studios, West Hampstead, London. Notes by Anthony Rooley in English, French, and German. Includes D9, D14, D15, D19, D26, D29, D34, D38, D40, D42, D52, D114, D115, D116, D117, D118, D119, D120, D121, D122, D123.

685 *Dowland: Lachrimae or Seaven Teares.* CD. Fuga Libera, 2013.

Performers: Hathor Consort [Romina Lischka (treble viol, director), Liam Fennelly (treble viol, tenor viol), Thomas Baeté (tenor viol), Anne Bernard (bass viol), Benoît Vanden Bemden (violone), Sofie Vanden Eynde (lute)]. Recorded June 25–28, 2013 at Notre-Dame de l'Assomption, Bra-sur-Lienne, Belgium. Notes by Annemarie Peeters in English, French, and Dutch. Includes D9, D14, D15, D19, D26, D29, D34, D38, D40, D42, D52, D114, D115, D116, D117, D118, D119, D120, D121, D122, D123.

686 *Dowland: Lachrimae or Seaven Teares.* CD. Hyperion, 1993, Helios, 2010.

Performers: The Parley of Instruments [Judy Tarling (violin), Theresa Caudle (violin, viola), Lisa Cochrane, Paul Denley (viola), Mark Caudle (bass violin)], Paul O'Dette (lute), Peter Holman (director). Recorded November 12–14, 1992. Notes by Peter Holman in English, French, and German. Includes D8, D9, D14, D15, D19, D26, D29, D34, D38, D40, D42, D52, D114, D115, D116, D117, D118, D119, D120, D121, D122, D123.

687 *John Dowland: Lachrimae, or Seaven Teares.* BIS, 1985.

Performers: Dowland Consort [Wendy Gillespie, Alison Crum (tenor and alto viols), Sarah Cunningham (bass and tenor viols), Richard Campbell (bass viol), Trevor Jones (great bass viol), Jackob Lindberg (lute)]. Recorded December 12–15, 1985 at Wik Castle, Uppsala, Sweden. Notes in English, Swedish, German, and French. Includes D9, D14, D15, D19, D26, D29, D34, D38, D40, D42, D52, D114, D115, D116, D117, D118, D119, D120, D121, D122, D123.

688 *John Dowland: Lachrimae or Seaven Teares 1604.* CD. Astrée, 1988, 1997, 2000, Alia Vox, 2013.

Performers: Hespèrion XX [Jordi Savall, Christophe Coin, Sergi Casademunt, Lorenz Duftschmid, Paolo Pandolfo (viols), José Miguel Moreno (lute), Jordi Savall (director)]. Recorded May 1987 at L'Église de Santa Maria de Sant Martí, Sarroca, Catalonia, Spain. Notes by Claude Chauvel in French, English, Spanish, Catalan, German, and Italian. Includes D9, D14, D15, D19, D26, D29, D34, D38, D40, D42, D52, D114, D115, D116, D117, D118, D119, D120, D121, D122, D123.

689 *John Dowland: Lachrimae or Seven Tears.* CD. Glasgow: Linn Records, 2016.

Performers: Elizabeth Kenny (lute), Phantasm [Laurence Dreyfus (treble viol, director), Jonathan Manson, Mikko Perkola, Emilia Benjamin (tenor viols), Markku Luolajan-Mikkola (bass viol)]. Recorded July 5–7, 2015 at Magdalen College, Oxford, UK. Notes by Laurence Dreyfus and Elizabeth Kenny. Includes D9, D14, D15, D19, D26, D29, D34, D38, D40, D42, D52, D114, D115, D116, D117, D118, D119, D120, D121, D122, D123.

690 *John Dowland: Lachrimae Pavanen Galliarden.* LP. Harmonia mundi, 1962, 1976, 1980.

Performers: Schola Cantorum Basiliensis [Eugen M. Dombois (lute), Hannelore Müller, Jan Crafoord, Johannes Koch (viols), August Wenzinger (viol, director)]. Recorded March 1962 in Stuttgart-Botnang. Also released as *Altenglische Gambemusik*. Includes D14, D15, D19, D26, D29, D34, D38, D40, D42, D52, D114, D115, D116, D117, D118, D119, D120, D121, D122, D123.

691 *Lachrimæ, or Seaven Teares.* CD. Fra Bernardo, 2013.

Performers: Gambe di Legno [Juan Manuel Quintana (treble viol), Francesco Galligioni (tenor viol), Carlo Zanardi, Paolo Zuccheri, Riccardo Coelati Rama (bass viols), Evangelina Mascardi (lute)]. Includes D15, D114, D115, D116, D117, D118, D119.

692   *Music by John Dowland.* LP, CD, Hyperion, 1981, 1987.

Performers: Extempore String Ensemble [Rosemary Thorndycraft (viols), Janet Trent (viols, violin), Peter Trent (lutes, viol, guitar), Robin Jeffrey (lute, theorbo), George Weigand (lute, orpharion, bandora, director)]. Recorded September 20–21, 1980. Notes by Diana Poulton and George Weigand. Includes D8, D15, D19, D26, D38, D47, D54, D55, D58, D62, D111, D120, D122, D123.

SACRED MUSIC

693   *Dowland: Mr. Henry Noell Lamentations 1597; Psalms & Sacred Songs.* LP. Florilegium series. Éditions de l'Oiseau-Lyre, 1979.

Reissued on CDs 6 and 7 in **600**. Performers: Consort of Musicke [Emma Kirkby (soprano), Glenda Simpson (mezzo-soprano), John York Skinner (countertenor), Martin Hill (tenor), David Thomas (bass), Bernard Thomas (flute), Catherine Mackintosh, Ian Gammie, Polly Waterfield, Trevor Jones (viols), Julian Creme (cittern), Jakob Lindberg (bandora), Alan Wilson (organ), Anthony Rooley (lute, director)]. Notes by Anthony Rooley in English, French, and German. Includes D142, D203, D204, D205, D206, D207, D208, D209, D210, D211, D212, D213, D214, D215, D216, D217, D218.

KEYBOARD MUSIC

694   *Dowland: Keyboard Transcriptions.* LP. Florilegium series. Éditions de l'Oiseau-Lyre, 1979.

Reissued as CD 5 in **600**. Performer: Colin Tilney, harpsichord. Notes by Anthony Rooley. Includes arrangements of D8 (Peerson), D10 (anon.), D15 (Byrd), D15 (Farnaby), D15 (Morley), D15 (Schildt), D19 (Bull), D23 (Wilbye), D23 (anon.), D42 (anon.), D42 (anon.), D48 (anon.), D95 (Siefert).

VIDEO DOCUMENTARIES

695   *The Journey & the Labyrinth: The Music of John Dowland.* DVD. Deutsche Grammophon, 2007.

Performers: Sting (voice and lute), Edin Karamazov (lute). Directed by Jim Gable and Ann Kim. Recorded at St. Luke's Church, Old Street, London. Bonus CD included (**651**). Features D15, D42, D60, D138, D149, D158, D174, D178, D201.

Secondary Source Author Index

Subject Index

For all topics, readers should consult **264** and **265**.

Composition/Collection Index

For all compositions, readers should also consult **264** *and* **265**. *Works list* **D** *numbers are presented in bold type.*

Performer Index

Made in the USA
Middletown, DE
15 September 2024

61005692R10117